Lloyd J. Ogilvie General Editor

THE

D1432365

PREACHER'S

COMMENTARY

ROMANS

D. Stuart Briscoe

THOMAS NELSON PUBLISHERS
Nashville

THE PREACHER'S COMMENTARY SERIES, Volume 29, *Romans.* Copyright ©
1982 by Word, Inc.

Published in Nashville, Tennessee, by Thomas Nelson, Inc.

Library of Congress Cataloging in Publication Data

The preacher's commentary (formerly The communicator's commentary).

  Includes bibliographical references.
  Contents: v. 29. Romans/D. Stuart Briscoe
  1.Bible. N.T.—Commentaries—Collected works.
I. Ogilvie, Lloyd John. II. Briscoe, D. Stuart.

BS2341.2.C65   225.7'7   81–71764
ISBN 0-7852-4804-8   AACR2

1 2 3 4 5 6 7 — 07 06 05 04 03

Printed in the United States of America

CONTENTS

EDITOR'S PREFACE

God has called all of His people to be communicators. Everyone who is in Christ is called into ministry. As ministers of "the manifold grace of God," all of us—clergy and laity—are commissioned with the challenge to communicate our faith to individuals and groups, classes and congregations.

The Bible, God's Word, is the objective basis of the truth of His love and power that we seek to communicate. In response to the urgent, expressed needs of pastors, teachers, Bible study leaders, church school teachers, small group enablers, and individual Christians, the Preacher's Commentary is offered as a penetrating search of the Scriptures to enable vital personal and practical communication of the abundant life.

Many current commentaries and Bible study guides provide only some aspects of a communicator's needs. Some offer in-depth scholarship but no application to daily life. Others are so popular in approach that biblical roots are left unexplained. Few offer compelling illustrations that open windows for the reader to see the exciting application for today's struggles. And most of all, seldom have the expositors given the valuable outlines of passages so needed to help the preacher or teacher in his or her busy life to prepare for communicating the Word to congregations or classes.

This Preacher's Commentary series brings all of these elements together. The authors are scholar-preachers and teachers outstanding in their ability to make the Scriptures come alive for individuals and groups. They are noted for bringing together excellence in biblical scholarship, knowledge of the original Greek and Hebrew, sensitivity to people's needs, vivid illustrative material from biblical, classical, and contemporary sources, and lucid communication by the use of clear outlines of thought. Each has been selected to contribute to this series because of his Spirit-empowered ability to help people live in the skins of biblical characters and provide a "you-are-there" intensity to the drama of events of the Bible which have so much to say about our relationships and responsibilities today.

The design for the Preacher's Commentary gives the reader an overall outline of each book of the Bible. Following the introduction, which reveals the author's approach and salient background on the book, each chapter of the commentary provides the Scripture to be exposited. The New King James Bible has been chosen for the Preacher's Commentary because it combines with integrity the beauty of language, underlying Greek textual basis, and thought-flow of the 1611 King James Version, while replacing obsolete verb forms and other archaisms with their everyday contemporary counterparts for greater readability. Reverence for God is preserved in the capitalization of all pronouns referring to the Father, Son, or Holy Spirit. Readers who are more comfortable with another translation can readily find the parallel passage by means of the chapter and verse reference at the end of each passage being exposited. The paragraphs of exposition combine fresh insights to the Scripture, application, rich illustrative material, and innovative ways of utilizing the vibrant truth for his or her own life and for the challenge of communicating it with vigor and vitality.

It has been gratifying to me as Editor of this series to receive enthusiastic progress reports from each contributor. As they worked, all were gripped with new truths from the Scripture—God-given insights into passages, previously not written in the literature of biblical explanation. A prime objective of this series is for each user to find the same awareness: that God speaks with newness through the Scriptures when we approach them with a ready mind and a willingness to communicate what He has given; that God delights to give communicators of His Word "I-never-saw-that-in-that-verse-before" intellectual insights so that our listeners and readers can have "I-never-realized-all-that-was-in-that-verse" spiritual experiences.

The thrust of the commentary series unequivocally affirms that God speaks through the Scriptures today to engender faith, enable adventuresome living of the abundant life, and establish the basis of obedient discipleship. The Bible, the unique Word of God, is unlimited in its resource for Christians in communicating our hope to others. It is our weapon in the battle for truth, the guide for ministry, and the irresistible force for introducing others to God. In the New Testament we meet the divine Lord and Savior whom we seek to communicate to others. What He said and did as God with us has been faithfully recorded under the inspiration of the Spirit of God. The cosmic implications of the Gospels are lived out in Acts and spelled out in the Epistles. They have stood the test of time because the eternal Communicator, God Himself, communicates through them to those who would be communicators of grace. His essential nature is exposed, the plan of salvation is explained, and the gospel for all of life, now and for eternity is proclaimed.

A biblically rooted communication of the gospel holds in unity and oneness what divergent movements have wrought asunder. This commentary series courageously presents personal faith, caring for individuals, and social responsibility as essential, inseparable dimensions of biblical Christianity. It seeks to present the quadrilateral gospel in its fullness which calls us to unreserved commitment to Christ, unrestricted self-esteem in His grace, unqualified love for others in personal evangelism, and undying efforts to work for justice and righteousness in a sick and suffering world.

A growing renaissance in the church today is being led by clergy and laity who are biblically rooted, Christ-centered, and Holy Spirit-empowered. They have dared to listen to people's most urgent questions and deepest needs and then to God as He speaks through the Bible. Biblical preaching is the secret of growing churches. Bible study classes and small groups are equipping the laity for ministry in the world. Dynamic Christians are finding that daily study of God's Word allows the Spirit to do in them what He wishes to communicate through them to others. These days are the most exciting time since Pentecost. The Preacher's Commentary is offered to be a primary resource of new life for this renaissance.

This volume, *Romans,* was written by one of the very outstanding and popular pioneers of this biblical resurgence in our time. A noted Bible expositor, speaker, and author, Stuart Briscoe was senior pastor of the Elmbrook Church of Brookfield, Wisconsin, a suburb of Milwaukee, for thirty years. This Bible-centered church has been distinguished for Dr. Briscoe's biblical sermons, for study groups centered in contemporary application of the Scripture to daily living, and for its emphasis on equipping the laity for ministry. What Dr. Briscoe discovered in weekly preaching of the Word to this large congregation is reflected in his many books, with their lucid and impelling explanation of the Bible. Dr. Briscoe's expository style of preaching and writing utilizes corollary Scripture, rich illustrations from history and contemporary life, and personal stories which expose his own experience of living what he proclaims. His delightful use of humor helps his readers and listeners enjoy the application of truth to their lives. He is an admired and emulated example for preachers, teachers, and those who seek to communicate Christ with joy and power.

This volume on Romans is a dynamic blend of penetrating scholarship and fresh insight. Dr. Briscoe has opened windows for us to look with new vision into familiar passages. We are introduced to the apostle Paul as man in Christ, theologian, determined and spiritual adventurer. We are led down the corridors of the apostle's mind and heart in this exposition of his greatest epistle. The outline of the commentary is extremely helpful, and the unfolding discussion provides rich treasures for the communicator in sharing the essence of the Christian faith. Here is Romans for our time done with an excellence that will stand the test of time.

—LLOYD J. OGILVIE

INTRODUCTION TO ROMANS

WHY ROMANS IS SO SPECIAL

Paul's Epistle to the Romans holds a special place in the life of the Christian church. F. F. Bruce wrote, "Time and again in the course of Christian history it has liberated the minds of men, brought them back to an understanding of the essential Gospel of Christ, and started spiritual revolutions."[1]

One of those liberated minds belonged to Augustine, who is universally acknowledged as one of the world's most influential theologians. One day as he wept under a fig tree, in deep distress of soul desperately convicted of his own sinfulness, he heard a young child singing, "Take up and read. . . ." Turning to a copy of Paul's writings which lay nearby he opened it and read, "Let us walk properly, as in the day, not in revelry and drunkenness, not in lewdness and lust, not in strife and envy. But put on the Lord Jesus Christ, and make no provision for the flesh, to fulfill its lusts" (Rom. 13:13–14). He believed and obeyed, and the great mind was liberated for the glory of God and the good of mankind.

Centuries later Martin Luther, the serious, ardent scholar of Wittenberg, came under the influence of Romans and his life was also transformed. As he delivered a series of lectures on the epistle, he grasped for the first time in his life what he called "the righteousness by which through grace and sheer mercy God justified us through faith." His explanation of his experience bears repeating. "Thereupon I felt myself to be reborn and to have gone through open doors into paradise."[2] This liberating discovery led him not only into the peace for which he had searched so long, but also into a ministry that changed the face of Europe and the fate of thousands.

John Wesley, whose cultured mind was matched only by his spiritual sensitivity, servant attitude and social concern, returned to England from Savannah, Georgia, a discouraged man. He had run into rough water in his dealings with the colonists, and he encountered even more troubled seas on the voyage home. Both experiences led him to the awesome discovery that he had no assurance of his acceptability to the God he loved and served. In this frame of mind he went one evening, most reluctantly, to a meeting where Luther's preface to the Epistle to the Romans was being read, and during the reading his "heart was strangely warmed." He recorded in his journal, "I felt I did trust in Christ, Christ alone for salvation; and an assurance was given to me that He had taken away my sins, even mine, and saved me from the law of sin and death."[3] Armed with this message he embarked on forty years of ministry that beggars description and gladdens the heart. So mightily did the Spirit of God use him that revivals blazed in England and America throughout the eighteenth and nineteenth centuries and the course of history was changed.

Frederick Louis Godet was not exaggerating when he stated in the Introduction to his classic *Commentary on Romans*, "The probability is that every great spiritual revival in the church will be connected as effect and cause with a deeper understanding of this book."[4] And John Calvin of Geneva was no less enthusiastic when he wrote, "When anyone gains a knowledge of this Epistle he has an entrance opened to him to all the most hidden treasures of Scripture."[5]

THE PARTICULAR RELEVANCE OF ROMANS TO CONTEMPORARY SOCIETY

The modern reader might be tempted to wonder if an epistle of such antiquity, while eminently suited to Rome in the first century and even to the days of Reformation in Europe and Revival in England and America, might not be irrelevant to the contemporary world. To this we can only reply by pointing out that the timeless truths of God's eternal Word are always relevant. And we might add that the particular condition of modern society indicates a special need for a restatement of the truths outlined in Romans.

For instance, contemporary society has divorced itself so completely from divine revelation that it has little or no concept of the reality of God's Person. Many who believe He exists have a picture of Him that ranges from the outright bizarre to the downright blasphemous, while those who choose to believe He does not exist are beginning to wallow in the morass of their own making. Modern man's love affair with himself has produced such incredible self-centeredness that we are now variously called the "me-first generation" or the "narcissistic society." Such has been the emphasis on human rights that uncomfortable subjects like personal responsibility have been shelved. Modern man's inbred feeling that he has every reason to expect happiness to be his abiding experience has produced an inordinate desire for that which is "comfortable, popular and profitable." Anything that gets in the way of these cherished desires must be banished at all costs. That which is "good and true and right" must of necessity be discarded if it interferes with the achieving of the ultimate goal of human happiness.

Ironically, in the midst of this culturally acceptable and phenomenally expensive pursuit of happiness there is a brooding sense of foreboding, an unspoken feeling that all is not well. Modern man yearns for leadership that will take him only where he wants to go. He insists on arriving painlessly, he knows not where, and on the journey to this ill-conceived and ill-defined objective he fears lest the events of his uncontrollable world finally overtake him in the ultimate disaster, the terminal catastrophe.

To this kind of society the ancient epistle speaks in trenchant terms. Man is exposed as the shameful sinner his actions clearly demonstrate him to be. God is revealed as at once just, merciful, and gracious. The possibility of salvation from the consequences of sin and emancipation from the pernicious dynamic of sin is clearly set forth. The principles of salvation are stated unequivocally in terms of grace and faith. Human history is declared to be the arena in which the cosmic plan of the Sovereign God is moving relentlessly to its eternal conclusion. And the clarion call to commitment to the God of our salvation in terms of sacrificial yielding of ourselves to Him in glad gratitude for unmerited grace is shown to be more than a pious concept. It is in fact a call to a dynamic lifestyle. The committed Christian is given clear instruction concerning his consecrated behavior in the home, the church, the political arena, and the marketplace. The epistle ranges effortlessly from awe-inspiring expositions of the majesty of God to deeply intimate statements concerning His compassion for sinners. On the one hand the degradation of a fallen race is exposed in all its sordid detail; yet, on the other hand, the way of love and the possibilities of human understanding, tolerance, gratitude, and sacrifice are clearly delineated. Man as an individual, naked before his God, guilty and without excuse, is also shown to be a creature of infinite worth capable of functioning through divine grace as leader, encourager, and responsible community participant. The erstwhile sinner is pointed unerringly to the path of the saint; the fallen sons of Adam's helpless race are lifted joyfully into the very presence of God and launched on the breathtaking life of "heirs of God and joint heirs with Christ" (Rom. 8:17). The hopeless and the helpless are introduced to the gospel of hope and the Giver of help. In short, Romans is a marvelous statement of the message our society needs.

SOME HELPFUL BACKGROUND TO ROMANS

The Author

The epistle has traditionally been attributed to Paul, the great apostle to the Gentiles. Even when many other biblical books were coming under close scholastic scrutiny, which questioned many of the traditional assumptions relating to authorship, the Pauline authorship of the Roman Epistle was rarely questioned. Professor Bruce dismisses those who did question Paul's authorship as "erratic schools of thought."

The significance of Paul's authorship, however, goes far beyond purely academic considerations. The unique status of the apostle, both as pioneer missionary-evangelist and supreme teacher-theologian, demands that his carefully thought-out treatise be treated with the greatest respect. This epistle, in the opinion of many people, is the great apostle's greatest work, his most complete statement of the gospel specially delivered to him by the Lord of the church. His background as a Jewish scholar and Roman citizen who had been constantly exposed to Greek culture not only made him eminently suitable for the work of an apostle in the first century, but it fitted him uniquely to address the specific situation of the Roman church. Composed as it was of Jews from the Dispersion and Romans from all walks of life, all of whom had been influenced to some degree by Greek thought, the church at Rome needed the authoritative understanding voice of a Paul. When he addressed the Jews about their particular outlook, they attended to his words very carefully, if for no other reason than that they knew Paul was himself a "true-blue" Jew. When he switched his attention to the particular status of the non-Jew, his readers listened sympathetically because they knew he knew their situation as did few other people. And when he addressed his hearers concerning their attitude to law and order, freedom and government, they recognized this was no "wild-eyed" radical or "dyed-in-the-wool" conservative speaking, but a Roman citizen with a true sense of privilege and a deep regard for his Roman status.

The Destination of the Epistle

The careful work of New Testament scholars has led to the discovery of a number of interesting facts relating to the epistle. They have pointed out that the words "in Rome" recorded in verses 5 and 17 of the first chapter do not appear in some of the early texts. In addition, the Doxology of Romans 16:25–27 and the Benediction of Romans 16:24 appear in a variety of positions in different texts, while in one important text the entire fifteenth and sixteenth chapters are not included. These facts have stimulated much discussion and many theories concerning the possibility that the epistle circulated in a variety of forms to different destinations. If this should be true, as appears likely, there is no reason to doubt that the epistle was intended primarily for the believers in Rome, but was also circulated to other churches without the passages exclusively relevant to the Roman church.[6]

Paul had not visited Rome at the time he wrote the epistle and so, of course, had played no direct role in the founding of the Christian community in the Imperial City. How the gospel first came to Rome and how the believers joined together for worship and service nobody knows for sure, but there are a number of considerations that may be helpful to us in gaining some understanding of the dawn of Christianity in Rome.

On the day of Pentecost, when great crowds gathered in Jerusalem to hear the message of Peter and thousands believed and were converted to Christ, we know there were "visitors from Rome, both Jews and proselytes" (Acts 2:10) in the crowd. It is quite possible that these people returned to their homes with the message of the Risen Lord on their lips and the evidence of His transforming power in their lives. Some scholars are skeptical of this possibility because they feel that even if some of the visitors from Rome became followers of Christ they would not have had time to learn enough to effectively minister in their own city. This objection, however, may not be valid when we remember that they were well versed in the Old Testament, had received the illumination of the Holy Spirit and, quite possibly, stayed on in Jerusalem after the Passover for a time to attend the teaching sessions of the apostles. In addition, because all roads led to Rome in those days, there was a constant stream of people from the provinces passing through the city, and no doubt their number contained not a few believers.

The cherished tradition that Peter founded the church is not to be regarded too highly because Paul made no mention of Peter having been in Rome or of any ministry that he might have had in the city. In addition, we know that Peter was still in a position of eminence in the church of Jerusalem at the time of the conference recorded in Acts 15 (ca. A.D. 50), while there is good reason to believe that the church of Rome was already in existence before that date.

The Date of the Epistle

If we assume that the last two chapters of the epistle were part of the original document, there are clear indications that Paul wrote from Corinth. The people mentioned in the final greetings include some who are known to have been Corinthians. From the fifteenth chapter we also know that the epistle was written after Paul had concluded his long-drawn-out work on the collection for the church in Jerusalem and was planning to leave for that city immediately in order that he might minister to the believers and deliver the offering. These factors enable us to ascertain that in all probability the epistle was written toward the end of the third missionary journey (see Acts 20) and, as nearly as we can tell, this took place somewhere between A.D. 57 and 59 when Nero ruled in Rome and the Pax Romana prevailed around the shores of the Mediterranean.

The Purpose of the Epistle

The apostle clearly wrote the epistle to alert the Roman believers to his plans, which included an immediate journey to Jerusalem, a proposed trip to Spain, and a long-delayed visit to Rome itself. It is quite obvious, however, that he had much more in mind, because he alerted his readers to considerably more than his itinerary! The full exposition of the Christian gospel which is contained in the epistle must be taken into account when we endeavor to ascertain his reasons for writing. Some scholars who believe that the church in Rome was primarily Jewish are of the opinion that Paul was intent on showing them how their understanding of the gospel needed enlarging to incorporate the greatness of God's plan of redemption for Gentile as well as Jew. Others who are equally convinced that the church was primarily Gentile feel that he was trying to pour oil on potentially troubled waters by showing the place of both Jew and Gentile in God's gospel of grace. Both views stand or fall on the opinions concerning the make-up of the church and as we cannot be sure on this point, we must beware of undue dogmatism. There is no question, however, that for some reason the apostle felt it necessary to set out a reasoned presentation of the Christian gospel. We can only surmise what his reasons may have been. Perhaps he felt that the strategic nature of Rome demanded that the church there be particularly well equipped in its understanding of the truth. On the other hand, it is quite possible that he may have felt that his journeys to Jerusalem and Rome were fraught with difficulty and it would be wise for him to set down in writing the gospel he had delivered so faithfully in spoken form. Whatever his reasons, we must thank God that in the midst of a busy schedule he found the time to write down the epistle which has had such far-reaching impact on the church through the ages.

A Personal Word

From a purely personal point of view I must admit that this epistle is one of my favorite parts of Scripture. My bias is reflected in the fact that I have read through it on numerous occasions, preached through it slowly and deliberately in the church I serve as pastor, taught it over and over again in a Bible school for young people in England, and generally shared from it around the world. Wherever I have tried to share my enthusiasm for Paul's masterpiece I have discovered believers who have dipped into it sporadically, and heard sermons from isolated passages occasionally, but rarely have they studied it systematically and grasped the whole of its argument. I hope this volume may assist some who have never worked through the epistle to do so for the first time.

The resources available to the student of Romans are boundless, and I will show my indebtedness to many of the gifted teachers of this and other generations as I proceed. As you have opportunity, I trust that you will read what the old masters like Luther, Calvin, and Godet had to say. Take time to study the material of such men as Barnhouse, Griffith Thomas, Murray, Bruce, and Lloyd-Jones, and anything else you can lay hands on. If this much less scholarly and much more humble book stimulates you assiduously to read Paul and those who have exposited his work through the years I will be well pleased, and I trust that whether your study is linked to personal enrichment, pulpit proclamation, or small group participation you will be deeply enriched.

NOTES

1. *Zondervan Pictorial Encyclopedia of the Bible,* 5 vols. (Grand Rapids: Zondervan Publishing Co., 1975), 5:161.

2. *Luther's Works,* Weimar ed., vol. 54 (1928), pp. 179ff.

3. *The Journal of John Wesley* (Chicago: Moody Press), p. 64.

4. Frederick Louis Godet, *Commentary on Romans* (Grand Rapids: Kregel Publications, 1977), p. 1.

5. John Calvin, *Calvin's Commentaries on Romans* (Grand Rapids: Eerdmans, 1947), p. xxix.

6. For a full discussion, see Donald Guthrie, *New Testament Introduction* (Downers Grove, Ill.: InterVarsity Press, 1973), pp. 400–14.

An Outline of Romans

I. An Apostle's Attitudes: 1:1–17
   A. Paul's Realistic Appraisal of Himself: 1:1–6
   B. Paul's Deep–Rooted Appreciation of His Message: 1:1–6
   C. Paul's Warmhearted Interest in People: 1:7–12
   D. Paul's Enthusiastic Commitment to His Work: 1:13–17

II. First, the Bad News: 1:18–32
   A. Man's Suppression of Truth: 1:18–20
   B. Man's Rejection of God: 1:21–22
   C. Man's Substitution for Creation: 1:23–28
   D. Man's Appreciation of Evil: 1:28–32

III. The Judgment of God: 2:1–16
   A. The Inconsistency of Human Judgment: 2:1
   B. The Integrity of Divine Judgment: 2:2–10
   C. The Inevitability of Divine Judgment: 2:11–16

IV. The Dangers of Religion: 2:17—3:8
   A. Profession Without Performance: 2:17–24
   B. Ritual Without Reality: 2:25–29
   C. Privilege Without Perception: 3:1–2
   D. Objections Without Objectivity: 3:3–8

V. All Together Now: 3:9–20
   A. All Under Sin: 3:9–18
   B. All Under Law: 3:19
   C. All Under Pressure: 3:20

VI. The Genius of God: 3:21–31
   A. The Divine Dilemma: 3:21–26
   B. The Universal Solution: 3:21–26
   C. The Eternal Benefits: 3:21–26
   D. The Common Denominator: 3:27–31

VII. Facing Up to Faith: 4:1–25
   A. The Father of Faith: 4:1–4
   B. The Forgiveness of Faith: 4:5–8
   C. The Family of Faith: 4:9–16
   D. The Factors of Faith: 4:17–25

CHAPTER ONE—AN APOSTLE'S ATTITUDES

ROMANS 1:1–17

Scripture Outline

Paul's Realistic Appraisal of Himself (1:1–6)

Paul's Deep–Rooted Appreciation of His Message (1:1–6)

Paul's Warmhearted Interest in People (1:7–12)

Paul's Enthusiastic Commitment to His Work (1:13–17)

Men of great achievement are usually men of special attitudes. A study of those whose lives live on, whose actions have changed the course of human experience, will show that they achieved what they did because they believed deeply in what they were doing and thought uniquely about the lives they were living. Paul the apostle, the former Saul of Tarsus, was such a man. Without him the message of the risen Christ could conceivably have found its place among the little known legends of the Middle East and been relegated to the position reserved for stories of fancy loved by poets and romantics, but largely ignored by men of action and purpose. But to a great extent because of Paul's life this was not to be. From one end of the Roman Empire to the other he traveled—preaching, teaching, founding churches, instructing leaders, nurturing the faltering, rebuking the disorderly, organizing, sustaining, challenging, and comforting. Wherever he went, people believed, groups of remarkably dedicated disciples were formed, and with unbelievable speed and effectiveness the church of Christ was taken from the position of a troublesome sect of Judaism to a lively force of committed people throughout the known world.

From Paul's fertile mind and fluid pen flowed letters of abiding value. Inspired as they were by the Holy Spirit, they have become the basis for preaching and teaching in the Christian church through the centuries. Where Paul has been taught, cultures have been changed. In places where churches stand and speak for the lifestyle purchased and provided by Christ and broadcast by Paul, society shows the indelible imprint of the great apostle. More than any of us will ever realize, our lives have been touched and transformed not only by the Son of God, but also through the converted Pharisee, the proud son of Tarsus.

What were the motivations and attitudes that drove him? Where did he find his vision and revive his spirit? In the opening verses of the Roman epistle we may find answers to these questions.

> **1:1** Paul, a bondservant of Jesus Christ, called to be an apostle, separated to the gospel of God [2] which He promised before through His prophets in the Holy Scriptures, [3] concerning His Son Jesus Christ our Lord, who was born of the seed of David according to the flesh, [4] and declared to be the Son of God with power according to the Spirit of holiness, by the resurrection from the dead. [5] Through Him we have received grace and apostleship for obedience to the faith among all nations for His name, [6] among whom you also are the called of Jesus Christ;
>
> *—Romans 1:1–6*

It was customary in first-century correspondence to commence with the writer's name, to state the name of the recipient, and to bring greetings. Paul did this and much more, for in between the traditional and formal *"Paul, a bondservant. . . To all who are in Rome. . . grace to you and peace. . ."* he wrote much that presents to us fascinating glimpses of his heart and mind and then allows us to learn much of his personal attitudes. There are four to which I would direct your attention.

PAUL'S REALISTIC APPRAISAL OF HIMSELF

It was during his first missionary journey in Asia Minor with Barnabas that the apostle became known as Paul rather than Saul. While some people see in this change of name an expression of humility (Paul means literally "little") wrought in the proud Pharisee by the risen Lord, it is more likely he adopted this Roman name to facilitate his travels throughout the empire—a practice not uncommon in those days.

His careful choice of the words *"a bondservant of Jesus Christ"* in verse 1 is without doubt a clear statement of humble attitude and deep devotion. The Greek word *doulos* (translated "bondservant" in the NKJV) can be translated "slave" and, while there is no necessity to limit Paul's use of the term to this meaning, he certainly saw himself as one obliged to serve Christ, and as a person without exclusive rights to his own life but as one who had been bought with a price. If Paul had not seen himself in this light but had concentrated more on his own rights and desires, he would never have accomplished what he did. Times without number his circumstances dictated that he should think of his own safety and well-being; yet he pressed on with phenomenal determination and total disregard for himself for no other reason than that he was not his own master—he was a servant of One who had never drawn back, even from a cross.

If there is a ring of humility in the use of the word "bondservant," there is a balancing note of authority in the following phrase—*"called to be an apostle."* The status of apostle was something to which Paul held tenaciously. He knew that in this role he had the responsibility of founding churches in areas where Christ was unknown and, therefore, he had not only to speak with authority, but to be seen to act with authority. When he dealt with problems and countered error, he did not hesitate to remind his readers and hearers that they would disregard what he was saying at their own peril. They were dealing, he assured them, not with a "run-of-the-mill" itinerant preacher but with a divinely chosen apostle. To Paul, being "called" meant being selected and commissioned for a task by God Himself.

We should not overlook Paul's delightful balance here. If he had spoken exclusively of himself as servant, he would, no doubt, have been disregarded by the rebellious and discounted by the skeptical, but if he had thundered constantly concerning his apostleship, the timid would have been terrified. He was the "servant apostle" who lived in the challenging tension between personal humility and derived authority, in which, to a lesser extent, all of Christ's disciples are called to live.

Paul also had a sharply defined sense of destiny. He firmly believed that he was *"separated to the gospel of God."* There is a sense in which the word "separated" can relate to human actions, such as the consecration of a building to a special purpose or the ordination of a person to a specific ministry. Paul was "separated" or ordained along with Barnabas to the special ministry of outreach which the Holy Spirit had indicated to the church at Antioch that they were to fulfill. But this separation was not specifically what Paul had in mind. Writing to the Galatians, he said that his separation was "from [his] mother's womb" (Gal. 1:15)—an act that only God could accomplish. His conviction was that God had set him apart from the day of his birth to be a "gospel of God" man. This meant, of course, that he looked at his heritage, his education, his personality, and his gifts as being part of the divine plan; and, while he never recovered from the horror of his abuse of privilege and the consequences of his brutal mistakes before he came to Christ, he saw even in these events factors that could equip him uniquely to make the gospel known. To Paul it was no accident that he had Roman citizenship, Greek culture, and Jewish training. God had separated him from the womb. The earliest days spent in cosmopolitan Tarsus, the student days at the feet of Gamaliel, the turbulent days invested in a burning desire to eradicate the mistaken followers of the usurper Jesus of Nazareth had not only left their scars; they had built into his character the very traits that would send him and his gospel to people living in ignorance of the salvation of God. For Paul no tantalizing horizons beckoned, no long-cherished dreams drew him on; he was a one-goal man. With fierce intensity and unshakable determination, he knew himself to be a man fashioned by God for a task formidable in the extreme yet glorious in its purpose.

Far from being overwhelmed, however, Paul demonstrated his sense of adequacy under the most trying circumstances and in the most discouraging situations. This deep-rooted sense of competence came from his understanding that he had *"received grace and apostleship"* (Rom. 1:5). The apostleship, as we have seen, was the position of privilege and responsibility; the grace was the divine enabling for the task in hand. Grace was one of Paul's favorite words, and we will discover he used it in a variety of ways but always with the thought that it was a gift of God to undeserving people. To the apostle it meant that, along with the awesome responsibility of apostleship, he was also given by God all it would take to fulfill the responsibility. During World War II Churchill cabled Roosevelt, "Give us the tools and we'll finish the job." God had cabled Paul and said, "I've given you the tools (grace), now finish the job (apostleship)."

The extent of this job was made clear to Paul even as brave Ananias came to him in Damascus after the transforming encounter with the risen Christ. As Christ ministered to the stricken Saul, Ananias made it clear that the new apostle was to go as God's chosen instrument to the Gentiles. To Paul this meant simply a ministry *"among all nations"* (Rom. 1:5). From the early days in Damascus, into Arabia, Cilicia, and Syria, he had seen people who needed Christ come to know Him. On into Achaia, Macedonia, and Galatia he had moved relentlessly, ranging by any means available from one region to the next with the great goal of "all nations" before him. Now at the time of this writing he was planning not only to press westward to Rome but on into Spain. Wherever he went the objective was the same—to bring people to *"obedience to the faith."* It is important to note that for Paul "faith" was considerably more than an intellectual assent or even an attitude of trust. Faith, in his preaching, constituted a lifestyle of obedience, so wherever he went he presented truth to which people should assent, promises they should trust, and commands they should obey. His goal and burning desire was to bring people to the point where they would *"trust and obey"* Jesus Christ.

PAUL'S DEEP-ROOTED APPRECIATION OF HIS MESSAGE

In addition to Paul's view of his own special position in the purposes of God (Rom. 1:1–3), the apostle had an undying confidence in the validity and relevance of the message he endeavored to communicate. On numerous occasions I have met salesmen who have been so enthusiastic about their products that they have been most convincing in their presentation. But often I have been amazed to discover them a few months later working for their former competitors. When I have inquired about their abandonment of their former superlative product and their subsequent endorsement of what was previously regarded as inferior, I have discovered their commitment was more to their percentage than their product. Paul could never be accused of such behavior. He showed himself to be unshakably loyal to the *"gospel of God"* (v. 1).

The Greek word *euangelion* was used to convey the excitement and thrill associated with the announcement of good news. In the Greek translation of the Old Testament, the Septuagint, it is interesting to notice that *euangelion* is the word used to describe the announcement of the end of Babylonian captivity and the good news that former captives were now free to return to the beloved homeland from which they had been exiled for many bitter years. The Good News to which Paul was committed had a message even greater and grander—an exhilarating, exciting announcement that God Himself had procured liberty for people in spiritual bondage and reconciliation for those in spiritual exile. Wherever he went, Paul saw himself as the messenger of the kind of news that people needed to hear if they were ever to become free to be the people God intended them to be.

There was always criticism of Paul's message, particularly from his fellow Jews, who, as a result of the Dispersion, were scattered all over the regions in which he traveled. Many of them accused Paul of manufacturing his own message, but he was at great pains to show his critics that, far from being a new fad, his message was the one which God had *"promised before through His prophets in the Holy Scriptures"* (v. 2). Using the only Bible available in those days, the Old Testament, Paul delighted to do what his Master had done with the troubled disciples of Emmaus: "beginning at Moses and all the Prophets, He expounded to them in all the Scriptures the things concerning himself" (Luke 24:27). The fact that Paul was able to show his critics that the gospel he preached was the fulfillment of what the prophets had predicted went a long way toward establishing the credibility of both messenger and message.

The central point of his gospel was that to which the Old Testament had pointed unerringly. From the earliest promise of God to Eve that her seed would bruise the serpent's head, down through the tortuous history of God's special people through whom the bruiser of Satan would come, the point of emphasis had never changed. Through solemn festivals, innumerable sacrifices, the giving of the Law, the deliverance from Egypt, God had spoken persistently through type, symbol, and figure of the blessing to be made available through the One who would come. Prophets who had bemoaned the condition of Israel and Judah had tempered their criticisms and sweetened their dire predictions with promises concerning One whose coming would introduce a new era of blessing. Nothing delighted Paul more than to take the Holy Scriptures and show that God's dealings and promises were all *"concerning His Son Jesus Christ our Lord"* (v. 3) who indeed had come.

This coming of the Lord Jesus Christ had, of course, a human aspect, for He *"was born of the seed of David according to the flesh"* (v. 3)—something that was easily proven by His genealogies such as the one found in Luke's Gospel. But Paul's message did not center around a mere man, even a man of such royal status as the House of David, for Paul knew that the significance of the gospel of Christ lay in the Person of Christ. If Jesus were only a man, His death was nobler than many and more gruesome than most—but nothing more. But the gospel of God has had as its central point One who was, in addition to being born of the seed of David, *"declared to be the Son of God" (v. 4)*.

The church of Christ has wrestled with the basic Christian doctrine that Jesus was both seed of David and Son of God for centuries. In early years the church fathers wrote learned treatises on the subject, arguing endlessly about the meaning of the Incarnation. The Gnostics, who believed that matter was essentially evil and spirit intrinsically good, were appalled at the suggestion that God should inhabit human flesh. For them the idea was so unthinkable that they went to great lengths to avoid the conclusion they had already rejected. Some insisted that the man Jesus was invested with the Spirit "as a dove" at the time of His baptism but the Spirit "returned to the *Plērōma*" before the Crucifixion. Others maintained that when Christ was born "he passed through Mary like water through a tube." Try as they would, they were unable to avoid the clear statement of Paul and the strong teaching of John that the inexplicable miracle took place in which God assumed our humanity, was tempted as we are, was touched with the feelings of our infirmities, and stooped to the point of bearing our sins in His own body on the tree.

Having contrasted *"the seed of David"* with the *"Son of God"* (vv. 3, 4), Paul showed that the grounds for believing in the deity and humanity of Christ must be clearly understood. Christ, he said, was *"declared to be Son of God" (v. 4)*, and the word "declared" meant not only that a declaration was made about His deity but that certain things happened which clearly established His deity. First, His position as Son of God was established *"with power,"* second, *"according to the Spirit of holiness,"* and third, *"by the resurrection from the dead" (v. 4)*. The extraordinary power of the Lord Jesus was exhibited in many instances, as He conquered sin, death, disease, natural elements, spiritual forces of wickedness, and even Satan himself. The powerful work of the Holy Spirit in whose blessed fullness He lived and through whose eternal enabling He was able to offer Himself as a sacrifice for sin was constant evidence of the uniqueness of His being. But it was in the *"resurrection from the dead" (v. 4)* that both the power and the Spirit were seen to greatest effect in His experience. Man had done his foul worst and taken Christ into death via a cross and a tomb, but God had intervened and in a superlative display of the power of the Spirit had done His best. Man's worst produced a dead Savior—God's best, a risen Lord. With arms outstretched, the Christ of Calvary had intercepted Saul on the road to Damascus and in living testimony to His risen power had exploded all Saul's objections and shown Himself to be unequivocally the Son of God.

In his powerful explanation of the Resurrection addressed to the Corinthians, Paul made the uncontestable statement "if Christ is not risen, then our preaching is empty" (1 Cor. 15:14). In the ongoing proclamation of the gospel he stated the converse—since Christ is risen, our preaching and our faith have validity, because in the Resurrection God clearly placed before a watching world the unique Son of God who was dead but now lives in the power of an endless life. That Christ was alive Paul did not doubt—how could he after being confronted by Him on the Damascus Road?—and having no doubts about the Resurrection, he had no doubts about Christ and the Good News of God centered in the person and the work of the One whom he delighted to call Jesus Christ our Lord.

PAUL'S WARMHEARTED INTEREST IN PEOPLE

[7] To all who are in Rome, beloved of God, called to be saints:

Grace to you and peace from God our Father and the Lord Jesus Christ.

[8] First, I thank my God through Jesus Christ for you all, that your faith is spoken of throughout the whole world. [9] For God is my witness, whom I serve with my spirit in the gospel of His Son, that without ceasing I make mention of you always in my prayers, [10] making request if, by some means, now at last I may find a way in the will of God to come to you. [11] For I long to see you, that I may impart to you some spiritual gift, so that you may be established— [12] that is, that I may be encouraged together with you by the mutual faith both of you and me.

—Romans 1:7–12

It is not uncommon for a hard-driving man like Paul to be singularly unsociable. Driven as they are by hidden forces neither known nor desired by other people, they tend to isolate themselves from all but those who share their motivation or contribute to their goals. It would not be surprising to discover, in Paul, an aloofness related to position and a detachment attributable to his vision, but this was not the case. While he was not prepared to surrender his apostleship or to deviate from the sometimes unpleasant responsibilities of his office, Paul nevertheless displayed the great love for people without which a minister of Christ is severely handicapped.

Even his formal greetings (v. 7) were touched with a warmth that indicated his attitude toward the Roman believers whom he had never met: *"To all who are in Rome, beloved of God, called to be saints: Grace to you and peace from God our Father and the Lord Jesus Christ."*

In the same way that he reveled in his own sense of calling he recognized that they were also called. He, like them, had been *"called of Jesus Christ"* (v. 6), and while he was specifically called to be an apostle they were *"called to be saints"* (v. 7). They shared a common calling, acknowledged a common Lord, and knew something of the privilege of being set apart for a special task, as in Paul's case, or simply set apart to be special people in their case—for such is the meaning of *"called to be saints."*

In addition both he and they were conscious that, while God loves His whole creation, those who acknowledge His Son are specially "beloved of God." To Paul it was obvious that he should develop a deep relationship with those with whom he shared so much. No wonder he expressed himself as we read in verses 8–12.

Ever the evangelist and missionary—as well as theologian and teacher—Paul loved to hear about churches that were actively engaged in the propagation of the gospel. This was certainly the case at Rome, for, as he said, *"your faith is spoken of throughout the whole world"* (v. 8). Evidently the church at Rome was a topic of Roman conversation. The constant stream of people from the "eternal city" no doubt circulated stories about the life and witness of this remarkable group of believers over a wide area. It seems almost as if the church of the first century had a quality of life and a vitality of witness that made them a talking point in their immediate environment, and, in the case of Ephesus, Thessalonica, and Rome, over a much greater area.

It is a sad reflection on today's church that this is not always the contemporary experience. Neither, we might add, is the total lack of reservation in Paul's thanksgiving about their effectiveness. Not for him any questions about their integrity, innuendoes about their orthodoxy, or similar disparaging remarks which one has almost come to expect from those who comment on fellowships outside their sphere of influence. The fact that the Romans were not his converts and that the church at Rome was not one he had founded did nothing to diminish his genuine delight in what God had done in their midst. He exhibited the same spirit in later years when from his prison cell he wrote to the Philippians about his joy in the fact that Christ was being preached by his opponents. To Paul there was a grandeur about the gospel that should never be hidden in the murky mists of petty feud or professional jealousy.

Thanksgiving and intercession are inextricably bound up in each other as Paul demonstrated in a number of his letters. The praise for what had been accomplished often led to petition that more would be done, while sometimes the deep longings for blessing expressed in intercession were of necessity interspersed with glad outbursts of praise for blessing received. Using what to us may appear to be extravagant language to confirm an apparently minor point, he said, *"for God is my witness. . . that without ceasing I make mention of you always in my prayers"* (v. 9). To call God as a witness to a statement about praying may seem unnecessary to us but it occurs to me that that may be a reflection on our casual approach to prayer rather than a question about the intensity of Paul's approach. Perhaps more missionaries would be prayed for if modern Christians asked God to witness their solemn commitments to pray rather than the somewhat flippant promises which are so readily made and forgotten. His prayer was specific: he was asking God to make it possible for him to get to Rome. But there are interesting aspects to his prayer that should not be overlooked. He stipulated *"some means,"* which presumably meant he was open to all possibilities! There is a faint note of weariness and longing in the words *"now at last"* but there is still the doggedness and determination so characteristic of his whole approach as he adds *"I may find a way. . . to come to you."*

Notwithstanding weariness, openness to all means, doggedness and determination and deep longing to get to Rome, one thing shines through his prayers: he was only interested in getting there *"in the will of God."* Sometimes out of frustration we try to manipulate our circumstances and, not infrequently, out of earnest zeal and enthusiastic commitment, we leave no stone unturned in our efforts to accomplish what we desire to see accomplished. But there is always the danger that our manipulations may lead us into situations inferior to God's best and circumstances related more to our design than to God's will.

There is a safeguard against our own willfulness not only in submission to God's will but also in commitment to the well-being of others. This was delightfully illustrated by Paul's touching words, *"For I long to see you, that I may impart to you some spiritual gift, so that you may be established"* (v. 11). In the vertical dimension, he wanted to visit Rome to do God's will. On the horizontal, his desire to visit Rome was to do them good, leaving little room for selfish desire. After years of ministry Paul still had an insatiable desire to be with people and to see them blessed through the imparting of a spiritual gift. Godet comments, "A *'charisma'* (gift) is a concrete manifestation of grace *('charis')*. The epithet 'spiritual' shows the nature and the source of the gift which he hopes to impart to his readers (the spirit, the *'pneuma'*)."[1]

As we have already seen, in his traditional greeting Paul had expressed a desire that *"grace and peace"* should be the experience of those to whom he was writing. But when he used these terms he invested the traditional with spiritual content because he genuinely wanted them to experience God's grace through the exercise of the spiritual gifts in the fellowship. On numerous occasions as I have traveled in South Germany, Austria, and parts of Switzerland, I have been greeted by the solid natives of those beautiful areas with the traditional *"Grüss Gott"* (literally, "God bless you") and I have often wondered if those who so greet me have any idea how their formal wishes may become actual in my experience. For Paul, formality gave way to intense practicality as he made plans to exercise and share with the believers in Rome the gift of the Spirit with which he had been entrusted.

Of course, we must be careful to note that the exercise of these gifts was to take place with the very definite objective that they would be "established" or strengthened. There can be a tendency among Christians for gifts of teaching or preaching and other spiritual gifts to be used to entertain or intrigue, to fascinate or amuse; but this is a gross abuse. When the gifted man of God comes to town he should come in the will of God for the strengthening of the people. When the people come under the influence of his gift they should be open to the strengthening ministry of the Spirit. When the servant of God leads a congregation in worship through music, entertainment should never be the prime objective—the establishing of believers should be the goal of both the one ministering and those being ministered to. The understanding of this on the part of God's people would lead to an immeasurable improvement in much spiritual activity.

Perhaps the most delightful touch from Paul is seen in his transparently honest statement, *"that is, that I may be encouraged together with you by the mutual faith both of you and me"* (v. 12). The great apostle, intent on ministering in Rome for the church's benefit, was careful to let the Roman believers know that his coming was not only going to result in their benefit but also in his blessing. No doubt they would expect to be blessed by his ministry, but they may never have considered that they could help him. Some ministers with apostolic pretensions are careful to preserve an aura of detached sufficiency that leads people to believe that the blessing flows only one way—but these ministers are sadly mistaken.

Years ago, as a young preacher, I was invited to share the ministry at a convention with Dr. Paul Rees, who for years had been to me a model both as believer and minister. You can imagine that I approached the series of meetings with mingled apprehension and anticipation—anticipation of the joy that would be mine to sit at his feet for a week; apprehension that he might sit at mine! He never missed a meeting at which I spoke, never failed to express appreciation for the message I brought—and to my intense amazement and embarrassment never failed to take copious notes! He showed me there is always a mutuality of blessing among the people of God and that like his namesake he could be strengthened through a "no-name" believer just as much as he could be used of God in his strengthening ministry.

PAUL'S ENTHUSIASTIC COMMITMENT TO HIS WORK

Human frailties must be recognized in all human endeavor. People get tired, discouraged, bored, and disillusioned, with the result that both they and their work suffer. At the time of writing the Roman epistle, Paul had been actively engaged in his ministry for almost thirty hectic, energy-sapping years. He had endured enough hardship and been exposed to enough trauma and excitement to last most people for half a dozen lifetimes. Great triumphs had attended his labors, but persistent problems dogged his steps. Nevertheless, his enthusiasm had in no way abated. As we read of his plans to travel to Rome, it is easy to forget that he was almost sixty years of age—such is the vigor and vision of his thought and expression.

13 Now I do not want you to be unaware, brethren, that I often planned to come to you (but was hindered until now), that I might have some fruit among you also, just as among

the other Gentiles. [14] I am a debtor both to Greeks and to barbarians, both to wise and to unwise. [15] So, as much as is in me, I am ready to preach the gospel to you who are in Rome also.

[16] For I am not ashamed of the gospel of Christ, for it is the power of God to salvation for everyone who believes, for the Jew first and also for the Greek. [17] For in it the righteousness of God is revealed from faith to faith; as it is written, *"The just shall live by faith."*

—Romans 1:13–17

It is possible that the Roman Christians had expressed some concern to Paul that the apostle of the Gentiles had not seen fit to visit the great Gentile center. Paul must have been most anxious to assure his Roman colleagues that his failure to minister in their city was certainly not by design but was the result of circumstances outside his control. His desire to *"have fruit"* among them as he had in other cities was as deep and enduring as his sense of calling to Gentiles the world over. In fact, he labored under a great sense of obligation, seeing himself as *"a debtor both to Greeks and to barbarians, both to wise and to unwise"* (v. 14).

There is something almost frightening in the intensity of Paul's statement about being a *"debtor."* It is as if he felt that God had revealed the gospel to him not so much for his own benefit as for the benefit of the Gentiles—a situation not unlike that of a trustee banker or stockholder to whom securities are entrusted by an elderly grandparent for the benefit of minor grandchildren as yet too immature to handle their own financial affairs. To the degree in which the trustee holds the securities in his own name he is indebted to the one for whom they were made available. Paul's compelling sense of indebtedness to God for His grace and to people because of his ministry meant that he was never free to feel that his work was done. It is hard to imagine how Paul was able to live with such a constant load of spiritual responsibility; yet, at the same time, it is harder to grasp how many believers are able to live complacently without any sense of obligation.

The fact that Paul placed no limits on his ministry, in the sense that he endeavored to reach all types of people, is, I believe, of major significance. He felt obliged to minister to Greeks, barbarians, wise, and unwise. That means those who had the benefit of exposure to Greek culture, those without such exposure, those who were sophisticated, and those utterly devoid of education—in fact, everybody! In days of more and more specialization, it is perhaps necessary for us to remind ourselves that we are called to reach people in general, not exclusively our own kind of people. Paul, the educated and sophisticated product of Tarsus, would, no doubt, have felt much more in common with the Greeks and the wise than with the barbarians and the unwise, but to him this was a matter of no consequence. If they were people, that was all he needed to know. He was prepared to find ways of bridging the gaps between himself and them in order that the message of the gospel might be brought to them.

On top of the sense of his obligation rested a great eagerness to go to Rome. *"So, as much as is in me, I am ready to preach the gospel to you who are in Rome also"* (v. 15). I'm sure that we know ourselves and others well enough to recognize that the obligated people of this world are not necessarily the most eager people under the sun! In fact, the sense of obligation often produces a disgruntled attitude and a minimal acceptance of responsibility. Not so for the apostle—he was desperately anxious to "evangelize" in Rome. It is worth noting that his objective was to go much further than to encourage and establish the church, but also to proclaim the gospel to those outside the fellowship of faith.

Warming to his theme, Paul went on to insist that he was *"not ashamed of the gospel"*—not that anyone ever had grounds for thinking that he might be! Why should he be ashamed of a message which was to him so obviously *"the power of God to salvation"?* The Greek word *soteria,* meaning "salvation," is related to *sos,* meaning "safe and sound," reminding us that what God had made available to mankind through Christ was the possibility of spiritual safety and deliverance and wholistic soundness. Safety for all eternity—soundness for all of life.

Why, reasoned Paul, should anyone be deferential or apologetic about such a message, particularly when it was not just an enchanting philosophical concept but rather a reality backed by nothing less than *"the power of God"?* In his travels he had seen God's power at work through the gospel, making every conceivable type of person "safe and sound." So without hesitation he proclaimed this gospel as a powerful life-changing agent *"for everyone who believes, for the Jew first and also for the Greek"* (v. 16).

Marvelous as it is that the gospel is the means of blessing to mankind, Paul was careful to alert his readers to the fact that the gospel is also the means whereby *"the righteousness of God is revealed from faith to faith"* (v. 17). From a purely human point of view, it is understandable that the interest of human beings in the gospel may be limited, initially, to what God is prepared to do for people. But the gospel goes beyond that and reveals what God is like as well as what God will give. It demonstrates who He is in addition to what He does. The *"righteousness of God"* which the gospel reveals is an expression so full of meaning that it would be true to say that the rest of the epistle is designed to explain it. At this juncture we will content ourselves with the understanding that the *"righteousness of God"* in Romans means, primarily, that God is always "in the right" and can be relied upon, therefore, to do what is right, for the simple reason that what is right can be determined only with reference to Him. Flowing from the fact that God will always be in the right, Paul explained how the gospel reveals the way in which God makes men and women who are "in the wrong" to be "in the right" without jeopardizing His own righteousness.

How does this come about? By faith, insisted the apostle, and to undergird his introductory statement he quoted Habakkuk 2:4: *"the just shall live by his faith"*—a reminder that men are justified (made right) by faith in order that having been made right by faith they might live rightly by faith—or as Paul expressed it *"from faith to faith"* (v. 17).

As you will see, Paul has slipped out of his introduction into the main theme of his teaching, and we have slipped in with him! Before we go on, however, may I remind you that the introductory verses of the epistle radiate with the beauty of the apostle's attitudes to himself, his message, his brethren, and his work. They not only present great insight into the author but confront us with the great challenge to examine our attitudes also.

NOTES

1.   Godet, *Commentary on Romans,* p. 87.

CHAPTER TWO—FIRST, THE BAD NEWS
ROMANS 1:18–32

Scripture Outline

Man's Suppression of Truth (1:18–20)

Man's Rejection of God (1:21–22)

Man's Substitution for Creation (1:23–28)

Man's Appreciation of Evil (1:28–32)

Paul, as we saw in the previous chapter, had a boundless enthusiasm for his work as a proclaimer of the gospel of Christ. He was overwhelmed with eagerness to get to Rome by any means and share the Good News both with those in the church who knew and believed it and those among the teeming masses of the city who were unaware of the fact that God's righteousness had been revealed.

This righteousness of God is the theme of both the gospel Paul preached and the epistle he wrote to the Romans. Accordingly, this will play a major part in our thinking as we proceed with this study. The fact that God is righteous—or always "in the right"—is both a challenge and a comfort. The challenge comes to mankind through the realization that the rightness of human action must be determined not by the fluctuating moral standards of a volatile society but by the unchanging revelation of an eternal God. The comfort of knowing that God is always "in the right" is found in the experience of the humble person who, in consistently turning to the Lord for wisdom when surrounded by a cacophony of contradictions, discovers that truth can be known and that right still exists. Comfort, however, is short-lived because, knowing what is right and doing what is right are so far from each other. The closer a man gets to the rightness of God, the more uncomfortable he becomes about the unrighteousness of himself. The gospel, however, recognizes this, and in its revelation of the righteousness of God shows how the one who is not "in the right" before God can have his situation rectified. There is a legal note in the word "righteousness" and thus Romans, at times, gives off an air of the courtroom. Strictly speaking, the way in which the unrighteous become righteous through the action of the righteousness of God is through man standing before the bar of God and being declared righteous by God Himself. Nothing could be finer than for a man who knows in his heart that he is far from being "in the right" to be told by God that he is, after all, in the right. But, as in all courtroom scenes, before the person standing in front of the judge can be declared righteous, charges have to be made against him and evidence presented to substantiate the charges. In effect, this means that before we can hear the Good News with a degree of comprehension, we must first grasp the measure of the bad news—the charges against us. This Paul proceeded to do in his systematic presentation to the Roman believers. He charged that while the righteousness of God has been revealed there has also been a revelation of the *"wrath of God."*

> 18 For the wrath of God is revealed from heaven against all ungodliness and unrighteousness of men, who suppress the truth in unrighteousness, 19 because what may be known of God is manifest in them, for God has shown it to them. 20 For since the creation of the world His invisible attributes are clearly seen, being understood by the things that are made, even His eternal power and Godhead, so that they are without excuse,
>
> *—Romans 1:18–20*

The moment we embark on a study of the Roman epistle we are confronted with the statement that the wrath of God is part of the righteousness of God—a concept so unnerving to many and distasteful to others that innumerable attempts have been made to avoid the subject. Even a cursory glance at Paul's argument, however, will show that any attempt to avoid what he had to say about the wrath of God at the beginning of his presentation of the gospel would be disastrous. The answer to the problem of the "wrath of God" is to be found in understanding it, not avoiding it. To human beings, who periodically either give way to wrath and feel subsequently embarrassed or are subjected to wrath and feel hurt and humiliated, wrath is a most reprehensible human characteristic. But divine wrath should never be confused with human anger for it contains none of the uncontrolled passion, the unreasonable outbursts, the self-vindication that are the unfortunate ingredients of human wrath. God's wrath is "right": it is a holy response to the unholy, a just reaction to the unjust, a pure rejection of the impure. In fact, for God not to express wrath at much of what goes on in our world would be wrong. Not only is His wrath intrinsically right—failure to respond in wrath would be intrinsically wrong. We know this is true because we believe that imperfect man is not only capable of righteous anger, but also has a moral responsibility to express outrage in certain circumstances. If he fails to express it he is seen to be less than a desirable person. But what human actions and attitudes have moved God to wrath?

MAN'S SUPPRESSION OF TRUTH

Modern man, so sophisticated in technology and skilled in managing the complexities of the modern world, is uncharacteristically content to live in self-imposed unsophistication in the area of the spiritual. All too often he feels comfortable expressing ignorance of spiritual things and even goes so far as to suggest that he doesn't have the time or the ability to unravel the mysteries of God. Indifference and complacency are, therefore, commonplace, and may even be coupled with a sense of well-being based on the assumption that because truth is so hard to come by and one doesn't have the time to come by it, one cannot be reasonably expected to know more than one does.

Paul totally opposed this position. He insisted that man is not ignorant of truth because it is so difficult to discover but because he has "suppressed the truth" that is uncomfortably clear. Man's problem is not a lack of spiritual sophistication leading to confusion but an unrighteous and ungodly response to the truth leading to rejection. It isn't what man did not know but what he will not do that is the root of the matter. The word "suppress" means "to hold firmly," and it can be used both in a positive sense, as in "let us hold fast the confession of our hope without wavering" (Heb. 10:23) and negatively "to hold down, resist, or suppress." In secular Greek, the word was used to describe a helmsman "holding" the course as his boat battled through wind and current. Paul was careful in using the word to convey the sheer determination on the part of mankind to stand firmly against truth and to hold rigidly to this position of opposition to the truth. Note carefully that his position is a product not of an unfortunate lack of information but a deliberate rejection of the information given. This God will not tolerate.

It was Pilate who put into words the attitude of many when he asked Christ, "What is truth?" The answer, of course, was standing right in front of him. No man ever had a greater opportunity to know the truth than the Roman who sat in judgment of the Galilean, for Christ consistently had proclaimed Himself to be the truth. This thought was picked up by the apostle Paul when he explained that "the truth" is *what may be known of God.*" Part of the suppressive activity of man is seen in his commitment to regarding MAN as the center of reality or truth and relegating GOD either to a position of relative unimportance or total irrelevance. It cannot be overemphasized that all reality is to be found in the "knowledge of God"; failure to recognize this is what Paul calls the suppression of the truth.

When Copernicus, the Polish astronomer, started to study the heavens, he gradually came to the conclusion that the earth was not the static center around which the universe revolved but, rather, was a moving planet which itself revolved around the sun. He was, however, strangely reluctant to publish his findings, no doubt because he knew what a battle he would have trying to convince his contemporaries that man and his world are not the center of all existence. Man has always felt that he is the center and everything revolves around him. To be told otherwise, whether by an astronomer or a theologian, has always presented man with extreme problems. To insist that the core of truth is in "Him" rather than "us" and that we find our significance revolving around Him rather than the converse, poses a problem similar to that of Copernicus, because man, frankly, doesn't want to know this kind of thing. This is part of the truth that he suppresses.

Some men would vigorously deny this, arguing either that God is not knowable, or that man is so limited in his capability and God is so vast in His being that man can hope to accomplish little more than struggle to the best of his ability to discover as much as he can of God. Paul, however, insisted that the truth *"is manifest in them, for God has shown it to them.*" The use of the Greek aorist tense for the words translated "has shown" points to a definite, powerful, and unequivocal act of God in which knowledge of God has been made available to man in the inner recesses of his being. Some see evidence of this in the in-built sense of morality common to all men. Others point to the fact of man's innate "religiousness."

Calvin wrote, "There is no nation so barbarous, no race so brutish as not to be imbued with the conviction that there is a God. Even those who, in other respects, seem to differ least from the lower animals constantly retain some sense of religion."[1] He quoted Plutarch (whom he called a "heathen"): "You may find cities without walls, or literature, or kings, or houses, or wealth, or money, without gymnasia or theaters. But no one ever saw a city without temples and gods."[2] Similar evidence of man's inbuilt sense that truth is in some way connected with the being of God has been presented in more recent times by our ubiquitous pollsters. They inform us that while most people in America have no deeply felt spiritual experience or commitment, practically all of them still insist that they believe in the existence of God.

When Paul spoke of God having shown the truth about Himself to mankind he was not referring solely to an inner subjective experience in which man had an intuitive sense of God. God has revealed Himself in the created world in such a way that *"His invisible attributes are clearly seen, being understood by the things that are made"* (v. 20). From this statement it is apparent that man's intelligence and observational powers, as well as his moral insight and spiritual intuition, are all involved in God's self-revelation to man. I remember on one particularly stormy night flying with two friends in a light aircraft from Tennessee to Wisconsin. A massive storm stretched across our path and our pilot elected to press on regardless. First we looked for a break in the storm but found none. Then we tried to fly over the storm but found it went higher than we could! So we attempted to fly under the problem, but this was not possible, so we took a deep breath and flew straight through! Air currents of unbelievable force picked up our small plane and literally hurled it around the sky. The crash of thunder was so loud at times it drowned the noise of the engine, and the lightning was so intense that we were blinded by its persistent flashes crackling all around us. I have never been so glad to put my two big feet on terra firma as when we finally arrived at our destination. But I came out of the experience enriched. As never before I had seen the sheer immensity of the power of nature, but I had also been able to interpret this power as a demonstration of God's *"invisible attributes . . . even His eternal power and Godhead."* This ability to translate what theologians call "general revelation" into the knowledge of God's invisible attributes is a gift of God without which man would see, feel, hear, and experience only inanimate, impersonal forces and respond to them as such. Fortunately, human experience shows that man in all types of civilizations has looked at such forces with much greater insight and has been able to see behind them (however imperfectly) that which points to God Himself.

The word "Godhead" (Greek, *Theiotēs*), which is not uncommon in secular Greek usage, appears only once in the New Testament. It has been defined as "the quality of the divine: that which shows God to be God and gives Him the right to worship."[3] There is enough evidence available to man through the revelation of creation and man's God-given abilities to observe, understand, and interpret such revelation, to know not only *that* God is, but also *who* He is. This powerful conviction of the apostle was forcefully illustrated in his address to the philosophers of Athens. He described God as the "God who made the world and everything in it . . . and He has made from one blood every nation of men to dwell on all the face of the earth, and has determined their preappointed times . . . so that they should seek the Lord . . . for in Him we live and move and have our being . . ." (Acts 17:24–28). The Athenians, despite this, had embarked on a variety of religious exercises which included worship of "the unknown god." Paul had endeavored to declare that God and Father of the Lord Jesus was knowable, and to them, but without much discernible response. No doubt, he saw this as a further suppression of the truth. This he regarded as inexcusable; in fact, he regarded the whole race as without excuse. The Greek at this point allows a translation suggesting either that God's intention in revealing Himself was that man might be without excuse or that the result of such revelation is that man can never satisfactorily claim he had no knowledge of God.

There is a chilling severity about the bad news that God's revelation of Himself had been so callously rejected by man, that God's righteous anger at such behavior has been revealed and that, try as he may to avoid the situation, man is without excuse.

MAN'S REJECTION OF GOD

21 because, although they knew God, they did not glorify Him as God, nor were thankful, but became futile in their thoughts, and their foolish hearts were darkened. 22 Professing to be wise, they became fools,

—Romans 1:21–22

Paul not only insisted that God has revealed Himself to mankind, but he went so far as to assert that, *"although they knew*

God, they did not glorify Him as God, nor were thankful." The knowledge of God that even the most primitive man has available to him is enough to lead him to an attitude of glorifying and thanking God. Ideally a man in the normal course of events would be so sensitive to all that he is learning of God that he would make the transition from knowledge to response. The reality of the situation, however, is that man chooses not to respond adequately and accounts for his actions by stressing his inadequate knowledge in contrast to God's assertion that the problem is inadequate response. The situation is not unlike that with which all parents of small children are familiar, when youngsters confronted with certain unsatisfactory actions claim ignorance rather than responsibility.

Man's refusal to glorify God as God is as unacceptable to God as the suppression of the truth. To glorify God as God means, as Godet wrote, "to draw from the contemplation of the work the distinct view of the divine order; then, in the way of adoration to invest this sublime being with all the perfection which He displayed in His creation."[4] Failure to do this can be the result of mental laziness, moral irresponsibility, willful disregard, or any one of a wide variety of actions and attitudes common to man. The Greeks of Paul's day, despite their unquestioned brilliance, had taken the truth revealed to them and, instead of allowing it to lead them to a knowledge of the true God, had arrived at a pantheon of gods whose characters were little more than glorified enlargements of the Greeks themselves. The Romans were no better.

Objections may be raised on the grounds that not all people have the mental capability to start with an observation of creation and come to such an accurate view of the Creator that they begin to glorify Him, but whatever merit there may be in this argument, there is no doubt that all people are capable of being thankful. God's awful indictment of the human race is that they were not even prepared to respond to Him in expressing the gratitude that even a child can show to a parent, or a helpless invalid to a nurse.

Nature, as we know, abhors a vacuum, and the same thing can be said of the human spirit. Man's unwillingness to glorify and thank God in the way that he was created to function has left in his innermost being a great void which cannot stay empty. Into this void has poured all manner of spiritual disease, and men and women *"became futile in their thoughts, and their foolish hearts were darkened. Professing to be wise, they became fools"* (Rom.

1:21, 22). Thought life became controlled by futility, aspirations and desires were shrouded in the darkness of egotism, folly conquered wisdom, and man didn't even seem to know what was happening.

The word "fool," which is so common in Scripture, needs to be carefully studied. In modern language, a fool may be an uninhibited person who is the life and soul of the party, an unfortunate person who is deficient in intelligence, or someone given to unwise actions. But the fool in Scripture is a person who willfully makes moral decisions contrary to God's instructions—a person who has adopted a stance in opposition to God's position, one who has said in his heart, *"There is no God"* (Ps. 14:1).

Paul had lived and worked in the world where the philosophical speculations of the Greeks played an enormous role in the thought-life and the lifestyle of the people. The Greeks were so sure of themselves that they tended to regard all others as "barbarians." Yet with all their wisdom, philosophy, speculation, and rational debate, they had arrived at a point of total confusion as far as spiritual insights were concerned. Paul did not hesitate to point this out to the Athenians when he told them he had observed the shrine to "the unknown God"—an experience which tacitly affirmed what he was teaching, that "the world through wisdom did not know God" (1 Cor. 1:21).

Kenneth Prior has illustrated how their "wisdom" was "foolishness," not only in the realm of theology: "Take for example chemistry. One view which was current among them was that everything comes ultimately from water. Another theory propounded by one of their philosophers was that air was the primary substance of the material world while another philosopher came to the rival conclusion that fire was the fundamental principle. Finally there was the great Aristotle himself, who settled for four elements—earth, fire, air and water!"[5] Prior saw the failure of the Greeks to advance human knowledge of physics, chemistry, and other sciences in the same light as their failure to discover God, and he attributed both to the Greek's love affair with human reason which is futile "even when it is the mind of a Socrates or an Aristotle that is engaged in it."[6] Modern illustrations of the fertility and futility of human wisdom abound. Contemporary ideas and philosophies flourish in bewildering profusion, but so many of them say little that is new because they are simply parading the ideas of old in a new dress. How old can be seen when we consider the third reason for God's wrath.

MAN'S SUBSTITUTION FOR CREATION

[23] and changed the glory of the incorruptible God into an image made like corruptible man—and birds and four-footed animals and creeping things.

[24] Therefore God also gave them up to uncleanness, in the lusts of their hearts, to dishonor their bodies among themselves, [25] who exchanged the truth of God for the lie, and worshiped and served the creature rather than the Creator, who is blessed forever. Amen.

[26] For this reason God gave them up to vile passions. For even their women exchanged the natural use for what is against nature. [27] Likewise also the men, leaving the natural use of the woman, burned in their lust for one another, men with men committing what is shameful, and receiving in themselves the penalty of their error which was due.

[28] And even as they did not like to retain God in their knowledge, God gave them over to a debased mind, to do those things which are not fitting;

—Romans 1:23–28

God has shown Himself to man "since creation," but it is true to say that man began to reject the obvious revelation from the earliest times. He *"changed the glory of the incorruptible God into an image made like corruptible man—birds and four-footed animals and creeping things"* (v. 23).

The similarity between the lists of idols Paul gave and the branches of creation described in Genesis 1:20–25 is not accidental. Neither is the obvious link between Paul's use of the words "image" and "like[ness]" and the well-known verse "Let us make man in our image, after our likeness. . ." (Gen. 1:26).

The thrust of Paul's words is inescapable. From earliest times man has not only suppressed the truth and rejected God as God, but he has totally reversed the divine order by making God in his own image after his own likeness and then, to add insult to injury, has stooped to the point of making God in the image of the lower echelons of creation. It is this blatant audacity of man's actions in substituting his own order and creation for that of God which is so insulting to God. Of course, the root of the problem is in man's utterly arrogant preoccupation with himself. Tourists from all over the world have viewed the wonders of ancient Rome, Greece, and Egypt without realizing that much of the magnificence was man's tribute to himself and an insult to God. We should never forget that many of the statues that grace our museums, pleasing our aesthetic senses and sparking our curiosity, provoke God to wrath. Neither should we overlook the fact that ancient idolatry is alive and well in the modern world. The article on "Idolatry" in the *Zondervan Pictorial Encyclopedia of the Bible* lists some of the better-known gods of the Mesopotamian pantheon: Ishtar, goddess of love; Nabu, the patron of science and learning; Nergal, the god of war and hunting.[7] Today we sit in Ishtar Cinema, study in Nabu University, and yell our heads off in Nergal's Stadium—modern places and attitudes of worship.

This is not to suggest that the modern world does not produce much that is wonderful any more than it is to dare to suggest that many of the ancient achievements were less than stupendous. But behind the splendor of all man's achievements so often lies a deification of himself which is idolatry. The seriousness of this cannot be described more pungently than in the words of the apostle, *"Who exchanged the truth of God for the lie, and worshiped and served the creature rather than the Creator, who is blessed forever. Amen."* (v. 25). The apostle found the thought of the depths to which man had fallen so distasteful that he felt obliged to include his own doxology to the Creator. As if to disassociate himself completely from "the lie" that man's ingenious ignorance had foisted on the race, Paul "blessed the Lord" who, in contrast to the creatures who will mix their remains with the dust of their idols, lives "forever."

The Hebrews had been aware from ancient times that God had said, "You shall have no other gods before Me. You shall not make for yourself a carved image—any likeness of anything that is in heaven above, or that is in the earth beneath, or that is in the waters under the earth; you shall not bow down to them nor serve them" (Ex. 20:3–5). And yet, despite these clear prohibitions, God's people had been influenced more by the idolatry of their neighbors than by the commands of their Lord. The prophets persistently condemned such aberrant behavior, and their successors in the Christian era, such as Paul, were deeply offended by the idolatrous practices so common in their day. In the second century Tertullian wrote in his work "On Idolatry" that it is "the principal charge against the human race, the world's deepest guilt, the all-inclusive cause of judgment."[8] No doubt the contemporary church needs to address the subject of man's idolatry with more of the intensity of the prophets and the fathers, bearing in mind, as we have seen, the cause of such behavior and the inevitable consequences, namely, the wrath of God.

When we think of the wrath of God there is a tendency to project into the future as if divine action against man's sins is being reserved for a coming day. Paul taught that the wrath was already being dispensed in ways which many would not recognize as the wrath of God. He explained that the divine reaction was to be seen in that *"God also gave them up to uncleanness, in the lusts of their hearts, to dishonor their bodies among themselves. . . . God gave them up to vile passions. For even their women exchanged the natural use for what is against nature. Likewise also the men, leaving the natural use of the woman, burned in their lust for one another, men with men committing what is shameful, and receiving in themselves the penalty of their error which was due. . . . God gave them over to a debased mind. . ."* (Rom. 1:24–28).

The triple use of the expression *"God gave them up to"* or *"over"* is an obvious clue to understanding what Paul meant by his statement that the wrath of God is revealed. The reaction of God in response to the action of mankind was not to send fire and brimstone on the defenseless heads of pagan idol worshipers any more than He is doing that today. He did something far more subtle and infinitely more appalling—He gave man the absolute right to choose his own course of action and then gave him the perfect freedom to live with the consequences. There is an awful rightness about this—so right it cannot be repudiated; so awful it must not be denied. Yet the tragedy of humanity is that it fails to recognize the wrath of God and the righteousness of God at work in everyday experience.

Man used his God-given freedom to remake God in his own image—an act of such arrogant self-centeredness that it elevated the human above the divine and placed the physical and visible above the spiritual and invisible. Accordingly, the human heart and its lusts take precedence over the divine being and His plan, and physical experiences become more important than spiritual realities. This can lead only to *"uncleanness"* which will lead people to *"dishonor their bodies among themselves."* In modern times this has been called the sexual revolution, but it would be better if those who are living with the consequences of their action could see through the glamor of their promiscuity something of the wrath of God in their own emptiness and loneliness and ultimate lack of satisfaction.

Two things—freedom and pleasure—captivated the thinking of the people of Rome. Their freedom, safeguarded by their remarkable armies, was spent in pleasure. The more free they felt, the more pleasure they desired, and as freedom and pleasure reigned hand in hand, ironically both freedom and pleasure were forging their own chains. They became slaves to freedom, in bondage to pleasure. Freedom must be protected, but pleasure distracts from the disciplines of protection, so freedom perishes. Pleasure needs satisfying, but the search for new satisfaction becomes a burden that denies freedom. Believing that life was to be found in self-produced freedom and self-gratifying pleasure, the Romans, like many succeeding generations, exchanged the truth of God for the lie: "the lie" being that man has his own destiny in his own hands and is capable of providing the "good life" for himself.

Because sexual freedom and pleasure have always been dear to the heart of man, when freedom and pleasure become "liberated" from the truth of God and subjected to "the lie," it is in the area of sexual morality and behavior that the consequences can be seen starkly and unmistakably. The sexual behavior that was common in Paul's time both in Greece and Rome was a scandal even to pagan thinkers. Barclay, referring to Romans 1:26–32, wrote: "It might seem that this passage is the work of some almost hysterical moralist who was exaggerating the contemporary situation and painting it in colors of rhetorical hyperbole. It describes a situation of a degeneracy of morals almost without parallel in human history. But there is nothing that Paul said that the Greek and Roman writers of the age did not themselves say."[9] Similar, powerful criticism of a contemporary Western moral degeneracy has long been heard through the preaching of many a concerned pastor and the careful teaching of Christian moralists. But recently even secular film critics have raised their voices in alarm, some sociologists have begun to express concern, and political leaders have spoken out against what they see as a chronic social malaise.

Another interesting parallel between the Rome of Paul's day and the contemporary society in which we live is seen in the place that homosexuality holds in the thinking of both civilizations. Barclay described ancient Rome in striking terms: "Vice did not stop with the crude and natural vices. Society from top to bottom was riddled with unnatural vice. Fourteen out of the first fifteen Roman Emperors were homosexuals."[10] The Kinsey Report on *The Sexual Behavior of the Human Male*, published in 1948, and its counterpart on the female, published in 1953, stated most clearly that the incidence of homosexuality was much greater than has been imagined. The findings of these reports, the teachings of

Sigmund Freud, and the strong insistence on human rights—including the rights of homosexuals—have served to bring homosexuality into the public consciousness. Reactions have been predictably varied. Dr. Don Williams in his helpful book *The Bond That Breaks* makes a strong plea for people not to be moved away from a biblical base as they attempt to work out their responses. He also insists that homosexuality will only be understood when human sexuality is understood. He adds: "God gives us the gift to be male *or* female . . . then calls us to live as male or female. . . . This call, however, may be rejected. Sin disrupts God's order, and homosexuality bears witness to that disruption. Paul shows in Romans 1:26ff that the homosexual person no longer knows that God has created him to live as male or female. Nature is thereby violated in homosexual acts."[11]

This "violation" was described by Paul in the strongest possible terms such as *"vile passions," "burned in their lust," "shameful,"* and he added that those engaging in such behavior were *"receiving in themselves the penalty of their error which was due."* It is particularly unfortunate that the word "gay" has become a synonym for "homosexual" because both biblical truth and practical observation point to the fact that there is more evidence of "penalty" than "gaiety" in those who live homosexually.

The logic of Paul's argument should not be missed. Those who reject what they know of God in so doing divorce themselves from truth and reality. This means, among other things, that a person out of touch with the reality of God is out of touch with reality, period, including the truth about humanity. To be out of touch with the meaning of humanity means a crisis of identity which is demonstrated in many ways, not least in confusion concerning sexuality. When sexuality is misunderstood, the sheer power of unrestrained sexual drive and uneducated sexual insight will produce all manner of aberrant sexual behavior. In short, confusion about God breeds confusion about man, which breeds confusion about sexuality, which produces sexual confusion and chaos. Far from being, as was fondly imagined by many, an enlightened age of sexual freedom, Paul showed his contemporaries that they lived in a dark day of divine wrath.

While Paul made a particular statement concerning homosexuality at this point in his argument, it would be a serious mistake to assume that he limited his remarks to this particular area of human experience. He went on to show that the confusion about humanity which shows itself in sexual chaos is also clearly demonstrated in societal disintegration. In a broad sweep of human relations he said,

> [28] And even as they did not like to retain God in their knowledge, God gave them over to a debased mind, to do those things which are not fitting; [29] being filled with all unrighteousness, sexual immorality, wickedness, covetousness, maliciousness; full of envy, murder, strife, deceit, evil-mindedness; they are whisperers, [30] backbiters, haters of God, violent, proud, boasters, inventors of evil things, disobedient to parents, [31] undiscerning, untrustworthy, unloving, unforgiving, unmerciful; [32] who, knowing the righteous judgment of God, that those who practice such things are deserving of death, not only do the same but also approve of those who practice them.
> —Romans 1:28–32

Without going into the details of the record of human misdemeanors listed here, we cannot avoid seeing that the societal malaise that abounds on every hand in our day was common in Paul's time too. In the home, the family, the marriage, the place of business, the stadium, the temple, there was and is overwhelming evidence of human disorientation Godward resulting in disintegration manward. The shame of the situation ought to be overwhelming. A sense of repentance and grief ought to permeate the human scene. A great reaching out for righteousness, restoration, and renewal ought to be the greatest human longing, but such is not the case. The appalling truth is that those who could reasonably be expected to react towards God in such a way do exactly the opposite, as Paul states in verse 32. This leads us to consider one more negative attitude of man.

MAN'S APPRECIATION OF EVIL

It is not only the absence of repentance which troubles the apostle, but the presence of celebration. Far from being overwhelmed with a sense of failure and responsibility, a carnival air of casual enjoyment prevails in human society. Instead of acting as guardians of each other's souls, people tend to function as encouragers of each other's destruction. Where mourning might be expected, rejoicing is to be seen; instead of wholesome disapproval of sin, there is a wholesale approval of unrighteousness.

Remember that all the confusion and the perversion, all the disgrace and the inappropriate response, the chaos, and the disintegration are, according to Paul, clear evidence that "the wrath of God" has been revealed. He has cataloged this sordid state of affairs as evidence of God's reaction to man's actions with the intention of showing those who recognize the truth of the bad news the glory of the Good News. Those to whom the wrath of God has been revealed are the ones most likely to be concerned that the righteousness of God has been revealed too. To those people Paul has much more to say.

NOTES

1. *Calvin's Institutes* (Grand Rapids: Associated Publishers), *Institutes of Christian Religion* I. III. 1.

2. Ibid., Index to Footnotes I. III. 1.

3. *Theological Dictionary of the New Testament,* 10 vols., ed. Gerhard Kittel and Gerhard Friedrich (Grand Rapids: Eerdmans, 1964-1976), 3:123.

4. Godet, *Commentary on Romans,* p. 104.

5. Kenneth F. W. Prior, *The Gospel in a Pagan Society* (Downers Grove, Ill.: InterVarsity Press, 1975), p. 68.

6. Ibid., p. 70.

7. *Zondervan Pictorial Encyclopedia of the Bible,* 3:243.

8. G. W. Bromiley, *Historical Theology* (Grand Rapids: Eerdmans, 1978), p. 30.

9. William Barclay, *The Letter to the Romans* (Edinburgh: St. Andrews Press), p. 23.

10. Ibid., p. 25.

11. Don Williams, *The Bond That Breaks* (Ventura, Calif.: Regal), p. 116.

CHAPTER THREE—THE JUDGMENT OF GOD
ROMANS 2:1–16

Scripture Outline

> The Inconsistency of Human Judgment (2:1)
> The Integrity of Divine Judgment (2:2–10)
> The Inevitability of Divine Judgment (2:11–16)

When Paul dictated the Roman letter to Tertius (Rom. 16:22), he obviously felt very deeply about the things he was saying. Scholars have shown that the Greek of the epistle is disjointed and ungrammatical at times, and on occasions sentences are not even completed. This suggests to me that Paul was pacing up and down pouring out his heart in the hearing of Tertius, who was trying his hardest to get the apostle's thoughts down on paper!

It must have been particularly difficult when the apostle adopted the literary style called the "diatribe"—a sort of debate conducted between the author and a nonexistent imaginary critic. He first appears at the beginning of the second chapter:

> **2:1** Therefore you are inexcusable, O man, whoever you are who judge, for in whatever you judge another you condemn yourself; for you who judge practice the same things.
> —*Romans 2:1*

THE INCONSISTENCY OF HUMAN JUDGMENT

Anonymous though Paul's critic may have been, there is no doubt that he represented a class of people who refused to be identified with those who were so scathingly denounced in the first chapter. It was not that they disagreed with Paul's evaluation of the

53

moral and spiritual degeneracy of the pagan world; they wanted to put as much distance as possible between themselves and those whom Paul had exposed. Obviously, the broad, sweeping generalities of the denunciation left plenty of room for individual exceptions even among the pagans themselves. Not all of them went to the extremes that Paul had outlined, and some of them were almost as outspoken in their objections as he. But it is unlikely that he had in mind such individual "enlightened" Gentiles when he introduced his imaginary debating opponent. In all probability, the spokesman was representing the Jewish people who were appalled by the idolatry of the Gentiles and all its associations. With their deep-rooted monotheism and their abhorrence of idols, they not only rejected the philosophical and moral degeneracy of the Gentiles but they regarded themselves as philosophically, morally, and spiritually superior. They would insist on being disassociated from anything and everything that might tarnish their reputation or prejudice their position.

It must be admitted that there is no clear identification of the Jewish people in the early part of this chapter, but in the tenth verse Paul speaks of the *"Jew first and. . . the Greek"* and in the seventeenth verse he specifically identifies and addresses a Jew. Perhaps he "eases" gradually into this identification because of the particularly delicate nature of the subject matter he wishes to introduce. Of all the subjects that are difficult to address, hypocrisy is probably one of the most difficult. How do you tell a person who feels, probably on what might appear to be good grounds, that he is morally superior to another, that in actuality his life is equally unacceptable? One method is to blurt it out bluntly and encounter his righteous indignation and total rejection!

This approach Paul disdained. It appears that he introduced a broad generality first of all with which most people would agree; that is, there are a lot of people who sit in judgment of others who are far from perfect themselves. Then, when this had been established and agreed upon, he more clearly identified those who were adopting such an attitude. Before going on with the details of Paul's exposure of the Jewish situation we need to look at the broad generalities on human judgment that he made. His fundamental concern was that man often has the capacity to evaluate and criticize the behavior of his fellow without recognizing that his evaluation is tainted because of his own inconsistency. In other words, human judgment, which is often necessary, sometimes helpful, and occasionally correct, is fundamentally inconsistent.

In a strictly legal sense, many people are deeply offended by the lack of freedom and the absence of justice even in countries which speak loudly and often about "liberty and justice for all." Illustrations of corruption, double standards, human abuse, and miscarriage of justice abound even in the "free" nations, and in those countries where ideology is more important than individuals, gross injustice and abuse prevail. But at another level, in the arena of interpersonal relationships, there is no lack of judgment and criticism, much of which is thoroughly inconsistent.

It is this that Paul addresses and exposes. He is particularly concerned about those people who feel that their lives are beyond reproach because they eschew the great extremes of others. This produces a brand of righteousness based on the faulty logic that says because I don't do what he does I'm better than he and because I'm better than he I'm all right. This is self-righteousness of the worst kind. It is as ludicrous in its assumptions and conclusions as thinking that says that because you owe a million dollars and I only owe half a million dollars, I don't owe as much as you, so therefore I'm free from debt!

Paul insisted that those who did not go to the excessive extremes of the Gentiles must be very guarded in their judgment because they, themselves, were by no means without fault. He went so far as to say "you who judge practice the same things." This did not mean that the overt actions were the same but that the covert attitudes were fundamentally similar. To the degree in which covert attitudes are similar, despite the dissimilarity of overt activities Paul identified a common condemnation. Furthermore, where the one condemned the actions of the others while harboring similar attitudes himself, that amounted to self-condemnation.

All this is designed to show the inconsistency of human judgment and condemnation and serves as a superb introduction by way of contrast to:—

THE INTEGRITY OF DIVINE JUDGMENT

2 But we know that the judgment of God is according to truth against those who practice such things. 3 And do you think this, O man, you who judge those practicing such things, and doing the same, that you will escape the judgment of God? 4 Or do you despise the riches of His goodness, forbearance, and longsuffering, not knowing that the goodness of God leads you to repentance? 5 But in accordance with your hardness and your impenitent heart you are treasuring up for

yourself wrath in the day of wrath and revelation of the righteous judgment of God, [6] who "will render to each one according to his deeds": [7] eternal life to those who by patient
continuance in doing good seek for glory, honor, and immortality; [8] but to those who are self-seeking and do not obey the
truth, but obey unrighteousness—indignation and wrath,
[9] tribulation and anguish, on every soul of man who does evil,
of the Jew first and also of the Greek; [10] but glory, honor, and
peace to everyone who works what is good, to the Jew first and
also to the Greek.

—*Romans 2:2–10*

Paul's introduction of the subject of divine judgment in
Romans 2:2 is abrupt, and his assumption that his readers recognize its reality is such that he sees no necessity to argue the "ifs
and buts" of the subject.

We have no way of knowing whether this means that Paul's
contemporaries were more prepared to accept the fact of divine
judgment than twenty-first-century man or that Paul saw no
necessity to argue the subject. Whatever the reason, he stated the
fact that God's judgment (literally, "sentence") is a fact of human
existence that must be reckoned with if people want to escape the
realm of fantasy and live in the real world.

Naïve assumptions such as "God would never condemn anybody" or "a loving God must accept everyone" or "I'll take my
chances and I think they're as good as the next man's" are so common today that Paul's approach to the subject of divine judgment
is largely rejected. Yet those who reject the concept rarely consider
the alternatives. If God does not judge a man ultimately, that
means that his actions have no ultimate value, and the man
whose actions lack ultimate value has little alternative but to view
his life as being devoid of meaning and his existence as totally
inconsequential. Those who wish to free people from the awesome thought of divine judgment need to remember that they
often liberate people into the awful bonds of meaninglessness and
emptiness. Is it not far better, with Paul, to believe that the fact of
divine judgment points to the intrinsic value of humanity? For if
God regards what we *do* important enough to judge, He certainly
must regard what we *are* as important enough to matter.

Not only is there strange comfort in the judgment of God in
that it shows God's evaluation of our worth, but there is also comfort in the fact that contrary to man's judgment, which is so

inconsistent, the judgment of God is *"according to truth"* (v. 2). We can at least be sure of a fair trial!

That God's judgment is related to truth means, first, that God himself is true and therefore will be totally unprejudiced, and, second, that the evidence will be real and therefore there can be no thought of a mistrial.

Even the best legal systems in the world ask for nothing more than a verdict "beyond reasonable doubt." In a court of law everyone knows that the evidence is open to question, the witnesses are prone to error, the jury can be misled, and the judge is quite capable of making a mistake. But in the court of God there will be no misunderstanding, no misrepresentation, no miscarriage of justice, no misdemeanor, and no mistakes—all will be according to truth.

The solemnity of this meaning is particularly noticeable when we bear in mind the attitude of those whom Paul was addressing at this point. They were priding themselves in being acceptable to God because of their moral superiority to the pagans while discounting the reality of their own heart condition. Any man can observe external actions and maybe even rightly evaluate the inner motives, but only God can be relied upon rightly to judge the innermost being of both the uninhibited pagan and the disciplined moralist hidden behind what Calvin called "the mask of a feigned piety."

Second, the judgment of God is inescapable (v. 3). One of the major complaints of human beings is that so often the innocent suffer and the guilty escape. In modern society there is a strong feeling that there is one law for the wealthy and another for the poor. Certainly there is no shortage of cases where it would appear that those who can afford the best lawyer capable of exploring every nook and cranny of the law often fare much better than the destitute man whose case is being handled by a public defender who may be overworked, understaffed, and inexperienced. In many crimes the criminals concerned escape judgment because their crimes are not even discovered, and in others, even though the crimes are discovered the criminals are never caught. There are cases of criminals who are caught but escape from the authorities before they are brought to trial, and there are those who are truly guilty but escape conviction on sheer technicality. All these people escape the judgment of the court.

While nobody seriously thinks he can escape detection by God or resist arrest when death, God's agent, comes to arrest him, and while there is no one who would expect to be able to hire lawyers who could find loopholes in God's laws or even get him off on a technicality, still people think they can escape the judgment of God. In particular, the religious Jew of Paul's day thought that there was one rule for the Jew and a different rule for the rest. Trypho, in his dialogue with Justin Martyr, stated the Jewish conviction clearly as follows: "They who are the seed of Abraham according to the flesh shall in any case, even if they be sinners and unbelieving and disobedient towards God, share in the Eternal Kingdom."[2] Paul clearly announced the unpalatable truth that *all* people—Jew and Greek—can anticipate the judgment of God, for no one will escape.

Third, the judgment of God is cumulative (vv. 4, 5). In the first chapter of the epistle, Paul stated that the wrath of God was already in evidence in human behavior, but now he adds the further thought that in the present day there is not a complete demonstration of wrath and judgment and that there is more to come *"in the day of wrath and revelation of the righteous judgment of God."* The awful evidences of divine wrath that abound on every hand in the present age are to be recognized as nothing more than a foretaste of the complete demonstration yet to come.

Some people, the Jews included, have misunderstood the absence of a full demonstration of divine judgment, seeing it either as evidence that God does not judge or that the judgment is not severe and can, therefore, be disregarded. Paul, however, insists that the true reason for the delay in the dawn of the day of wrath is God's *"goodness, forbearance, and longsuffering."* Holst wrote: "'Makrothumia' (longsuffering) can never imply irresolution on the part of God as though He could decide only after a period of waiting. Nor does it imply compliance or indulgence. God's patience does not overlook anything. It simply sees further than man. It has the end in view. It has the true insight which knows best."[3]

These beautiful attributes of God, when known, are intended to lead people to repentance. When it dawns upon the human soul that God is tolerating human sin a little longer out of kindness, not weakness, and is withholding His holy judgment on sin out of determination, not irresolution, mankind is supposed to be grateful and demonstrate the gratitude in turning from sin. But unfortunately such is not the case. Rather, man *"despises"* the kindness and uses the freedom for more sin. Instead of a warm, generous response to the gracious goodness and generosity of God, man has exhibited *"hardness"* and an *"impenitent heart"* from which more sin has flourished. The net result has been, therefore, for many people, that the day of grace instead of being an experience of loving gratitude and warm submission has been spent in more sin, which, in turn, has meant a *"treasuring up"* of more condemnation and guilt. Human destiny, which is replete with stories of abuse, has no sadder story to tell than the abuse of divine goodness, forbearance, and longsuffering. History, which is full of tragic incidents, has no greater tragedy to document than that of man's using the day of grace for more sin when it was granted for more acts of repentance. Barclay said, "It is one of the most shameful things in the world to use mercy and love's forgiveness as an excuse to go on sinning."[4]

Fourth, the judgment of God is based on man's actions. When Paul gets particularly excited about his subject, his sentences have a marked tendency to stretch out, making it a little more difficult to follow his line of thought. Such is the case when he explains how the judgment of God is related to the deeds of man in verses 6–10. Clearly he teaches at this point of the epistle that a man will be judged on his works and that his works are most definitely related to his motivations. Some people have seen in this passage a contradiction to the message of the rest of the epistle, namely, that man is justified by faith, not works. It should be understood that the contradiction is more apparent than real.

Some people whose hearts and minds are set on *"glory, honor, and immortality"* have a genuine desire deep within to live on earth in the light of heaven, to be men before God, and to spend time always with eternity in mind. The glory of God is their concern; the honor that comes from God is their goal; the incorruptible presence and enjoyment of God is that to which they aspire. The reality of their heart's desire and orientation is measured not by their protestations and professions but by their *"patient continuance in doing good"* (v. 6). These people, when they stand in the judgment, will be among the justified but not because they were good enough to merit justification. Rather, they will be among the justified because they were earnest enough, as evidenced by their lives, to be open to being shown what it means to be brought to faith. For them eternal life is their glorious portion.

Cornelius, the Roman, is a beautiful example. He is described as *"a devout man and one who feared God with all his household, who gave alms generously to the people, and prayed to God always"* (Acts 10:2). God intervened in his life and sent Peter to him. As Peter preached, "whoever believes in Him will receive remission of sins," he was amazed to see that, "the Holy Spirit fell upon all those who heard the word" (Acts 10:43, 44).

In stark contrast there are those whose works exhibit not a deep desire for God but an inveterate *"self-seeking"*—they *"do not obey the truth, but obey unrighteousness."* The self-seeker places his own desires before the commands of God; he regards his own self-gratification as more important than the needs of others. Accordingly, his life is a sad saga of one evil deed after another; evil in that it contravenes the holy law of God; evil in that it elevates the self to the central place in the universe which is God's alone; evil in that it despises and ignores the people God created and cherishes; evil in that it is fundamentally detrimental to human well-being and destructive of God's handiwork; evil in that it callously rejects truth and warmly embraces unrighteousness. The life invested in such pursuits receives in the day of judgment an awful dividend— *"indignation and wrath, tribulation and anguish"* (vv. 8, 9).

It is crucially important that we notice that Paul presents only two alternatives. There is a universal human tendency to introduce at least a third alternative into matters of this nature. This third alternative is usually the place reserved for the person establishing it. It is a place of quiet immunity—a tranquil area in which what happens to the rest of the world can't happen to me! But Paul denies everyone the privilege of such a position. We all come under one or the other position; we all adopt one or the other lifestyle; we will all reap one or the other harvest. No excuses, no exceptions, no exemptions.

Fifth, the judgment of God is impartial:

> 11 For there is no partiality with God.
> 12 For as many as have sinned without law will also perish without law, and as many as have sinned in the law will be judged by the law 13 (for not the hearers of the law are just in the sight of God, but the doers of the law will be justified;
> 14 for when Gentiles, who do not have the law, by nature do the things in the law, these, although not having the law, are a law to themselves, 15 who show the work of the law written in their hearts, their conscience also bearing witness, and between themselves their thoughts accusing or else excusing them)
>
> —*Romans 2:11–15*

The absolute justice of God and His unswerving commitment to righteousness are more than abstract qualities. They have concrete manifestations in the way He deals with people and in the manner He dispenses judgment. This is particularly true in His handling of the Jewish people. That they were specially privileged and specifically called to play a major role in the divine plan cannot be denied. But it would be an insult to the divine integrity to suggest that the privileged position of the Jew meant he could expect special exemption from the consequences of his sin. Paul's oft-used expression, *"to the Jew first and also to the Greek"* shows that there is a clear difference in God's eyes between Jew and Greek—that the Jew has a position of primacy—but this position of primacy also includes a primacy of judgment. The Jew who believes, with some justification, that he comes first in God's thinking must remember that the first place means first in judgment too. If he wants to believe he is first he must believe he is first in everything! Paul clearly stated this when he said, *"tribulation and anguish, on every soul of man who does evil, of the Jew first and also of the Greek"* (v. 9).

If there is no partiality toward the Jew because of his privileged position, it is equally true there is no partiality to the Gentile for his lack of privilege. The Jew who has the law and sins against it is responsible for his sin; the Gentile who does not have the law but sins anyway is equally responsible for his sin. This is eminently fair. The unfairness would be if Jews were treated as if they didn't have the law or if Gentiles were treated as if they did. The judgment of God is based on the light that people have received and their reaction to it and is never based on the light they have not received.

In the same way that some people who have privilege abuse it, there are always those who, lacking privilege, rise above it. Paul speaks of the Gentiles who were never given the privilege of having the law of God, yet who had such sensitivity to what they knew of God that their consciences were keen and alert and in touch with reality.

The important thing for everyone to understand, Jew or Gentile, is that the judgment of God has no place for favoritism or exceptions but is based strictly on the response of the individual to the knowledge of truth that has been made available. That obviously means that the more privilege a person has, the more responsibility he holds.

THE INEVITABILITY OF DIVINE JUDGMENT

Like drowning men who grasp at straws, men confronted with the thought of divine judgment clutch hold of any possibility of its not happening. I find in my pastoral ministry that many people don't really think that the judgment will happen. Some question God's character, some avoid thinking it will happen to them, some don't think about it at all, some treat it with scant regard and assume everything will turn out all right in the end, and many hold onto the hope that the final day of judgment will be averted in some way or another. Paul's statement concerning the inevitability of divine judgment needs to be understood:

> 16 in the day when God will judge the secrets of men by Jesus Christ, according to my gospel.
>
> *—Romans 2:16*

The emphasis is on the word *"will."* God will judge the world. Of this there need be no doubt.

Paul includes two very important details of the final judgment. First, it will be a judgment of *"the secrets of men"*—a statement which, when coupled with the earlier statements concerning the judgment of "deeds," reminds us that the external deeds are seen in their true light only when the secret motivations are known. Conversely, the hidden secrets of men often become visible through their actions, particularly in unguarded moments or pressure situations. Deeds in the light of secrets will be judged in that final day.

Second, the judgment will be *"by Jesus Christ."* Anyone who has a picture of Christ which does not include Him as Judge of the earth is laboring under a serious misapprehension of the true identity of the Savior. The babe in the manger, the healer of the sick, the One who welcomed the children, the teacher of parables, the silent prisoner in the judgment hall, the pitiful victim on the Via Dolorosa, the agonizing sacrifice on the Cross, the resplendent Lord in the garden, the triumphant leader in the Upper Room—all are pictures of a Lord that, in one form or another, appeal to something in the human heart. But Jesus as Judge is foreign to many. Yet this should not be, because he repeatedly announced His own Judgeship during the days of His ministry. No doubt, many heard Him speak about it but chose not to believe, as was the case when Paul told the Athenians that God "has appointed a day on which He will judge the world in righteousness by the Man whom He has ordained. He has given assurance of this to all by raising Him from the dead" (Acts 17:31).

Paul's explanation that the Resurrection is an evidence of God's appointment of Christ as Judge needs to be considered.

The Resurrection was the Father's unmistakable stamp of approval on all that the Son had been and had done. This approval extended to His right and ability to preside in the final judgment day. That He has the right to judge is beyond dispute since it is the Father who has appointed Him, and His ability is without question when we consider the life that He, as man, lived among us. His insight into human nature was such that "He knew what was in man" (John 2:25). Nicodemus' need was obvious to Him, the woman of Samaria's condition was not hidden from Him, Judas' dark schemings were clear to Him, Peter's twisted loyalties were uncomplicated to Him—He truly knew what was in man. Yet this knowledge of man's true nature was touched with a compassion which came from His deep empathy with man in all his struggles, for He, too, had lived and struggled, been tested and tried, and yet had never succumbed. He was Himself not only the ideal Judge, but He was in Himself the very standard by which judgment should be made, in that He had fulfilled all the law's demands.

It seems almost out of place for Paul to conclude his explanation of so somber a subject as the judgment by saying that it was "according to my gospel."

Gospel, as we have seen, means "Good News." Many people, when confronted with news of judgment, look long and hard for any evidence of Good News. But one thing we must always remember: before we can adequately understand the Good News we must grasp first the bad news. Then the wonder of the message of grace is seen in all its fullness and glory.

NOTES

1. *Calvin's New Testament Commentaries, Romans,* p. 41.

2. Barclay, *The Letter to the Romans,* p. 35.

3. *Theological Dictionary of the New Testament,* ed. Kittel and Friedrich, 4:382.

4. Barclay, *The Letter to the Romans,* p. 37.

CHAPTER FOUR—THE DANGERS OF RELIGION

ROMANS 2:17—3:8

Scripture Outline

Profession Without Performance (2:17–24)

Ritual Without Reality (2:25–29)

Privilege Without Perception (3:1–2)

Objections Without Objectivity (3:3–8)

The establishment and maintenance of the Roman Empire was a phenomenal achievement. Starting from their obscure location on the Tiber, the industrious Romans extended their influence to the limits of the known world. Building roads and aqueducts that exist to this day, establishing laws that still obtain, they brought to society a measure of stability the like of which has rarely been equaled. The brilliant Greeks were included in the list of Roman conquests, but it has been well said that "captive Greece captured her conquerers"[1] to such an extent that the Greek language and Greek thought permeated Roman life. Together Greece and Rome worked out a relationship that dominated the world of Paul's day, with one major exception—the Jews.

As a result of the tragedies that had befallen their nation, the Jews had been dispersed from their homeland in every direction. Thus wherever Rome and Greece ruled supreme, Jews lived, too. Industrious, proud, and different, they had stubbornly refused to be assimilated into the cultural patterns dictated by the "superpowers." They were respected without being appreciated because of their fierce rejection of the cultural norms of their day. They preserved their distinction by differences in dress, diet, and demeanor which neither the might of Rome nor the scorn of Greece could erase. Despite the evidences of grandeur on every hand, they were unmoved by the accomplishments of others, being singularly convinced that they were the chosen people and all others, however prominent, were "the heathen." Their distaste for the ornate temples and their associations was well known: they worshiped the true God who was far removed from such pagan excesses. They were unimpressed by the secular empire of Rome because they looked forward to the day when Messiah would establish the real kingdom that would restore the people of Israel to their rightful preeminent place among the nations.

When we recognize this typical Jewish attitude toward the Romans and Greeks, Paul's scathing denunciation of Gentile society comes as no surprise. He had learned such attitudes at his mother's knee and refined them at Gamaliel's feet. But his attitude to his own people—the Jews—is a major surprise. He wrote:

> [17] Indeed you are called a Jew, and rest on the law, and make your boast in God, [18] and know His will, and approve the things that are excellent, being instructed out of the law, [19] and are confident that you yourself are a guide to the blind, a light to those who are in darkness, [20] an instructor of the foolish, a teacher of babes, having the form of knowledge and truth in the law. [21] You, therefore, who teach another, do you not teach yourself? You who preach that a man should not steal, do you steal? [22] You who say, "Do not commit adultery," do you commit adultery? You who abhor idols, do you rob temples? [23] You who make your boast in the law, do you dishonor God through breaking the law? [24] For "the name of God is blasphemed among the Gentiles because of you," as it is written.
>
> —*Romans 2:17–24*

It is important that we note the difference between Paul's criticism of the Jews and that which he leveled at the Gentiles. The Gentiles, he said, suppress the truth in unrighteousness—the truth available to them by observation and interpretation of the world around them. The Jews, however, had a much fuller knowledge of God available to them, which they recognized and in which they took considerable pride. But they had failed lamentably to apply this knowledge to their lives, and therein lay their sin. The Gentiles were living in the hazy dawn of knowledge when compared to the brilliant glare of the Jewish knowledge, and while the Gentiles willfully stumbled in their haze, the Jews were falling on their noses in the brightness of noonday.

They were guilty of a number of false behaviors.

PROFESSION WITHOUT PERFORMANCE

Originally the name *Jew* described a member of the tribe of Judah, an inhabitant of the land of Judea. Over the centuries the meaning has broadened considerably, but it has never failed to be deeply significant. No people in history have clung more tenaciously to a name and its related ethnic, social, and religious connotations. It is doubtful if any name has been more vilified by some or more respected by others. Paul was thinking of the Jews as the people of God chosen to be the special agents of His earthly activity. The Jews to whom Paul spoke had no difficulty seeing themselves in that light and were not slow to boast of their unique status. To them the name was a title of privilege and a matter of pride.

They were also proud that God had made the "law" available to them. Paul used the Greek word *nomos* ("law") over seventy times in the epistle, and it is important to remember that the usage varied. Usually he was referring to the specific instructions that God handed down to His people through Moses or other Old Testament writers. Occasionally he appeared to mean the immense body of rabbinical teaching that had become attached to the biblical literature in an effort to explain and apply the inspired writings. At other times *nomos* was used to describe certain principles of operation either in God's economy or man's experience.

In the law, God had revealed great details of His own nature, His expectations for human behavior, and the fundamental requirements for a healthy society. This meant that the Jews were second to none in their ability to *"boast in God and know His will."* Because they were equipped to *"approve the things that are excellent,"* they had the potential to evaluate things in terms of God's estimation and compare things in the light of His absolute standards. These considerable capabilities were available to them as to no other people.

The sense of pride stemming from these privileges had, unfortunately, produced an attitude of superiority which, while understandable, had led to the Gentiles becoming antagonistic and the Jews becoming unrealistic in their self-evaluation. It is not surprising that when a Jew let it be known that he regarded himself as a *"guide to the blind. . . an instructor of the foolish, a teacher of babes"* that some of those who were unceremoniously characterized as blind, foolish babes resented those who had elevated themselves to the position of guides, teachers, and instructors. Even more seriously, the superior view that the Jews had of themselves led often to an erroneous sense of their own importance. Professing to be more than they were, they overlooked the glaring inadequacies of their own performance and lived in self-induced blindness to their own inconsistencies. Many of the teachers of babes were themselves babes, and not a few of the guides of the blind were more blind than they imagined.

To avoid the possibility that the seriousness of his statements might be submerged in a sea of generalities, Paul pinpointed four particulars from the law given to Moses. He spoke of honoring God and of abhorring idols, stealing, and committing adultery. The orthodoxy of Jewish teaching on these subjects was not in question, but the practical obedience to the teaching by some of the teachers was very much open to question. Everyone knew of cases where the orthodox left loopholes in their business deals to allow for a little refined stealing. Even some of the better-known rabbis were charged with sexual immorality. The Jewish distaste for idols and pagan temples based on God's prohibition against the manufacture of "graven images" was well known and deeply resented. Ironically, the Gentiles called the Jews "atheists" on the false assumption that because their places of worship had no visible gods they worshiped no god. Evidently Paul knew of cases where the Jews, while making their strong statements about the temples, were not at all averse to reaping some pecuniary benefit from those temples, possibly by receiving stolen goods from them. This kind of behavior, Paul insisted, led not only to the Jews being despised but also to the law they taught being disregarded and the God they represented being blasphemed.

When I was in business, I was placed in a position where I had to deal with a man who had embezzled a considerable sum of money from the bank for which we both worked. The reason for his embezzlement was that he had two wives and families and was trying to run two homes. When he was apprehended and dismissed from the company, he stunned everyone in the room by saying, "I am very sorry for what I have done and I need to know whether I should fulfill my preaching commitments on Sunday in our local church!" As a practicing Christian, I spent a considerable amount of my time in the ensuing weeks undoing the damage done by this man's blatant inconsistency. To my chagrin, I discovered that my colleagues not only despised the man in question but because of his behavior were quick to dismiss the church he belonged to as a "bunch of hypocrites," the gospel he professed to believe as a "lot of hogwash," and the God he claimed to serve as "nonexistent."

Paul's explanation of the Jewish position clearly outlined three dangers that confront all religious people. First, the danger of failing to live according to knowledge and profession; second, the danger of being responsible for unbelievers being misled and confused by inconsistent behavior; and third, the danger of God's name being despised because of this confusion.

RITUAL WITHOUT REALITY

Having addressed two hallowed areas of Jewish thought and life—the name and the law—Paul turned his attention with equal candor to the rite of circumcision. The Jews delighted in tracing their traditions and practices to their ancient origins. With great conviction they told the story of Jehovah's choice of Abraham to be the father of the nation through whom Messiah would make His earthly entrance. Avidly they spoke of the covenant that God had made with Abraham, committing Himself to be the nation's God and promising them their land. They never tired of telling their children how God had also stipulated, "This is My covenant, which you shall keep, between Me and you and your decendants after you: Every male child among you shall be circumcised" (Gen. 17:10). From God's standpoint, the essence of the covenant was "I will be their God," and from the peoples' perspective, the proper response was to submit to circumcision as a sign and a seal of their acceptance of God's mastery over their lives and their expectation that He would be as good as His word.

Paul was convinced that the sign had lost its significance to many of his kinsmen and the rite was completely devoid of reality.

25 For circumcision is indeed profitable if you keep the law; but if you are a breaker of the law, your circumcision has become uncircumcision. 26 Therefore, if an uncircumcised man keeps the righteous requirements of the law, will not his uncircumcision be counted as circumcision? 27 And will not the physically uncircumcised, if he fulfills the law, judge you who, even with your written code and circumcision, are a transgressor of the law? 28 For he is not a Jew who is one outwardly, nor is circumcision that which is outward in the flesh; 29 but

he is a Jew who is one inwardly; and circumcision is that of the heart, in the Spirit, not in the letter; whose praise is not from men but from God.

—*Romans 2:25–29*

This was not a new insight because the prophets had complained loud and long about the same thing. Jeremiah had cried, "Circumcise yourselves to the LORD, and take away the foreskins of your hearts . . . lest My fury come forth like fire, and burn so that no one can quench it, because of the evil of your doings" (Jer. 4:4).

To insist rigidly on circumcision and then to disregard the covenant was to be no different from the neighboring tribes who also practiced circumcision without any divine connotations whatsoever. Paul's statement must have sounded like a thunderclap of heresy to those who had been taught by the rabbis, "All the circumcised have part in the world to come."[2] The apostle went even further when he added that if the circumcised could be classified with the uncircumcised because of the lack of reality in their relationship to the Lord, those outside the Jewish fold, the uncircumcised, could rightfully be regarded as members of the covenant if they had a valid heart commitment to the Lord. *"For,"* as he stated trenchantly, *"he is not a Jew who is one outwardly. . . but he is a Jew who is one inwardly."*

There are many people alive today who, like the Jews of Paul's day, have an excess of religion that borders on superstition. They gladly engage in ritual and avidly adhere to ecclesiastical rules and regulations regarding signs and symbols without resting in the One to whom the rite points or committing themselves to the One whom the sign signifies. To do this is to qualify for the wrath of God alongside the pagan who suppresses the law of God in his conscience and throws himself heartily into the confusion that results. Charles Haddon Spurgeon hit the right note in his beautiful communion hymn when he wrote:

> If now, with eyes deified and dim,
> We see the signs but see not Him,
> O, may His love the scales displace,
> And bid us see Him, face to face!

Concluding the passage, the apostle emphasized the difference between ritual and reality by contrasting not only inward attitudes and external signs, spiritual reality and physical symbolism, but also the difference between satisfying men and receiving praise from God. It is quite possible that when he wrote, *"whose praise is not from men but from God,"* he was making a somewhat subtle reference to the fact that the name "Judah," from which "Jew" is derived, means "praise" and, therefore, whenever a Jew rejoices in aspects of his Jewishness he needs to be thinking about whose praise he desires and what praise, if any, he will ultimately receive from God.

PRIVILEGE WITHOUT PERCEPTION

> **3:1** What advantage then has the Jew, or what *is* the profit of circumcision? **2** Much in every way! Chiefly because to them were committed the oracles of God.
>
> —*Romans 3:1–2*

There is always a danger that when we try to make a point we do so by emphasizing one aspect of the truth at the expense of another. Democrats and Republicans are superb exponents of this art form, particularly in election year! That Paul was sensitive to this possibility is apparent by his question in Romans 3:1.

Having shown clearly the dangers of an unbalanced approach to privilege, he was most anxious that the baby should not be thrown out with the bath water. Anyone listening to his arguments concerning the law, the name, and the rite would expect his answer to his own question to be, "Forget the whole business. There are no advantages; the things we thought important are totally irrelevant." But surprisingly, Paul says exactly the opposite. From every viewpoint the Jews have advantages but *"chiefly because to them were committed the oracles of God"* (Rom. 3:2). Whatever their failings, the Jews were God's special people, the law He gave them was His unique word, and the rite of the covenant was His chosen sign; therefore, they all had deep significance despite the fact that the Jews had to a great extent misread them.

Privilege, to be rightly handled, must be correctly perceived. When Queen Elizabeth, the Queen Mother, celebrated her eightieth birthday, the British, who have not been reticent to criticize members of the royal family at times, expressed so much affection for the Queen Mother that they took most people by surprise. Many commentators endeavoring to analyze the reasons for this public reaction pointed to the Queen Mother's attitude to her privileged position. She perceived her position as a platform for service, and her commitment could be measured by the fact that she had not missed a single engagement through illness for over twenty-five years.

Religious people must always wrestle with the possibility that they might misunderstand or misapply their privileges, either by disregarding the importance of the privilege or by exaggerating their own importance.

OBJECTIONS WITHOUT OBJECTIVITY

In his long and arduous ministry, Paul had made repeated overtures to his own people, with mixed results. Sometimes they had come to repentant faith in Messiah, but more often they had reacted unfavorably to him and his message, even to the point of violence. This is understandable because, when deeply held views are challenged, reactions are predictably strong. Think of the events surrounding early attempts at school integration. Remember the outrage at the flag burners of the Vietnam era, and observe the impassioned debate both for and against the Equal Rights Amendment. The stronger the position is held, the deeper the passions will flow. Unfortunately, the deeper the passions flow, the further the arguments stray from objectivity. Paul had heard all the arguments against his position and had observed the lack of objectivity firsthand. He used both in the diatribe that follows:

3 For what if some did not believe? Will their unbelief make the faithfulness of God without effect? 4 Certainly not! Indeed, let God be true but every man a liar. As it is written:

"That You may be justified in Your words,
And may overcome when You are judged."

5 But if our unrighteousness demonstrates the righteousness of God, what shall we say? Is God unjust who inflicts wrath? (I speak as a man.) 6 Certainly not! For then how will God judge the world?

7 For if the truth of God has increased through my lie to His glory, why am I also still judged as a sinner? 8 And why not say, "Let us do evil that good may come"?—as we are slanderously reported and as some affirm that we say. Their condemnation is just.

—Romans 3:3–8

This is not one of the easiest passages to understand, but it will help if we regard it as a typical discussion that had often taken place between Paul and irate opponents of his message:

"How can you possibly say in one breath that the Jews have failed so completely in their God-given role and then turn around and insist that they are still the privileged people? If they are as bad as you say they are, they cannot possibly be part of God's covenant, and if they have been removed, then God has broken His promise—He is unfaithful."

"On the contrary—the fact that God has exposed their sin and condemned it shows His justice in that He has treated everyone alike, even His chosen people. Far from showing Him to be unfaithful, He is seen to be strictly reliable and just. You remember when David wrote Psalm 51 he was concerned that God might be seen as the dispenser of justice and that His integrity would shine through every critical attack of man. This is exactly what has happened."

"Are you trying to tell me that God's condemnation of His people illustrates His justice? That means that He is using people to His advantage, and if He does that, He can hardly judge those He has used. Taken to its logical conclusion, what you are saying is an incentive to sin! If being bad makes God look good, let's be worse so he looks better! Is that what you're teaching?"

Except to respond that that kind of talk was slanderous, Paul did not pursue this argument further because he had demonstrated the total lack of objectivity in the objections. In fact, the arguments used against him served only to prove the point he was making—that his kinsmen were far removed from an understanding of the law delivered to them. With chilling brevity, he concluded his exposure of the Jewish position by stating that those who adopted such positions would have to accept their condemnation as just.

It is easy to forget the thread of Paul's argument in the weaving of his epistle, but we must remember that his brutal exposure of Jewish, or religious, sin, following his equally straightforward treatment of pagan degeneracy, was to show the guilt of the race before God and introduce them to the only answer to human guilt—the gospel of the Lord Jesus. Pagan and pietist alike must come to Christ.

NOTES

1. Michael Green, *Evangelism in the Early Church* (London: Hodder and Stoughton), p. 17.

CHAPTER FIVE—ALL TOGETHER NOW

ROMANS 3:9–20

Scripture Outline
> All Under Sin (3:9–18)
> All Under Law (3:19)
> All Under Pressure (3:20)

The Christmas spirit is a strange phenomenon. Every year for a brief period of time people seem to be overcome with a sense of cooperation not in evidence for the rest of the year. Hostilities are terminated for a set period, feuds are put on ice and conflicts placed on hold, and for a few days or hours an almost surrealistic air of "togetherness" prevails.

This was particularly true in Christmas 1968. Millions of people around the world, glued to their television sets, were waiting with bated breath and crossed fingers for the latest word from Apollo 8, the frail, intricate spacecraft in which the first manned lunar orbit was being attempted. They were amply rewarded not only because they watched history being made but also because they witnessed breathtaking pictures of earth, the tiny planet which the human race inhabits suspended in black space. For the first time, as man was made aware that the sum total of his differences is lived out on a fragile fraction of the universe, "togetherness" of a totally new kind was experienced. Born of a sense of awe and nurtured through a sense of necessity, Christmas 1968 produced a oneness on earth never known before. Unfortunately, the familiarity which constant exposure brings quickly eroded the sense of wonder. The global togetherness disappeared almost as quickly as the annual Christmas spirit, and the human race got back to the business of fragmentation. Hopes that new insights into our minuteness would bring the race together were dashed, and many people began to wonder if there is such a thing as a unifying factor. Scripture insists that such a factor exists. Its components are fourfold.

ALL UNDER SIN

⁹ What then? Are we better *than they?* Not at all. For we have previously charged both Jews and Greeks that they are all under sin.
¹⁰ As it is written:
"There is none righteous, no, not one;
¹¹ *There is none who understands;*
There is none who seeks after God.
¹² *They have all turned aside;*
They have together become unprofitable;
There is none who does good, no, not one."
¹³ *"Their throat is an open tomb;*
With their tongues they have practiced deceit";
"The poison of asps is under their lips";
¹⁴ *"Whose mouth is full of cursing and bitterness."*
¹⁵ *"Their feet are swift to shed blood;*
¹⁶ *Destruction and misery are in their ways;*
¹⁷ *And the way of peace they have not known."*
¹⁸ *"There is no fear of God before their eyes."*
—Romans 3:9–18

Having shown at some length the obvious differences between Jew and Greek (or Gentile) and having compared their relative advantages and disadvantages, Paul asks if there really are any material differences. He answers his own question with a resounding "no." Overriding all differences of class, creed, and culture is the somber fact that all are *"under sin."* This statement is presented as a "charge," that is, a legal accusation presumably made in the name of God against His own created beings. The awful togetherness of the human race that takes precedence over every other similarity or dissimilarity is that before God we are all exposed in our sinfulness.

The force of the expression "under sin" should be carefully noted. Paul described the relationship between a schoolboy and his teacher in Galatians 3:25 as being "under a schoolmaster." In 1 Timothy 6:1 he said slaves were "under the yoke." In all these instances to be "under" means "to be dominated by or under the authority of."

There is a major difference between "sin" and "sins," so we must be careful not to confuse "doing things that are not right" with the fact that we are dominated by a fundamentally evil dynamic. The difference is not unlike that which exists between the symptoms of a disease and the disease itself. When this is understood it becomes obvious that the human predicament is not so much that we have done things wrongly but that we are "in the Christless state under the command, under the authority, under the control of sin and helpless to escape from it."[1] Accordingly, any solution to the human problem that fails to deal with the root cause of "sin" is no more a solution than cold compresses on a fevered brow are a cure for the infection causing the fever.

Paul's all-embracing "charge" requires substantiation, which he wastes no time in presenting. Drawing freely from a variety of Old Testament sources he writes a scathing denunciation in Romans 3:10–18.

As we saw in our discussion of Romans 1:17, "the righteousness of God" is the central theme of the Epistle. We pointed out that God's righteousness has to do with His always being in the right and, therefore, always doing that which is right because He, Himself, is the only criterion of rightness. In the same way that there is and can be only one magnetic North and that all other points of the compass find their identity in relationship to North, so righteousness is found solely in the character of God, and all other standards of righteousness must be determined with reference to Him.

It is against this definition of righteousness that the charge *"there is none righteous"* (v. 10) is made and can be readily justified. The charge is not a figment of Paul's fertile imagination nor is it a product of his disenchantment with the human race, as he clearly demonstrates by substantiating his position with quotations from Psalms and Isaiah. It is as old as God's dealings with mankind, and man's resentment and resistance to the charge are equally as ancient.

Those people who have no interest in God and those who blatantly live in opposition to God are, if we may press the analogy so far, heading south from God's north and are clearly at odds with Him. Other people stray from the north in as many directions as there are points on the compass. But sometimes the people most resistant to the charge of universal, no-exception unrighteousness are those heading conscientiously NNW or NNE. They may be close and they are definitely closer than most, but they are not heading north where the righteousness is to be found. To the world in general Paul proclaims, *"There is none righteous,"* adding for the benefit of those who think they are close, *"no, not one."*

The dominating effect of sin can also be seen in the confusion of both individuals and society. *"There is none who understands"* means that without exception the thought processes of men and women are so affected by sin that there will always be some degree of deficiency in their grasp of the truth as it is to be found only in the knowledge of God. This naturally leads to confusion in everything else because all things have their meaning in Him. The politician who is confused about God will be confused about God's world, which leads inevitably to a confused world view and inadequate political solutions. The sociologist who does not adequately understand God cannot thoroughly understand God's masterpiece—man—so he will be in error at some point in his sociology. The same kind of thing must be said about all areas of human endeavor which are based on a warped or withered understanding of God.

That the mind of man is not so depraved that it is totally incapable of any activity is obvious. But the extent of the depravity is such that even though it cannot understand God of itself, it can still recognize its own deficiencies and may even be capable of identifying the deficiency as basically spiritual. This does not mean, however, that man has a natural inclination to go looking for God to fill the void. On the contrary Paul insists, *"There is none who seeks after God."* I have often engaged people in conversations who profess to have a desire to know God but who, after careful thought, have agreed that their search is more for a good argument than for a living God. The Lord Jesus made it clear that those who "seek will find" but Moses said to God's chosen people ". . . you will find Him if you seek Him with all your heart and with all thy soul" (Deut. 4:29). It is this kind of "seeking" that man does not naturally engage in, as is evident from the word Paul used, which Wuest said means a "determined search after something."[2] Sin has left man with a warped will as well as a confused mind.

The inevitable consequence of the foregoing is that *"they have all gone out of the way"* (Rom. 3:12). In the same way that an automobile with a twisted axle will have wheels out of alignment giving it a tendency to go off line, so man with his sin-dominated mind and will has a natural tendency to move from the path of

God's choosing. Without exception, the human race has a bent to evil and a bias to disobedience.

Like a symphony in which the various themes are interwoven, with more and more instruments adding their special contribution to the volume and the tempo accelerating until the tension becomes practically intolerable, so God's case against human fallenness builds to a crashing climax.

To state that the race has become "unprofitable," as in Romans 3:12, is to make a most damning indictment. The Hebrew word used in the Psalm Paul quotes stresses the thought of corruption or "turning sour," while the Greek equivalent used by the apostle in Romans emphasizes the idea of "uselessness." As wineskins that rot become useless because they cannot hold wine, so fallen man through the corrupting power of sin in the totality of his being cannot function as intended. As meat that perishes and cannot be used for anything and as salt that "loses its savor" has lost its *raison d'être*, so mankind is pitiful in its deteriorated and disintegrated uselessness.

Inevitably this depraved condition leads to the conclusion that is so starkly set forth—*"There is none who does good."* This thought is violently rejected by many people who see no way that it can be true in the light of innumerable acts of courage, boundless evidences of sacrificial love, countless works of creative genius, and millions of ordinary everyday actions that demonstrate compassion and concern by the masses. Two things need to be stressed, however. First, the expression "does good" would be better translated if the word "habitually" were included, and, second, the concept of goodness is defined with reference to God Himself. This is the goodness that is the essence of His nature rather than the product of human activity however enlightened or noble.

Paul, in effect, says that without a single exception there is not a human being of any shape, size, or form from any culture, environment, or age who has habitually produced a life characterized by undeviating commitment to righteousness and unadulterated goodness. No, not one!

The rabbis had a teaching method called "*charaz*" which means "stringing pearls" where they would take verses from a variety of sources and develop an argument from them. This Paul proceeds to do as he turns from broad generalities about the human condition and deals with specific human activities. In the same way that James in his epistle stressed the immense power of the tongue to express all manner of evil and produce all types of chaos, Paul chooses to concentrate on the activities of the human voice to illustrate human sinfulness. *"Their throat is an open tomb"* (v. 13) is a striking, even disgusting, metaphor. Yet a moment's thought will show how the naked obscenity and depraved vocabulary used by so many allows the unfortunate hearers to catch a glimpse of the barren deadness of the speaker's experience from which the sentiments flow. An "open tomb" is an apt description of the inner realities of human experience where little remains but the rotting bones and corrupting flesh of once-noble bodies of opinion.

In total contrast, Paul's second pearl on the string is, *"With their tongues they have practiced deceit"* (v. 13). Far from being disgusting and obscene, the speech of some is sweet and smooth. Sugar-coated statements and well-buttered platitudes expressed in cultured, modulated perfection are no less demonstrations of human perversity because they are designed for deception. David, whose Psalm Paul quotes at this point, knew from bitter experience with King Saul how devastating hostility could be cloaked in smooth civility.

One day the King said to the young man, "Here is my older daughter Merab. I will give her to you in marriage; only serve me bravely and fight the battles of the Lord." For Saul said to himself, "I will not raise a hand against him. Let the Philistines do that!" (1 Sam. 18:17, NIV). Saul, while talking piously about the Lord's battles and touching the young man's heart at the vulnerable point of his love for a girl, was actually plotting David's destruction with a tongue which for a long time had *"practiced deceit."*

The asp, or Egyptian cobra, has a small sac of deadly poison in its mouth which can have a devastating, paralyzing effect on the victim of its bite. Paul's use of the phrase *"The poison of asps is under their lips"* (v. 13) describes in a chilling and graphic way the far-reaching destructive capabilities of words spoken from a sinful heart. Sometimes it is the frontal venomous attack of an irate enemy couched in violent, vitriolic verbiage which is so debilitating; at other times it is the sudden sharp sting of the unexpectedly bitten heel that produces an even more devastating result. James, expressing similar strong sentiments, said, "But no man can tame the tongue. It is an unruly evil, full of deadly poison" (James 3:8).

When man's throat is as ugly as an open tomb, it may indicate a deep self-loathing. If his tongue practices deceit it would indicate a commitment to self-advancement at the expense of integrity and honor. Ups that spit poison betray a heart bent on personal triumph, regardless of the destruction caused. But when man's *"mouth is full of cursing and bitterness,"* (v. 14) it shows the lengths to which man will go to remove from his path all obstacles that threaten the advancement of his own designs and the selfish development of his own person. The "curse" in New Testament times was not so much a "swear word" as we would think of it. It meant the use of words which of themselves held the power to bring about the desired effect of their malediction. Springing from a bitter root, this practice was prevalent enough to strike fear in the hearts of all, even to the point of death in some. Peter recognized that Simon the Sorcerer's interest in the Holy Spirit was not at all related to spiritual growth but a desire to possess the "power" of the Spirit so that he might gain even more control of people's fate through imprecation and curse. Accordingly he was bluntly told: "Repent therefore of this your wickedness, and pray God if perhaps the thought of your heart may be forgiven you. For I see that you are poisoned by bitterness and bound by iniquity" (Acts 8:22–23). The wicked human heart will employ its physical capabilities in an alarming variety of ways to further its own ends while at the same time exposing its own depravity.

Having dealt thoroughly with the four organs associated with speech, Paul turns his attention to "feet" and "eyes." The theme is the same; only the ways in which it is expressed differ: *"Their feet are swift to shed blood; destruction and misery are in their ways; and the way of peace they have not known. There is no fear of God before their eyes"* (Rom. 3:15–18).

The enthusiasm with which men's feet run to violence and the sad resultant trail of oppression and misery are not only clearly stated in Scripture; every day they are graphically illustrated through national and international events so that further comment is probably not necessary. The link between this behavior and the spiritual vacuum from which it springs may not be so obvious. Ignorance of "the way of peace" and absence of "the fear of God" are the factors which Paul insists must be recognized. The dynamic of sin is responsible not only for the presence of malevolent forces but also for the absence of benevolent forces. Sin has imparted the ability to do evil and has robbed man of the power to do good. Therefore, his insights are marred. This can be seen in his inability to grasp the real meaning of peace, his uncertainty as to where it can be found, and the resultant confusion in his efforts to discover it and live in the good of it. Every man's best and most noble efforts at peacemaking result so often in increased hostility.

It is sad that it is not uncommon for the peace he proudly proclaims to be little more than a cessation of overt acts of hostility without any real solution having been found. As the prophet reminds us: *"There is no peace," says my God, "for the wicked"* (Is. 57:21, NASB).

The dying thief was incredulous that his crucified partner in crime was still blaspheming even on the threshold of death. *"Do you not fear God,"* he said, *"seeing you are under the same condemnation?"* (Luke 23:40). He was on the cross at that moment because he had never feared God! To fear God and to keep that fear before the eyes means to respect God for who He is and to constantly keep that knowledge of Him before you in all activities of life. Failure to keep the majesty, grace, and judgment of God in mind leads people into all kinds of wrong objectives and false perspectives. Human beings who do not respect God as their Creator can never adequately understand the mystery of their own being. Those who fail to respect Him as Judge will never approach moral concerns with the seriousness they deserve, while those who do not know Him as Savior can never be motivated to love as those whose hearts have been overwhelmed with the love of God shown in Christ. Lack of respect for God produces an alarming vacuum in man.

Recently, in the Caribbean, I observed expert scuba divers at work. I was impressed by their sober assessment of the dangers related to their diving and the ways in which they made responsible procedural precautions to obviate the danger. This led to a very high degree of safety and a resulting high standard of efficiency and enjoyment. Others less knowledgeable tend to take terrible risks through lack of respect and finish up in dire danger and not infrequently suffer serious consequences. The more you know God and respect Him, the more conscious you are of the dangers inherent in ignoring who He is. But little knowledge leads to no respect, and that is the road to disaster.

It should be stated that the apostle does not mean to convey that all the characteristics of sin listed above are in evidence in every life. Godet has wisely written, "Some, even most of them, may remain latent in many men: but they all exist in germ in the selfishness and natural pride of the ego, and the least circumstance may cause them to pass into the active state."[3]

ALL UNDER LAW

Having completed the long "string of pearls" to substantiate his contention that all are "under sin" Paul adds:

¹⁹ Now we know that whatever the law says, it says to those who are under the law, that every mouth may be stopped, and all the world may become guilty before God.

—*Romans 3:19*

The Jews are the ones specifically "under the law" whether this refers to the law as given to Moses or the whole Old Testament. In the light of Paul's quotation of David and Isaiah instead of Moses, it would appear that the latter approach is what he had in mind. In either case, it is important to remember that the apostle's objective was to show both Jew and Gentile "under sin," and he concludes that those "under the law" are those who belong to "all the world" which is guilty and "every mouth" which is stopped. This would mean that the Gentiles without having the advantage of the law as given to the Jews were still guilty of the things outlined in the law and come under the same condemnation. The solidarity of the human race is to be seen not only in its common bondage to sin but its common guilt before the law of God.

ALL UNDER PRESSURE

Without going into any detail, Paul introduces two important pieces of information concerning the law in the statement:

²⁰ Therefore by the deeds of the law no flesh will be justified in His sight, for by the law *is* the knowledge of sin.

—*Romans 3:20*

First, Paul shows the impossibility of people being "justified" (a technical word which we will study more fully later) by fulfilling the demands of the law for the obvious reason that, as he has shown conclusively, they have already failed in this regard. Second, he announces that the law serves as a means of showing to sinful mankind the reality of sin. Here he uses one of his favorite words, *epignosis,* meaning "full knowledge," to describe the ministry the law has in revealing to men and women the true nature of their sinfulness. Through the law which we do not fulfill we really begin to understand fully the meaning of sin. This knowledge and the discovery that efforts to please God through self-effort are bound to fail put the race under immense pressure to discover the means whereby man might be reconciled to God. In this desperate sense of need and search, there is yet another evidence of human solidarity.

It is ironic that in its search for common ground the human race appears to have overlooked the fact that we are totally united in our subjection to sin, condemnation by God, and necessity for salvation.

NOTES

1. Barclay, *The Letter to the Romans,* p. 51.

2. Kenneth S. Wuest, *Word Studies in the Greek New Testament, for the English Reader, Romans* (Grand Rapids: Eerdmans), p. 55.

3. Godet, *Commentary on Romans,* p. 142.

CHAPTER SIX—THE GENIUS OF GOD

ROMANS 3:21–31

Scripture Outline

 The Divine Dilemma (3:21–26)

 The Universal Solution (3:21–26)

 The Eternal Benefits (3:21–26)

 The Common Denominator (3:27–31)

When I was a young man aspiring to be a preacher I was told by a veteran expositor to look out for the word "but." "It's a key word, Stuart," he said. "Always introduces a new thought, usually in marked contrast to what has gone before." This has proved to be good advice, and I rarely read the word "but" in my Bible without looking for the new thought it introduces.

There is no better illustration of this than the statement Paul makes after he has outlined the depth of the human condition and the inability of man to extricate himself. Having started his exposition of the Good News by showing the badness of the Bad News, he introduces the divine answer by one of the biggest "buts" in world literature.

21 But now the righteousness of God apart from the law is revealed, being witnessed by the Law and the Prophets, 22 even the righteousness of God, through faith in Jesus Christ, to all and on all who believe. For there is no difference; 23 for all have sinned and fall short of the glory of God, 24 being justified freely by His grace through the redemption that is in Christ Jesus, 25 whom God set forth as a propitiation by His blood, through faith, to demonstrate His righteousness, because in His forbearance God had passed over the sins that were previously committed, 26 to demonstrate at the present

time His righteousness, that He might be just and the justifier of the one who has faith in Jesus.

—*Romans 3:21–26*

THE DIVINE DILEMMA

One memorable day the Lord Jesus was confronted by a group of highly indignant religious leaders who interrupted Him as He was teaching in the temple. Thrusting an embarrassed woman into the center of the group, "they said to Him, 'Teacher, this woman was caught in adultery, in the very act. Now Moses, in the law, commanded us that such should be stoned. But what do You say?'" (John 8:4–5).

It was apparent that they had scant regard for the feelings of the woman and even less for the Lord. Deeply offended by her attitude to sexual morality, they were also incensed by their perception that the Lord's approach to the Law was considerably more liberal than theirs. Ever since He had healed a paralytic on the Sabbath, an act which they considered a blatant contravention of the Law's prohibition of work on the day of rest, they had been most anxious to expose Him as a law-breaker. Numerous other incidents had added fuel to the flames of their hostility, and they had brought the woman to Him before the crowds in an effort to force a showdown. If, as they suspected, He would decline to endorse the stoning of the adulteress, they felt they would have conclusive proof of His disdain for the sacred Law.

From the Lord's point of view, however, the matter of the woman's well-being had to be considered along with the integrity of the Law. To Him the woman's sin was a horrendous thing, her contravention of the divine law of grave importance, but He would not allow her to become a pawn in a religious-political power play or a meaningless nonentity in a cold impersonal struggle to prove a point. The terror in her eyes, the uncontrolled shaking of her body, the tremors in her voice spoke deeply to His heart, for she was more than a cipher—she was a person. Her sin was manifest and could not be disregarded, but her need was equally obvious and must not be ignored. The dilemma He was facing was that He had an obligation to honor the Law and a commitment to uphold it, but at the same time He was deeply drawn to the sinner and was intent on redeeming her. But in the eyes of His adversaries if He took steps to redeem the woman He would desecrate the Law, while His own convictions insisted that if He followed through on the letter of the Law He would be denied the opportunity to redeem her shattered life.

This incident in the life of the Lord illustrates in a specific sense the dilemma that confronts the Father on a divine scale. As we have seen, there is no question about human sin and guilt and equally no doubt about divine judgment and condemnation, but there is also unequivocal evidence of the Father's love for sinners and His clear commitment to their redemption. Paul states the Father's intention to be *"just and the justifier."* As this brief expression is so crucial, we must be clear in our understanding of the words used. There is a very definite link between "righteousness," a key word in the Epistle to the Romans, and the group of words clustered around "just and justification." This can be seen in the way Paul uses them in Romans 3. *"Righteousness"* (v. 21) is *dikaiosune*, *"just"* (v. 26) and *"righteous"* (v. 10) are *dikaios* and *"justifier"* (v. 26) is *dikaiou*. The root word from which all these others come is *dike*, the name of the Greek goddess of justice.

When Paul was bitten by a viper after his shipwreck on the beach at Malta, the superstitious islanders said, "No doubt this man is a murderer whom, having been brought safely through out of the reach of the sea, the goddess of justice did not permit to continue living."[1] When, to their amazement, he survived the snakebite, they promptly assumed that he must be a god whose powers exceeded those of *Dike*. His survival was conclusive evidence to them that his magic powers were of divine origin.

The relationship between justice (that which is right) and righteousness (being and doing right) is clear, and from this basic understanding we can move to a position where we see justification as a divine declaration that before God we are "right." When this declaration of justification is made by God He is revealed as "the justifier." For God to be "just" and "the justifier," He must be in a position to declare righteous those who have clearly broken His law and at the same time in a position to maintain His own integrity and preserve His own righteousness. This kind of dilemma appears to be far beyond human solution, but God's handling of the situation is a superb illustration of the genius of God, which He has revealed in the gospel of Christ.

THE UNIVERSAL SOLUTION

Considerable time has been spent showing Paul's contention that the whole world is under sin and divine condemnation. But Paul further underlines his conviction with the words, *"for all have sinned and fall short of the glory of God"* (3:23). He employs two athletically oriented terms to make his point: the verb for *"sinned" (hamartano)* is related to the idea of an archer's arrow falling short of the target while the expression *"fall short" (hustereo)* means to fall behind in a race. The objective which humanity fails to achieve, whether expressed as lagging in a race or missing the bull's eye, is *"the glory of God."* Throughout human history, man has shown himself remarkably adept at adopting goals, lofty or otherwise, whether it be the goal of survival, personal freedom, world peace, or making a million before age thirty-five. However noble man's goals have been, they all pale beside the God-given goal, which is to reflect something of the glory of God in life and after life "to glorify Him forever." Having failed totally to achieve this goal, man's greatest need is to find a remedy before God for the responsibility and guilt of his failure and also to discover the means whereby the goal might become realistic in terms of human capability.

In theory, at least, there are two options open to the person who wishes to be reconciled to God. Either he can set about living a life that will be so pleasing to God that he will be rewarded by reconciliation, or he may decide that is hopeless and trust God to give him a chance, although he neither earned it nor deserved it. Theologically speaking, the first option is called "justification by works" and comes in many and varied forms. Paul himself had been an ardent advocate of this method for many years and had been proud of his achievements in fulfilling the demands of the law upon which his religion and lifestyle were based. He came eventually to the point of discovering that if he was to earn God's approval through keeping the law he would need to keep all of it, all the time, in spirit as well as letter. The more he pondered this the more he realized that he had failed, and he knew that all his contemporaries had failed in their efforts to be justified by their works. Finally, he stated his position boldly: *"Therefore by the deeds of the law no flesh will be justified in His sight. . ."* (Rom. 3:20).

Paul, along with many of the people who lived and studied with him in the schools of the rabbis, was deeply in earnest in his desire to fulfill the dictates of the law, as have been countless thousands of peoples in religions around the world through the ages. Even people who have no particular love for religion, when asked what they feel about meeting God, will usually answer that they expect things will work out all right because what they have done has been pretty good and they estimate it will be good enough to make the grade with God. This is simply another approach to justification by works, and Paul is desperately trying to show that it just doesn't work—it simply isn't a viable option.

This leaves only one option, and the big question is, "What are the chances that God will grant justification to people who have not earned it and do not deserve it?" The answer comes loud and clear, that God has made His righteousness available "apart from the law" and that He has carefully shown this to be the case in His long dealings with His people through the law and the prophets. Further on in the epistle, Paul draws from the ancient writings of the Old Testament to show instances where God has consistently shown that human effort will never be satisfactory and that only humble faith will suffice.

When I was in training as a Marine, I remember one particularly grueling exercise where we were deposited in the center of Dartmoor, one of the bleakest parts of England, and told to make our way on foot to a certain point on the map more than fifty rugged miles away. As we had done a similar journey the previous day, slept out on the hard ground for a number of nights, and been brought slowly to the point of physical and mental exhaustion, we knew that it was going to be a long day. What we didn't know was that my partner's feet, which had a tendency to blister, would become so badly worn after a few miles that they would become like pieces of raw meat. When I realized he was in pain, I took his equipment and added it to mine. Later I supported him on my shoulder as he hobbled along, but it became increasingly plain to me and to the colleagues who caught up with us that he wasn't going to make it. But he was made of stern stuff and he insisted that he would keep going, that we should go on and stop worrying about him. After many more excruciating miles, however, he came to the point of admitting he was through, and then I was able to pick him up, put him across my shoulders, and carry him the rest of the way. He had no option but to trust himself to me to do for him what he was incapable of doing for himself. It was hard for him to be so humiliated, but it was his sole recourse, and it is hard for proud people like Paul and other earnest people to admit that there is no way of justification through self-effort, but only through "faith in Jesus Christ."

So far in the epistle we have been introduced to God as the God of wrath and righteousness and judgment, but now Paul introduces us to the God of grace. Behind the decision of God to provide the means of redemption for man through Christ lies a deep, beautiful facet of the character of God. It is because He is a God of grace that there is a gospel to proclaim and a Savior to extol. Far from tiring of His tiresome children, the Father chooses to deal graciously with them. While perfectly free to leave His errant creation to self-destruct, the Creator decides to offer forgiveness and reconciliation with no strings attached. Seated on His magisterial throne, the Judge of all the earth has all the evidence necessary justly to banish a guilty race from His holy presence. But instead He elects to grant a pardon, and this He does "freely by His grace." Mankind has for so long been so enamored of its considerable achievements and so confident of its own capabilities that it has a residual feeling it has some moral pull with God that makes it impossible for Him to be anything but gracious to us. After all, we have done a truly remarkable job with His creation—developing it, organizing it, exploring it, and generally harnessing it—and in all fairness we feel that God should at least acknowledge that He does owe us something. To think like this, even subconsciously, is to be out of touch with biblical reality but, more important, out of tune with the nature and character of God. He didn't have to do a single thing. We had no hold on Him whatsoever. He acted "freely" out of sheer grace.

"Grace" and its related words such as graceful and gracious all have warm positive connotations. That which is graceful, whether it be an athlete on the playing field, a bride walking down the aisle, or an eagle lighting on an eyrie, evokes admiration and appreciation. Gracious people tend to shine serenely in the midst of uncouth behavior; they silence the unrestrained and invest mediocrity with a degree of significance, and people are grateful. So it is with the graceful, gracious act of God in tempering justice with mercy, mixing holy wrath with divine restraint and blending condemnation with forgiveness. When men adequately understand grace, they no longer resist and resent God but long to draw near to Him. Confronted with inevitable wrath, they look desperately for the mountains to fall on them. But grace sends them with happy feet to the mountains to publish glad tidings.

On my first trip to the United States as a young and inexperienced preacher, I was taken into a men's store by a new friend who promptly disappeared after introducing me to the storekeeper. To my utter amazement and embarrassment, he started to take down my measurements. Looking around for my friend, who was nowhere to be seen, I stammered, "I think there must be some mistake. I just came in with my friend and I have no idea where he has disappeared." The storekeeper just smiled and went on merrily measuring, and then said, "You obviously haven't known Jim very long. He loves to bring preachers in here so we can fit them out with a new wardrobe." When Jim eventually returned and I tried to explain my embarrassment, he was highly amused and said to me, "I'm doing this for you because I want to." To me, a preacher of grace, that was a striking example of grace. Unmerited generosity for no other reason than the desire of the gracious one to be gracious. All I had to do was swallow my pride and graciously accept and then get busy expressing my gratitude!

If the grace motivation, from which our salvation flows, leaves us in a state of wondering gratitude, the means whereby the salvation becomes a reality is likely to render us speechless. It is through ". . . *the redemption that is in Christ Jesus, whom God has set forth to be a propitiation, through faith, in His blood. . ."* (3:24–25). This quotation includes three words which we need to examine closely. The first, "redemption," is vaguely familiar because it is used in financial dealings; the second, "propitiation," is totally unfamiliar outside theological circles; and the third, "blood," is troublesome because it seems incongruous to modern-day people.

In New Testament times the infamous slave market was a common sight. Hapless individuals were callously displayed before potential buyers who would examine them and, if satisfied that they had a bargain, would purchase the slave by paying a *lutron*—a ransom price. Fortunately, those days are long gone, but, sadly, we are living in days where similarly reprehensible tactics are employed for a variety of ends. We are all too familiar with hijackings, kidnappings, and hostage-taking, which so often are resolved only when innocent people pay exorbitant ransoms to release equally innocent captives. The word "redemption" in the Greek is *apolutrosis,* which means "to deliver by paying the *lutron* or ransom." Paul sees the human race which he describes as being "under sin" in a situation not unlike that of a slave or hostage held against his will under bondage and incapable of delivering himself. But Christ is portrayed as the One who, coming into the place of our bondage and observing our hostage status, freely offered to deliver us by paying the ransom Himself.

We must not forget that an adequate redemption must deliver people from the practicalities of living "under sin" and also be sufficient to deal with the just and holy wrath of an offended Deity.

A *lutron* of such proportions must, of necessity, be phenomenal—and indeed it is. Paul says that Christ's ransom price is "His blood."

Modern man is often uncomfortable with the emphasis on "blood sacrifices" in the Old Testament and the frequent references to "the blood of Christ" in the New Testament and understandably has poured scorn on hymns which ask such questions as:

> Are your garments spotless,
> Are they white as snow,
> Are they washed in the blood
> of the Lamb?

Theologians have been quick to denounce what they have called "the gospel of gore," and congregations have voted to ban hymns which extol the virtues of "the blood." It should be pointed out, however, that while the expression may sound strange to the modern ear, the meaning of the expression is imperative for the modern heart. So while we must insist that the term be translated into understandable phraseology, under no circumstances may we move from an acceptance of the meaning of "the blood." When the Bible uses expressions related to "the blood" it is employing readily understandable figures of speech for "a life being laid down." The price of human redemption is nothing less than the voluntary surrender by Christ of His life on the Cross.

The necessity for this stupendous act is explained in the word "propitiation" (Greek, *hilastērion*). Considerable theological debate has raged around the different understandings of *hilastērion*. When used in secular Greek, it referred to the sacrifices offered to pagan deities as a means of appeasing their displeasure and averting their anger. Some theologians have simply transferred this concept to the New Testament and seen Christ's sacrifice as a means of placating an angry God. Others have objected to this interpretation on the grounds that it demeans the character of God and demotes Him to the level of a petty pagan deity. A different view emphasizes the fact that *hilastērion* is used in the Septuagint—the Greek translation of the Old Testament—to translate the "mercy seat." In Hebrew ritual, the High Priest appeared before the ark of the covenant which contained the stone tablets of the law and sprinkled blood from a sacrifice on the gold lid of the ark which was called the mercy seat (*hilastērion*). The symbolism richly portrayed the fact that a broken law stood between a holy God and His children, but through the shedding of blood the place of judgment and estrangement became the place of mercy and reconciliation. Christ's death is therefore seen as the means whereby the legitimate demands of God for justice against a sinful race are fully met, leaving Him free to be merciful to those who formerly merited only judgment.

THE ETERNAL BENEFITS

People often ask about the status of those who lived before Christ. If Christ's death is the only means of reconciliation and propitiation, what hope is there for those who through no fault of their own predeceased Christ? Paul answers this question by showing that the death of Christ was as meritorious for those who died before Him as for those who live after Him. He states that it appears that nothing was done about those who sinned prior to Christ and it could, accordingly, be argued that God overlooked their sin while judging the sin of others. If this were true then God's justice and righteousness would be open to question. The apostle insists that God's integrity is unimpaired because the sins were not disregarded, but were related to an event which would take place at a later date, that is the Cross. There is a sense, however, in which this is not strictly true, because in God's way of looking at things, events do not happen in sequence as they do in time but rather they exist in a state of the ever-now because they exist in eternity. This means that in God's mind those who sinned a thousand years prior to Christ were no different in their sinning or in their justification than those who sinned today because the Cross of Christ, while it is an event of time and space, is more importantly an eternal event which is ever-relevant and efficacious. When men and women are finally translated from their time-capsule earth and liberated into eternal blessedness they will find to their intense delight that the Cross of Christ is an eternal reality, ever blessing and constantly the theme of praise and worship.

THE COMMON DENOMINATOR

[27] Where is boasting then? It is excluded. By what law? Of works? No, but by the law of faith. [28] Therefore we conclude that a man is justified by faith apart from the deeds of the law. [29] Or is He the God of the Jews only? Is He not also the God of the Gentiles? Yes, of the Gentiles also, [30] since there is one God who will justify the circumcised by faith and

the uncircumcised through faith. [31] Do we then make void the law through faith? Certainly not! On the contrary, we establish the law.

—Romans 3:27–31

Try to imagine a heaven full of people who had earned their right to be there rather like a political dinner where supporters pay $1,000 a plate. What arrogance and boasting—what cliques and class distinctions—what arguments and suspicions! Heaven would be no heaven at all! Through God's grace this cannot happen. There will not be a trace of boasting for the simple reason that entrance is limited strictly to those who have been justified by faith.

The entrance to the Church of the Nativity in Bethlehem is surprisingly low and for people my size decidedly inconvenient. Watching scores of visitors pass through one day, I inquired why such an impractical approach was retained. I was told that there used to be a large entrance but the nobility rode into the church on their horses.

The authorities decided that church was no place for horseback heroics and that a low entrance that brought everyone down to the same level was far more appropriate. I agreed and gladly folded myself through the door.

Only those who will, by faith, accept justification from the hand of a just God who made it all possible will enjoy its eternal benefits. Receiving something you could never earn and do not deserve is grounds for humility, not arrogance. Gratitude, not boasting, is the language of the redeemed.

NOTES

1. Kenneth S. Wuest, *The New Testament: An Expanded Translation* (Grand Rapids: Eerdmans, 1961), p. 345.

CHAPTER SEVEN—FACING UP TO FAITH
ROMANS 4:1–25

Scripture Outline

The Father of Faith (4:1–4)

The Forgiveness of Faith (4:5–8)

The Family of Faith (4:9–16)

The Factors of Faith (4:17–25)

There is a surprising resistance to the message of "justification by faith." Not infrequently I have been challenged by people who have said, "Do you mean to tell me that if a murderer-rapist repents and believes at the last minute before he dies he will be justified by God because of Christ, but a decent, honest, moral person who doesn't believe will not be justified?" There is nothing new about this difficulty as can be seen from Paul's introduction of God the Father of faith in verse 1 of Romans 4.

THE FATHER OF FAITH

4:1 What then shall we say that Abraham our father has found according to the flesh? [2] For if Abraham was justified by works, he has something to boast about, but not before God. [3] For what does the Scripture say? "Abraham believed God, and it was accounted to him for righteousness." [4] Now to him who works, the wages are not counted as grace but as debt.
—*Romans 4:1–4*

Opponents of Paul's message, particularly those who came from a traditional Jewish background would phrase the question slightly differently. "Are you saying that God will forgive Gentile reprobates who happen to believe in Jesus while our father Abraham who lived a superb life without knowing Christ will not be accepted?" There was, of course, no doubt about the caliber of Abraham's life—in fact, God called him, "my friend" (Is. 41:8) and said, "Abraham obeyed my voice, and kept my charge, my commandments, my statutes, and my laws" (Gen. 26:5). It was clear that Abraham had not lived his superb life because of his intimate knowledge of the risen Christ. He could not, therefore, be said to have been justified other than by his works because he had not so much as heard of Christ. Therefore, Paul's gospel was palpably false.

Abraham, having received such an endorsement from God, could presumably be well satisfied with his success and indulge in a little boasting about his accomplishments and God's unstinting praise. Paul, however, remarks that Abraham might be able to boast, *"but not before God"* (v. 2). In other words, the argument sounds great and is certainly most convincing except where it really matters, and that is *"before God."*

In verse 3, Paul is quoting Genesis 15 which records the dramatic conversation between the Lord and His servant. Speaking to Abraham in the quietness of his innermost being, the Lord reminded him that He was his "exceedingly great reward." Abraham's response was a startled, "How can you say that when I am constantly denied the one treasure I desire more than any other—a son who will perpetuate my name?" In a most remarkable reply, the Lord said, "Abraham, you will have your son—a real son, not an adopted son—and through him you will become the father of such a host of people that they will resemble the stars of the sky." Despite all the obvious difficulties bound up in such a promise Abraham believed God implicitly. With complete abandon he trusted himself and his most cherished ambitions to his God and what his God was committed to do, and it was "counted to him for righteousness."

Paul is able to show quite clearly from the Old Testament that Abraham's acceptance with God came through his faith, not his works, although his works were exemplary. Far from being the cause of his acceptance with God, Abraham's lifestyle was the result of his acceptance. God did not declare him righteous because he was so good, but rather Abraham lived a good life because God had freely justified him by faith.

The logic of all this is sometimes hard for Western minds to follow, so it is encouraging to discover that the Greek word for "counted" is *logizomai* which, besides having obvious connections with the English word "logic," means "to place to someone's account." God, out of grace, determines to make righteousness available to those who will humbly accept it by faith.

Shortly before I married his daughter, my father-in-law said to me, "Stuart, if you drive over to Austria and go to the little border town of Feldkirk, at a certain address you will find a person who has some funds which I have placed in your name. Go and collect them and you will have more than enough for three weeks vacation on the continent of Europe." I believed him, traveled over, met the person, in faith claimed what he had promised, and found that my father-in-law, in sheer grace, had actually placed the funds to my account.

For me to have traveled around Europe bragging about my newfound wealth and pretending that it was the product of my work would have been as insulting to my father-in-law as it would have been removed from the truth. If any boasting was permissible at all, it was limited to boasting about the generosity of another on my behalf. In the same way Abraham, the recipient of grace through faith, had nothing to boast about.

THE FORGIVENESS OF FAITH

5 But to him who does not work but believes on Him who justifies the ungodly, his faith is accounted for righteousness,
6 just as David also describes the blessedness of the man to whom God imputes righteousness apart from works:
7 "Blessed are those whose lawless deeds are forgiven,
And whose sins are covered;
8 Blessed is the man to whom the LORD shall not impute sin."

—Romans 4:5–8

Paul was not satisfied with proving his point from the experience of the great patriarch alone but also called in another Old Testament heavyweight—none other than King David—to further substantiate his argument. Quoting from Psalm 32, he showed that God imputes (the same word as "counted," noted above) "righteousness apart from the law," and this introduced those so enriched into a state of "blessedness" where sins are "covered," "forgiven," and "not imputed."

"Blessedness" is a word which, when used by ancient Greek writers, usually referred to the state of the gods. For instance, Homer, in his *Odyssey,* has Minerva rebuke the council of gods because apparently they are totally unconcerned about the desperate plight of Ulysses while living in *makarios*—eternal blessedness—themselves. In New Testament usage, the word has to do with the sense of spiritual joy and ecstasy that comes from participation in the gracious activity of God in human affairs.

As we have already seen, God's imputing has a positive side in that He counts righteousness to the ungodly, but the negative aspect of His imputing ministry is no less exciting for He also declines to impute sin to those who have broken His law when they come to Him in faith. A bookkeeper would look at it as if a generous donor was placing vast credits to our account and also refusing to debit the withdrawals but rather was placing them against his own account.

When Paul wrote to Philemon about Onesimus, the runaway slave whom Paul had met far from home, he asked Onesimus to receive him back again and promised to accept all responsibility for anything that Onesimus might owe his master. *"If he has wronged you or owes anything, put that on my account"* (Philem. v. 18). Onesimus must surely have experienced the *makarios* of the slave released from obligation in much the same way that people from Abraham through David and Paul down to our own day have rejoiced in the blessedness of the justified.

Human sinfulness is expressed in such a variety of ways that biblical authors in both Hebrew and Greek found it necessary to employ a variety of words to express their understanding of sin. Both David in Psalm 32 and Paul in his quotation of the Psalm in Romans 4 are good examples of this, and the expressions they used are full of significance. Delitzsch defined the Hebrew words for "lawless deeds" as "a breaking loose or tearing away from God"; "sins" as "deviation from that which is well-pleasing to God," and "iniquity" as "a perversion, distortion, misdeed." Forgiveness has as many facets as the sin it seeks to dispel, and Delitzsch describes it as "a lifting up and taking away. . . a covering so that it becomes invisible to God, the Holy One, and is as though it had never taken place."[1]

As we have seen, man's superficial attitude to sin and forgiveness can only be countered by an adequate understanding of the immensity and seriousness of the human problem. Those who find sin relatively unimportant find little difficulty in expecting that human effort, however half-hearted, may well merit forgiveness, but those who know what sin is also know that only divine action can deal with it. In the same way, those who regard "forgiveness" as a type of "forgetting" coupled with a shrug of the divine shoulders see no necessity for man to take his sin with anything more than a grain of salt. But those who realize that forgiveness entails "a taking away" and a "covering so that it becomes invisible to God" as well as the willingness of God to accept accountability for human sin while relieving man of responsibility, also know that this requires more than human activity—in fact, nothing less than divine intervention. Only the grace of God can initiate such an act of mercy and only the open hand of faith can receive such blessedness. Such is the forgiveness that comes through faith.

THE FAMILY OF FAITH

When God called Abram from Ur, told him of the Promised Land, and outlined His covenant, He clearly illustrated that, once more, He was taking the initiative and moving graciously into the affairs of man. Through this man He intended to move into the affairs of a family which, by His description, was going to be very large and far-reaching. Jewish people have, quite rightly, traced their roots to Abraham with great pride, but so also have the Arabs—the former, through Isaac, the latter through Ishmael. When Paul speaks of Abraham as "the father of us all," the family of which Abraham is father is neither the Jewish nor the Arab family but something that transcends both and incorporates far more. It is the family of all those who believe, the family of faith.

[9] Does this blessedness then come upon the circumcised only, or upon the uncircumcised also? For we say that faith was accounted to Abraham for righteousness. [10] How then was it accounted? While he was circumcised, or uncircumcised? Not while circumcised, but while uncircumcised. [11] And he received the sign of circumcision, a seal of the righteousness of the faith which he had while still uncircumcised, that he might be the father of all those who believe, though they are uncircumcised, that righteousness might be imputed to them also, [12] and the father of circumcision to those who not only are of the circumcision, but who also walk in the steps of the faith which our father Abraham had while still uncircumcised. [13] For the promise that he would be the heir of the world was not to Abraham or to his seed through the law, but through the righteousness of faith. [14] For if those who are of the law are heirs, faith is made void and the promise made of no effect, [15] because the law brings about wrath; for where there is no law there is no transgression. [16] Therefore it is of faith that it might be according to grace, so that the promise might be sure to all the seed, not

only to those who are of the law, but also to those who are of the faith of Abraham, who is the father of us all
—*Romans 4:9–16*

The somewhat tedious nature of this part of the epistle has led some people to avoid it. This is unfortunate because great and powerful truths are to be found in it. Continuing to use Abraham as an illustration of God's dealings with man, the apostle points to the chronology of events in this part of the divine human drama. When God had made His promise to Abraham, it had been believed with the result that justification by faith was experienced. Fourteen years later the Lord introduced the concept of circumcision. Paul's inescapable conclusion is that as Abraham was declared justified fourteen years before he was circumcised, he was quite obviously not justified because he was circumcised. Therefore God is not interested in a man's circumcision but in whether or not he is a man of faith. There are, in the divine way of looking at things, uncircumcised believers and circumcised unbelievers. The former are justified; the latter are not justified. In a similar passage in Galatians, Paul stated that the law was given to Moses 430 years after Abraham had been justified by faith, and therefore neither Abraham nor anybody else would ever be justified by keeping the law but only by believing unto righteousness. In fact Paul says bluntly, *"The promise. . . was not to Abraham or to his seed through the law, but through the righteousness of faith."* He adds that "the law brings about wrath."

These truths, when applied, lead to the discovery that there is one thing God is looking for in the confused and convoluted world of human religion, tradition, and culture. Is that man in the midst of all the accumulated weight of the Jewish tradition a humble believer in the God who justified the ungodly? Is that Muslim who professes to pray five times a day, to give to the poor, to visit Mecca, to observe Ramadan trusting in his ritual or in the God who justifies freely by His grace? Is the Buddhist who in his quest for enlightenment endeavors to practice right views, right desires, right speech, right conduct, right mode of living, right effort, right awareness, and right meditation really trusting in the eightfold path or in a God who through the blood of Christ freely forgives our straying from His path? The same can be said for Baptist, Seventh Day Adventist, Presbyterian, Episcopalian, all denominations. . . what are they looking to for salvation?

The British Commonwealth is a remarkable phenomenon not least because it survived the demise of the British Empire and found a unique identity of its own. Comprised of nations which differ in political ideology, religious persuasion, cultural identity, economic status, and geographical location, it still hangs together. At times its member nations have squared off against each other, misunderstandings have abounded, and all manner of political maneuvering which has taxed even British diplomacy has characterized the scene. What makes it work? Some say "allegiance to the Crown," others more skeptical say "economic and diplomatic expedience," but, whatever it is, the Commonwealth manages to hold together what would in practically all other circumstances fall apart.

There is another phenomenon which defies all human explanation. It is known as the Christian church or the family of faith. I have traveled round the world many times, meeting with people whose backgrounds are so diverse and whose traditions are so opposed that it would appear that nothing, not even the Commonwealth, would ever get them together. And yet they *are* together—the Jew, the Muslim, the Buddhist, the agnostic, the Marxist. I've met them all, but these are not their prime characteristics. They preserve their national differences, they revere their cultural differences, but they place all these things in a subordinate position to their relationship to the justifying God and His Son. In so doing they allow other fragmenting factors to become irrelevancies in the light of their family status. They understand that the promise of God's forgiveness is to *"all the seed, not only to those who are of the law, but also to those who are of the faith of Abraham, the father of us all."* What a family!

THE FACTORS OF FAITH

[17] (as it is written, "I have made you a father of many nations") in the presence of Him whom he believed—God, who gives life to the dead and calls those things which do not exist as though they did; [18] who, contrary to hope, in hope believed, so that he became the father of many nations, according to what was spoken, "So shall your descendants be." [19] And not being weak in faith, he did not consider his own body, already dead (since he was about a hundred years old), and the deadness of Sarah's womb. [20] He did not waver at the promise of God through unbelief, but was strengthened in faith, giving glory to God, [21] and being fully convinced that what He had promised He was also able to perform. [22] And therefore "it was accounted to him for righteousness."

23 Now it was not written for his sake alone that it was imputed to him, 24 but also for us. It shall be imputed to us who believe in Him who raised up Jesus our Lord from the dead, 25 who was delivered up because of our offenses, and was raised because of our justification.

—*Romans 4:17–25*

With everything hinging on faith, it is no surprise that Paul analyzes the faith of Abraham so that there would be no confusion in peoples' minds as to what constitutes faith. First we must note that his faith was *confidence in a person: ". . . in the presence of Him whom he believed—God, who gives life to the dead and calls those things which do not exist as though they did"* (Rom. 4:17).

When it comes to the subject of faith it is amazing how vague people become. To have a "lot of faith" is applauded, and the need for "more faith" is often expressed. People of "strong faith" are revered, those of "another faith" are distrusted. In all these common expressions of contemporary understanding of faith there is one major misunderstanding. The object of faith is that which really matters more than anything else. Some people who had strong faith in thin ice never lived to tell the tale but died by faith. Others who had weak faith in thick ice were as safe as if they stood on concrete. Abraham's faith is not exemplary because of its strength or lack of it, but because its object was God. Through the years, people of faith in their own abilities have perished; men and women who believed implicitly that God was dead found out they were wrong. Their faith was sincere, but sincerely wrong, as was the case when my mother believed the bottle of medication contained something beneficial but when applied to my brother it proved to be acid! But she believed sincerely to the contrary. This is not to suggest that faith should be unintelligent.

Abraham's faith was clearly related to his knowledge of its object. In the same way that the man on thick ice knows about its thickness before he exercises faith in it, so Abraham knew two things about his God whom he trusted: *". . . he believed—God, who gives life to the dead and calls those things which do not exist as though they did; who, contrary to hope, in hope believed, so that he became the father of many nations . . ."* (Rom. 4:17–18). He was the God who specializes in breathing life into deadness and speaking the creative word which brings into existence things which previously were nonexistent. The magnitude of these concepts of God is so vast that they should not be overlooked because it is possible that some believers believe in a God who is far removed from the One revealed in Scripture. J. B. Phillips expressed this in the title of his book, *Your God Is Too Small!*

People all round Abraham believed in something, probably as fervently as he believed in his superlative God. But, of course, their experience was limited, not because of their faith, but because of the limitations of that which they believed. Belief sometimes is nothing more than empty superstition, but intelligent faith knows intimately that which it believes. We should also note that Abraham's faith was expressed by a hope which believed *"contrary to hope."* When we talk about hope we often convey a sense of hopelessness and desperation. We "hope" someone will show up or something will happen, but we have no real grounds for such hope. Abraham, naturally speaking, had no basis for believing that he would, in his old age, become the father of many nations. Frankly, it was a hopeless situation. Nevertheless he believed in hope. His "hope" was rooted in God and His word and, therefore, had a ring of confidence rather than a touch of desperation. His faith was confidence in a person.

Second, in Romans 4:19 we read that his faith, far from ignoring the practical realities of the situation and closing its eyes to the facts of life which surrounded him, was a faith that was *conversant with the problems.* It must be admitted that there are some textual problems in the manuscripts of this passage of the epistle which appear to say opposite things. Some would give the impression that he carefully avoided thinking about the facts of his own old age and his wife's infertility. Other manuscripts present Abraham as carefully considering both these factors, refusing to be intimidated by his circumstances but rather demonstrating the faith for which he was famous. I believe the latter interpretation is to be preferred.

Nothing is to be gained in terms of virile faith by ignoring those factors which militate against faith. On the contrary, strong faith triumphs over the difficulties it fully understands. Abraham was able to grapple adequately with the deadness of his own body precisely because he believed in a God *"who gives life to the dead"* (v. 17). His inadequacy, therefore, became the arena in which God's power was to be shown instead of the place where his faith would sink without a trace. The fact of Sarah's incapability to bear a son even in her youth was matched in Abraham's mind with the fact that God "calls the things that are not as being in existence."[2]

The nonexistent capacity of Sarah's womb was the very place to prove God's ability to make the barren womb capable of reproduction. Abraham showed that faith links its knowledge of the person (God) with the difficulties that stand in faith's way and throws in its lot with the reality of God in the situation.

The third aspect of Abraham's faith was that it was *consistent in its progress,* as Paul tells us in Romans 4:20. My father used to tell me that he was continually surprised that the same sun that hardens clay also melts wax. Obviously there is something about the composition of the two substances that produces the opposite results when exposed to identical conditions. Some people, when faced with delay and discouragement, "waver" in their faith, while others are strengthened by the delay. *Diakrithenai* ("to doubt or to waver") is a graphic word which means, literally, "to have two minds or opinions" and, therefore, to stagger and waver. When he considered his circumstances on the one hand, Abraham must have been tempted to sink into despair; yet when he considered the promise of God as it related to his circumstances he must have been euphoric. The tendency would have been to vacillate between the two extremes. This he refused to do, preferring instead patiently to trust God to work through interminable delays and disappointments. In so doing he quietly "gave glory to God." The more opportunities he was given to praise God in faith and be reminded of the promise of God irrespective of circumstances, the more he was led into a stronger trust in God. People who nervously board airplanes tend to settle down halfway across the Atlantic, not because God gives them more faith, but because the longer they sit on the plane and it stays up, the more they learn it is worthy of trust, and, accordingly, they trust it more. They are strengthened in their faith through the ongoing experience of the faithfulness of faith's object.

In the fourth place Abraham's faith was *convinced of the promises* (Rom. 4:21). When I was a young traveling evangelist I neglected my family, and my patient wife carried my burden in addition to her own. She occasionally suggested that I ought to take a family vacation, but, having agreed with her, I promptly forgot about it. One day I said facetiously, "Okay, if you want a family vacation, I'll take you all to Majorca in the Mediterranean for a couple of weeks." Her response was simply, "Stuart, that's not funny." Shortly after this conversation, I received a phone call from a friend who told me that he had made reservations for Jill, the children, and me to go to Majorca for a two-week vacation. To make sure that we would go he proposed coming with us. When I told Jill, her response was completely different. "Fantastic, wonderful, how exciting!" This response was elicited because when I said it she knew I did not mean it. Even if I did I could not afford it, and if I could have afforded it, I probably would not have spent the money! So why take that kind of statement seriously? When I said that Norman had promised, however, the situation was different because he meant it, could afford it, and had demonstrated his generosity to us previously. She, like Abraham, was fully convinced that what he had promised he was able also to perform.

It was this kind of faith that led to Abraham's justification, as Paul reminds us in Romans 4:23–25. When we read about the great heroes of the faith such as Abraham there is a tendency for us to feel that they had a special corner on God and thus it was easier for them to believe; if we had similar opportunities we would probably believe in similar fashion. Paul introduces a thought that explodes this idea completely. He reminds us that while Abraham believed in a God who could raise the dead, we have a record of an event which showed that God can raise the dead and that He *has* raised His Son from the grave. The object of the believer's faith is not only the God of Abraham but also the God and Father of our Lord Jesus Christ.

Paul's statement concerning the death and Resurrection of Christ shows that it was not the death of Christ alone which provides the basis upon which God justifies the believer, for if Christ had stayed dead, He would never have been regarded as anything other than another unfortunate martyr to a lost cause. But through His Resurrection, He was shown to be the "Son of God with power" and, accordingly, the divine answer to the human problem.

NOTES

1. Carl F. Keil and Franz Delitzsch, *Old Testament Commentaries,* 10 vols. (Grand Rapids: Eerdmans), *Nehemiah to Psalm LXXVII,* p. 1134.

2. Wuest, *Word Studies, Romans,* p. 71.

CHAPTER EIGHT—GOOD CHRISTIAN MEN, REJOICE
ROMANS 5:1–11

Scripture Outline

Rejoice in Your Present Position (5:1–5)

Rejoice in Your Future Prospects (5:1–5)

Rejoice in Your Personal Problems (5:1–5)

Rejoice in Your Spiritual Possessions (5:6–10)

Rejoice in Your God's Person (5:11)

The church I am privileged to serve as pastor is made up of people from a wide variety of backgrounds. Some come from church traditions which have a keenly developed sense of the majesty and holiness of God, and their worship and service has clearly reflected this in their preference for order, poise, and reverence. Many of our people, however, have had little or no previous church experience and until recently have lived their lives in varying degrees of disintegration because they have lived unrelated to the One who alone brings meaning and content to existence. On discovering Christ as Savior and Lord, these people have experienced such a dramatic, revolutionary change that their whole lives have taken on a fresh new aura of joy and celebration. For them anything to do with Christ and His church is exciting and exhilarating and shows itself in free, uninhibited expressions of joy and delight.

Many churches have split at the seams because of such differences, but our people have avoided this because they have recognized the validity of each others' position through study of the Scriptures. They have recognized that the Bible has much to say about the holiness of God and the necessity for God's people to approach Him with a deep sense of reverence and holy fear. They have also seen that a vital experience of the saving work of Christ leads people to ecstasies of delight which may well be demonstrated in uninhibited acts of worship and celebration.

The early chapters of Romans which expose the awfulness of the human condition in somber, solemn language are hardly designed to make people clap their hands and kick up their spiritual heels. Indeed, such a response would be quite out of keeping with the message being conveyed. But when the apostle switches to an exposition of the divine initiative in Christ which has procured justification and reconciliation through faith, it would be strange if those who believed the message were able to assimilate it into their lives and still sit on their hands and keep their faces from breaking into the widest of evangelical grins and expressions of joy!

It is clear that the apostle believed that believers in Christ should be both somberly reverent at times and joyfully exuberant at other times. In the fifth chapter of Romans, on three occasions he used the Greek word *kauchasthai,* which means "to triumph, to glory, to exult." In the second and eleventh verses it is translated "to rejoice" and in the third verse "to glory."

> 5:1 Therefore, having been justified by faith, we have peace with God through our Lord Jesus Christ, 2 through whom also we have access by faith into this grace in which we stand, and rejoice in hope of the glory of God. 3 And not only that, but we also glory in tribulations, knowing that tribulation produces perseverance; 4 and perseverance, character; and character, hope. 5 Now hope does not disappoint, because the love of God has been poured out in our hearts by the Holy Spirit who was given to us.
>
> —*Romans 5:1–5*

It is right and proper that Christian men should rejoice in whatever manner they feel is compatible with their experience of Christ and the wishes of the Christian community to which they belong.

REJOICE IN YOUR PRESENT POSITION

The relationship between mind and emotion, or heart and head, is important. Sometimes when we exercise our minds, the things we understand have such a profound impact upon us that the emotions are moved in response, and this leads to a healthy experience, provided, of course, that the information producing the emotional reaction is truth. On other occasions, emotions are allowed to govern actions either in direct conflict with the mind or without the mind being brought into play. When this happens, the result can be similar to a car's being parked on an incline without the brakes being applied or the gears being engaged. The sheer power of emotional response to situations when the mind is put out of gear can lead a life on a reckless uncontrolled journey to disaster. For instance, the teenager whose heart rules her head to such a degree that she marries the immature youth against the advice of loving supportive people may be courting trouble. Or the middle-aged woman who sinks into depression because she feels fat and ugly and useless, despite the fact that her husband and family constantly affirm her and express their love to her, is allowing her feelings to divorce her from the facts.

Christians are just as likely as other people to make mistakes in this area. If they embark on a spiritual experience unrelated to facts revealed to them by the Spirit through the Word of God, they will be the victims of every emotional stress known to man. But if they get their theology squared away, they stand a much better chance of being emotionally and spiritually stable.

I have officiated at many wedding ceremonies and so have had considerable experience of nervous brides and distracted grooms. Often they have been strained and inhibited throughout the service, but I have noticed that once they sign the register, a realization that their status has changed and that they are really married bursts upon them. Then bouquets fly through the air and satin gowns are gathered into scrunched-up bunches as the celebration begins. So it is with the person who begins to grasp that he has been "justified by faith." The realization of changed status and position is designed to bring exclamations of joy from the believer's heart.

This should be expressed in the private life of the believer as well as in the corporate life of the church. Often I find myself literally shouting for joy as I contemplate my justified status—even if I am driving along the freeway! Then when I meet with God's people in worship, I love to join my voice with hundreds of others proclaiming such sentiments as:

> Born of the Spirit with life from above,
> Into God's family divine,
> Justified fully through Calvary's love,
> O, what a standing is mine!
> And the transaction so quickly was made

When as a sinner I came,
Took of the offer
Of grace He did proffer—
He saved me,
O, praise His dear name![1]

Paul also reminds the Roman believers that *"we have peace through our Lord Jesus Christ"* (Rom. 5:1). Foerster helpfully writes, "The basic feature of the Greek concept of *'eirene'* is that the word does not primarily denote a relationship between several people, or an attitude, but a state, i.e., 'time of peace' or 'state of peace' originally conceived of purely as an interlude in the ever-lasting state of war."[2] It would not be stretching Paul's meaning too far to say that, through the work of Christ, mankind can be set free from the "everlasting state of war" between God and man and be at peace. One of the most vivid recollections of my youth was the ecstasy with which we Britishers welcomed VE Day in 1945. The lights which had been blacked out for years were allowed to shine freely, the church bells which had been silent for six long years rang cheerfully once more, and the people danced in the streets long into the night. There is great joy in being at peace.

Then there is the added incentive to joy in knowing that *"we have access by faith into this grace in which we stand"* (Rom. 5:2). Godet says that the word "access" (Greek, *prosagogē*) "sometimes signifies the act of bringing or introducing." Like most fathers of teenagers, I learned some time ago that the young people usually prefer the company of their peers to that of their elders. Accordingly, when we have friends of our age in the home, our young people are free to excuse themselves whenever courtesy allows. One day they not only wanted to stay around, but mysteriously, many of their friends appeared, too! The reason was not hard to find. Our guest was Billy Graham, and every kid in the neighborhood wanted to be introduced! Billy Graham would be the first to agree that being intro-duced to "grace" and being allowed to stand firmly and securely in the benefits of grace is the greatest introduction which produces the deepest joy.

REJOICE IN YOUR FUTURE PROJECTS

Predicting the future has always been as exciting as it is pre-carious. At a recent meeting of the National Committee for Monetary Reform, in New Orleans, over 5,000 people discussed trends and predicted consequences. Many widely divergent views were expressed. For example, one expert was so optimistic about the real estate market, he predicted a new boom. But another expert from the same field said, "The least safe place for money in the next four years is real estate," and another told his hearers to "kiss the recovery in housing good-by." In other words, the experts can't have any great certainty about the future, not only in real estate, but also in every other area of existence. This uncertainty produces anxiety, which naturally leads to many complications such as breakdown in confidence on a broad societal scale and all manner of individual maladies.

Paul insists that the believer can be delivered from apprehension into a state where he can *"rejoice in hope of the glory of God"* (Rom. 5:2). Having stated that man is constantly "coming short of the glory of God," Paul now teaches that those who have been justified can look forward with great anticipation to sharing in the glorious experience of all that God is, and all that He has for them in the future. Like Abraham's hope, this hope is rooted not in wishful thinking but in the gracious revelation by God of His eternal purposes.

When I talk with sick people, I see how much hope means to them. At first they hope nothing is wrong. When they discover that all is not well, they hope it is not serious. When that hope perishes, they hope something can be done, but if they are told eventually that there is "no hope," I, as a Christian, can remind them that there is hope even if death cannot be avoided. That hope is centered in the promise of life in the glory after death. Archbishop Leighton wrote, "The world dares say no more. . . than *Dum spiro spero* ('while I breathe I hope'); but the children of God can add by virtue of this living hope, *Dum exspiro spero."*[3] Even those people who do not know Latin can grasp the Archbishop's meaning. When uncertainty prevails anxiety reigns, but where future hope is rooted in the Risen Christ, joy rules supreme.

REJOICE IN YOUR PERSONAL PROBLEMS

One of the chief criticisms of Christianity is that it promises "pie in the sky when you die" but offers little for the present. Some preachers who talk rather exclusively about the future as if they were encouraging their people to survive on the promise that they would soon be out of the unpleasantness of the present may have contributed to this misunderstanding. But anyone reading Paul would recognize that the criticism is totally without merit.

Not only do believers rejoice in their position and their prospects, but they are encouraged to rejoice in their problems! Far from advocating escapism, the gospel of Christ offers realistic truth for living in the midst of difficult situations with joy, even to the extent of appreciating the problems.

Paul's gospel makes it possible to *"glory in tribulations also. . ."* (v. 3). He is not suggesting that there is merit in developing a martyr complex, and he is certainly not advocating a kind of masochism. Rather, he is showing that we live in an environment where troubles are inevitable but not insurmountable. The Lord Jesus clearly taught His disciples, ". . . In the world you will have tribulation; but be of good cheer, I have overcome the world" (John 16:33).

The word for "tribulation" means "pressure," and while most people would testify to the unpleasantness of pressure, believers are able to rejoice in the unpleasantness. This is not because they flippantly ignore it or psychologically block it out with loud exclamations of "Praise the Lord" but because they know what is going on and welcome it.

Paul sees a chain of events in the life of Christians which when adequately understood can lead only to thanksgiving. He says that *"tribulation produces perseverance"* (v. 3). Literally, *hupomenō*, the word, translated "perseverance," means to "abide under" and suggests that the believer not only learns to abide in Christ when all is well but also learns to abide in Him under the things that are producing pressure. There is always a temptation to quit when life becomes difficult, but when believers realize that difficulties instead of being the causes of quitting can be the means of abiding deeper in Christ, their attitude to difficulties can be radically altered. A Korean Christian once told me that when he and his friends were under great pressure from the Communists, they used to say, "We are like nails: the harder you hit us the deeper you drive us." This is perseverance.

The next link in the chain is *"perseverance [produces] character"* (v. 4). Our word "character" hardly does justice to the Greek word used here *(dokimē)* which incorporates the idea of the approvedness that comes from passing through a trial. Paul, writing to the Philippians, used the same word about Timothy: "But you know his proven character" (Phil. 2:22), referring to the stability which the young man had exhibited in the fiery furnace of evangelistic endeavor with Paul. The people in the church at Philippi were in a position to recognize the type of man he was by the way he had come through his ordeals.

When these qualities begin to develop as a result of tribulation and perseverance, they lead to the next link, which is that *"character [produces] hope"* (v. 4). As we have already noted, New Testament "hope" means "confidence." It is not hard to see how those who have come through ordeals on previous occasions can look much more confidently at those which are looming on the horizon.

The most important part of the process of character-building lies behind the pressures that produce the character. Is it evil gone berserk that sends the pressure? Does a mindless, heartless fate control the tender destiny of mankind? Or is God the God of pressure? Paul's answer to such questions is clear and unmistakable: not only is the pressure mandated by God, it is mandated in love. This understanding comes *"because the love of God has been poured out in our hearts by the Holy Spirit who was given to us"* (v. 5). When the Spirit of God enters the life of the redeemed, He opens blind eyes to the wonder of divine love and shows the believer that from now on his life is destined to be governed by this love and all circumstances will be related to a loving purpose. It is knowledge of the divine process and the loving purpose that equips believers for rejoicing in tribulations.

REJOICE IN YOUR SPIRITUAL POSSESSIONS

Should there be doubt in the troubled believer's mind about the love of God, particularly when the pressures seem to indicate that God may be uncaring or forgetful, there is one reminder of God's love which stands supreme.

> [6] For when we were still without strength, in due time Christ died for the ungodly. [7] For scarcely for a righteous man will one die; yet perhaps for a good man someone would even dare to die. [8] But God demonstrates His own love toward us, in that while we were still sinners, Christ died for us.
> —*Romans 5:6–8*

The love of God is shown in sharp contrast to man's love by the reminder that mankind is very reticent to lay down its life even for good causes and law-abiding people, but God's Son accepted the death of the Cross for those who are totally unworthy. Paul uses strong words to describe those whom God loves and for whom Christ died. Three of the words express the deficiencies of human beings; we are *"without strength,"* *"ungodly,"* and *"sinners."* We lack the power to live as we ought even though we may have the power to live as we wish because our standards are so low. We lack the attitude of reverence and holy awe which a correct understanding of God's person requires and demands, and we lack the capability to hit the mark or achieve the divine expectations. This pitiful description would hardly move mankind to love such failures, but God's love is demonstrated in the supreme sacrifice of the Son for such people.

The fourth word is quite different. Instead of expressing a deficiency it portrays an ability to be "enemies" (v. 10). In the Greek, the word translated "enemies" can be either active or passive, which means that it can refer to man's antagonism to God, or to God's antagonism to man. While both are true, we should, of course, not confuse the sinful antagonism of a man with the holy, pure antagonism of God to all that is offensive to His nature.

The link between what mankind is and what mankind does must not be overlooked. The people who are lacking in strength and godliness and capability to achieve the divine ends have amassed records of appalling spiritual failure for which they are responsible. The hostility of man toward God has produced catalogues of actions repugnant to the holy God. Therefore God's loving provision deals not only with what man is but also what he has done. Paul outlines this provision as follows:

> [9] Much more then, having now been justified by His blood, we shall be saved from wrath through Him. [10] For if when we were enemies we were reconciled to God through the death of His Son, much more, having been reconciled, we shall be saved by His life.
> —*Romans 5:9–10*

The death of Christ on behalf of sinful mankind has made it possible for man to be *"justified by His blood."* This deals thoroughly with what man has done. The consequences of man's sin led him to the certain expectation of divine judgment, but the love of God made it possible for man also to be confident that he would be *"saved from wrath through Him."* But Paul shows that there is *"much more"* to our salvation than being saved from what we have done. *"We shall be saved by His life"* refers to the fact that God has provided, in Christ, the answer to what we are.

That Christ died is clear, but that Christ lives is sometimes overlooked. I was reminded of that when my friend Ian Thomas gave me the manuscript of his first book to read. The title was *The*

Saving Life of Christ, and instinctively I thought that should be "The Saving Death of Christ." His emphasis on the fact of the risen Christ's ability to reside in the life of the justified believer was firmly based on the fact that God's loving provision for sinful man includes a living Christ as well as a dying Savior.

When man considers that he is without strength, he may be moved to discouragement. Once justified, he may become frustrated in his efforts to live the justified life. But God has provided the living Christ in order that he might "be strengthened with might by His Spirit in the inner man" (Eph. 3:16). This also means that the indwelling Christ can save him from the ungodly attitudes that formerly characterized his life and produce in him a more seemly attitude of reverence for the Lord. Sinners who cannot hit the target find that the sheer power of the living Lord can enable them to hit what once they consistently missed, and the old enemy attitudes begin to disappear as the Son of God begins to impart His life. When we consider the scope of God's provision for us in Christ, we rejoice in the greatness of the things we possess because He loved us.

REJOICE IN YOUR GOD'S PERSON

William Barclay calls the early verses of Romans 5 "one of Paul's great lyrical passages." There is an air of excitement about what he is saying and such a sense of rejoicing in his appreciation of the truth being conveyed that he seems almost unable to stop. This reminds me of Beethoven's apparent reluctance to conclude his Fifth Symphony, as evidenced by the length of the coda. When we feel that there can be nothing to add Paul writes:

> [11] And not only that, but we also rejoice in God through our Lord Jesus Christ, through whom we have now received the reconciliation.
>
> *—Romans 5:11*

There is a sense in which Paul has saved the best kind of rejoicing to the last. Certainly we rejoice in hope and in troubles, in salvation and in our spiritual position, but more than all this we *"rejoice in God."* While it is practically impossible for us to think of God without thinking of the benefits we receive from Him, there must be a place in our lives where we have a deep well of joy in the knowledge of who He is quite apart from what we have gained through knowing Him.

I was reminded of this one day when I arrived at Manchester Airport after being away from home for about five months. Looking forward to being reunited with my wife and children, I wondered what my children's first comments would be, but was somewhat taken aback when they rushed toward me shouting, "What did you bring us?" I laughed at their childish preoccupation with things rather than persons and thought rather ruefully of my own childish preoccupation with the things that God has brought me, sometimes at the expense of my appreciation for who He is.

There is boundless cause for rejoicing in the Christian experience. And the more thoroughly we appreciate what God has revealed of Himself and His work on our behalf, the more we can exhibit the joy of the Lord which is our strength.

NOTES

1. John W. Peterson, "O What a Wonderful, Wonderful Day" (© 1961 Singspiration, Inc. All rights reserved. Used by permission.)

2. Kittel and Friedrich, *Theological Dictionary of the New Testament,* 2:400–401.

3. Robert Leighton, *Commentary on First Peter* (Grand Rapids: Kregel Reprint Library, 1972), p. 30.

CHAPTER NINE—THE FOUR MONARCHS
ROMANS 5:12–21

Scripture Outline

> The Reign of Sin (5:12–21)
>
> The Reign of Death (5:12–21)
>
> The Reign of Grace (5:12–21)
>
> The Reign of Life (5:12–21)

The turbulent history of ancient Rome produced no more momentous year than A.D. 69. Nero, having contrived to alienate practically everybody because of his behavior, personality, and policies, finally lost his nerve and brought his shameful life to an ignominious end. His decease terminated a dynasty, and immediately a great power struggle ensued among the armies, the senate, and the patrician families of Rome. The result was much intrigue, tyranny, and murder which earned A.D. 69 the title of "the year of the four emperors."

Paul, in the unfolding story of God's dealings with mankind, now turns his attention to the cosmic struggle of the four monarchs—sin, death, grace, and life. In the passage we shall now consider, notice the four occasions on which the word "reign" appears:

12 Therefore, just as through one man sin entered the world, and death through sin, and thus death spread to all men, because all sinned— 13 (For until the law sin was in the world, but sin is not imputed when there is no law. 14 Nevertheless death reigned from Adam to Moses, even over those who had not sinned according to the likeness of the transgression of Adam, who is a type of Him who was to come. 15 But the free gift is not like the offense. For if by the one

man's offense many died, much more the grace of God and the gift by the grace of the one Man, Jesus Christ, abounded to many. [16] And the gift is not like that which came through the one who sinned. For the judgment which came from one offense resulted in condemnation, but the free gift which came from many offenses resulted in justification. [17] For if by the one man's offense death reigned through the one, much more those who receive abundance of grace and of the gift of righteousness will reign in life through the One, Jesus Christ.)

[18] Therefore, as through one man's offense judgment came to all men, resulting in condemnation, even so through one Man's righteous act the free gift came to all men, resulting in justification of life. [19] For as by one man's disobedience many were made sinners, so also by one Man's obedience many will be made righteous.

[20] Moreover the law entered that the offense might abound. But where sin abounded, grace abounded much more, [21] so that as sin reigned in death, even so grace might reign through righteousness to eternal life through Jesus Christ our Lord.

—Romans 5:12–21

THE REIGN OF SIN

On rare occasions I have been able to revisit the English Lake District where I spent the first twenty years of my life. In the intervening years I have traveled to the four corners of the world, but few places stir my emotions like the quiet unspoiled lakes and mountains of my youthful home. Nothing seems to change, life maintains its slow pace, and the quietness is almost tangible. Places like that are few and far between, and we are the poorer because of it—not only because we have less chance to draw refreshment from our environment but also because we find it harder to imagine Eden. if our tarnished world clouds our understanding of Paradise, how much more must our experience of mankind warp our understanding of man as he was created? Milton tried to recapture some of the grandeur when he described man as: "the master work, the end of all yet done; a creature who not prone and brute as other creatures, but endued with sanctity of reason, might. . . worship God Supreme who made him chief of all his works. . . ."[1]

There is no way to explain the pollution of Paradise and the perversion of man outside the doctrine of the Fall. That "sin entered into the world" is an incontrovertible truth, but it is not treated with the solemnity it deserves. Part of the problem is that in our preoccupation with sins and our struggle against them—which may be little more than behavioral manipulation—we have tended to ignore the underlying fact of sin. Adam's sin was a calculated decision to disobey God and to take the consequences of his own free action. Whatever debate may rage about the relative merits or demerits of the female propensity to delusion as exemplified by Eve, there is no debate about Adam. He was not misled; he walked right into rebellion with his eyes wide open and his mind made up. Paul describes Adam's action as "transgression," "offense," and "disobedience." The immensity of this action cannot be overlooked because it introduced into the *kosmos* something previously unknown.

Paul expresses the enormity of Adam's action by such expressions as: *"by the one man's offense many died," "as by one man's offense judgment came to all men,"* and in his first Corinthian letter he writes, "in Adam all die" (1 Cor. 15:22). Bruce calls this kind of thinking "the Hebrew concept of corporate personality"[2] something which our individualistic style of thought and life may find hard to grasp, even though we accept John Donne's famous adage, "no man is an island, entire of itself." Nevertheless the fact of the solidarity of the human race must be addressed.

When Albert Einstein published his theory of relativity, it is said there were only twelve men who were intelligent enough to understand its implications. Forty years later the number had risen to millions as the horror of Hiroshima unfolded. Relatively few could see great significance in $E = mc^2$, but even fewer failed to understand that through one man the race had been ushered into the atomic age. There was no going back and there were no exceptions, because in Einstein atomic reality had come upon all men. When a man introduces something new into human experience, the race will always be left to live with the consequences. So when sin entered the life of a man, it also entered the experience of a race as yet unborn. If it be objected that those locked up in Adam's loins could hardly be said to have been introduced to sin in Adam, it should be remembered that in Adam they were introduced to everything, for without him as source they had nothing, and if he had died they would not even have had life.

Sin having entered human experience, it then proceeded to "abound." Adam's sin, as we have seen, was a calculated denial of God's authority and a clear statement of his intention to go his own way. Godet describes it magnificently as "a decision whereby he adhered to the inclination rather than to the divine will, and thus created in the whole race, still identified with his person, the permanent proclivity to prefer inclination to obligation."[3]

Subsequently, through the Law of Moses, man was made aware in more detail of the divine will as it "came on stage alongside" (the literal translation of "entered," v. 20) his own adamic potential. We are all familiar with people who, having experienced emotional problems, have sought professional counseling. Under the skillful, patient and firm direction of the counselor, hidden things in the inner recesses of the counselee's mind and emotions have been exposed until, sometimes very suddenly, there has been an overflow of resentment or hostility, anger or grief. All these things were present before the counselor came on stage alongside and through careful exertion of pressure was able to make the things which had entered the life come to the surface and overflow. This is the kind of ministry that the "law" has exercised.

Paul goes on to show that sin, having entered and abounded, went on to "reign" in human society and experience. The use of this powerful word is a strong reminder of the dynamic control that sin exercises in people on both an individual basis and on a societal level. It is relatively easy for Christians to look at Marxist states which on the basis of atheist philosophies dominate the life of their subjects. The normal Christian response is to see this as the tyrannical reign of sin as it dominates the lives of millions and reigns in apparently irresistible force. But we need to look much closer to home and recognize the reign of sin in all types of society. If we regard sin as a conscious choice to "prefer inclination to obligation," then we can see that the prevailing attitude in much of our business principles, political choices, educational emphases, and cultural norms may be under a reign of sin so powerful we may not even recognize that we are being subjected to its control.

THE REIGN OF DEATH

Paul goes on to affirm that the solidarity of the human race means not only that all were exposed to sin as a principle because of one man's sin, but also that this sin introduced all to the horror of death. As sin entered, abounded, and reigned, so also did death. Adam's race is not only pathetically susceptible to sin but painfully exposed to inevitable death.

When God spoke to Adam about obedience He made it clear that disobedience spells death. There is no room for misunderstanding in His statement, "of the tree of the knowledge of good and evil, you shall not eat, for in the day that you eat of it you shall surely die"

(Gen. 2:17). The immediate death promised was obviously not physical, in that Adam survived that awful day for many years. It was spiritual death, or alienation from the life of God (Eph. 4:18) which Adam experienced and which the race is still experiencing. Whether Adam would have died naturally, as apparently other parts of creation were dying, or whether he would have been translated to glory without seeing death in the manner of Enoch and Elijah is open to debate. But that he died physically at a later date reminds us that physical death was also part of sin's consequence. Projected into eternity, the alienation from God experienced on earth becomes an experience called simply "the second death," yet another product of sin which confronts humanity. When considered in all its spiritual, physical, and eternal dimensions, it is not hard to see the entrance and abundance of death. Some theologians understand Paul to mean that mankind dies because of individual sin, while others point to his teaching on solidarity and insist that mankind dies because of Adam's sin. The expression *"death spread to all men, because all sinned"* (Rom. 5:12) at first sight seems to support the former view, but the succeeding verses lean more toward the latter. Paul's position appears to be that during the period between Adam's sin and the giving of the Law of Moses, sin was in the world but sin is not imputed where there is no law. *"Nevertheless death reigned. . ."* (v. 13–14). Mankind was not sinning like Adam in direct contravention of the divine law because there was no clear-cut law to contravene and, therefore, he could not be held responsible. But he still died, not as a direct consequence of personal sin, but because he was in some way involved in the sin and death brought into human experience by Adam.

The difficulty of this passage and the theological debate that has continued from the days of Augustine and Pelagius should not be allowed to distract our attention from the fact that, whatever our understanding of the mechanics of the entrance, abundance, and reign of sin and death, they are terrible realities and need a powerful answer. It is this answer which Paul is eager to expound.

THE REIGN OF GRACE

At the same time Albert Einstein was climbing the mountains of Bavaria, an athletic young Scot was roaming Ayrshire countryside. In his early days, Alexander Fleming was mainly preoccupied with farming and fishing, little realizing that he would one day become a world renowned microbiologist whose discovery of penicillin would revolutionize human experience.

In the same way that the solidarity principle introduced the race to the possibilities of atomic destruction through Einstein, Fleming was the man in whom the race was introduced to healing on an unprecedented scale. Without casting the former as a modern-day Adam or the latter as a contemporary messiah, the analogy helps us to see how Paul saw the human race introduced to grace through Christ, having already been introduced to sin and death in Adam.

Paul calls Adam *"a type of Him who was to come"* (v. 14) and develops the idea to show that through "the one man's offense many died," and also, through "the one Man, Jesus Christ, grace has abounded to many." Having taken great pains to show the similarity between the first man, Adam, and the second man, Christ, Paul now sets about showing their marked dissimilarities with particular reference to the superiority of Christ and His work over Adam and his sin. Adam brought "offense," Christ brought "free gift"; the "offense" meant "death"; the "free gift" provided "justification"; the "disobedience" made many sinners, but "obedience" made many "righteous." The quiet healing of penicillin is in no way similar to the scorching blast of Hiroshima, even though both were introduced by one man.

By applying the same words—"abound" and "reign"—to describe the action of sin, death, and grace in human experience, Paul uses the reality of sin and death, which are clear to see, as an illustration of the reality of grace, which is not always easy to understand. Sin's reign is evident every time we open a paper or turn on the TV. Stories abound of overcrowded prisons, escalating divorce statistics, dramatic increase in the incidence of crime, not only in the traditional urban areas but in the respectable suburbs and the heartlands of the rural areas. Death's reign is painfully evident in expanding cemeteries, burgeoning funeral parlors, and proliferating nursing homes. Sin knows no bounds; death, like time and tide, waits for no man. Both march on in relentless, overpowering domination of the bleak human scene. But Paul says that all is not bleak, that grace is equally as real, just as powerful and pervasive. For every sin that robs and destroys another particle of human experience, there is grace to build and restore. For every grave opened by sin and death, there is a door opened in heaven by grace. While mourners mourn over loved ones laid to rest, angels rejoice over sinners coming to repentance.

There is a quality of grace that even this analogy does not express adequately. Paul says that *"the law entered that the offense might abound. But where sin abounded, grace abounded much more"*

(Rom. 5:20). Taken in its most obvious application, the Law (of Moses) applied to the people of Israel. As children of Adam's race, they were under the reign of sin, but when the law was applied to their lives, it pressured the latent sin out into the open in a great overflow of sins. This was seen in its most appalling demonstration in the rejection of Jesus as Messiah with the collective cry, "Crucify him, crucify him." When Pilate in his last-ditch effort to extricate himself washed his hands of the Christ controversy, the leaders of the Jews uttered the awful words, "Let his blood be on us and on our children." Sin at that moment overflowed its banks for the people of the law, the benighted members of "Adam's helpless race," but at the same moment that sin was abounding, "grace abounded much more." The very acts and attitudes of sin that nailed Him to the Cross were being dealt with in grace by the subjection of Christ to that cross. The Cross in its horrible illustration of overwhelming sin was in itself a demonstration of superoverwhelming grace. Sin at is blackest moment on Calvary was touched by grace at its most golden.

When the soldiers hammered in the nails, sin was abounding, but when the quiet victim said, "Father, forgive them," grace was abounding much more. One of the thieves who insulted Him engaged in a surfeit of sin, but lived long enough to hear superabounding grace say, "Today you shall be with Me in Paradise."

No one was more touched by a sense of the overabundance of grace than the writer of the Epistle to the Romans. He insisted that he was the chief of sinners and the least of apostles. He felt deeply that he was not worthy to be an apostle and was overwhelmed that he should be entrusted with the gospel. He even went so far as to describe himself as an *ektrōma* (abortion or miscarriage), which Thayer says means "that he is as inferior to the rest of the apostles as an immature birth comes short of a mature one, and is no more worthy of the name of an apostle than an abortion is of the name of a child."[4] Yet Paul went on to insist on his high calling and attributed it to nothing more than the grace of God. To the Corinthians he wrote, "But by the grace of God I am what I am. . ." (1 Cor. 15:10) and to Timothy he wrote, "I was formerly a blasphemer, a persecutor, and an insolent man; but I obtained mercy because I did it ignorantly in unbelief. And the grace of our Lord was exceedingly abundant. . ." (1 Tim. 1:13–14).

In his eagerness to convey grace in all its beauty and charm Paul adds one more expression and employs yet another contrast: *"So that as sin eigned in death, even so grace might reign through righteousness to eternal life through Jesus Christ our*

Lord" (Rom. 5:21). A friend of mine was working in one of Havana's luxury hotels in 1959 when Fidel Castro came to power. For some time he was not allowed to leave the country and was required to work for the new regime. Eventually he was granted an exit permit and headed home with a great sense of relief. While he understood that the powers which Castro overthrew left much to be desired and that the revolution was being greeted with considerable public acclaim, my friend had no desire to stay in Cuba, because he could see the direction that Castro's administration was going to take. He much preferred to live in his native Switzerland and enjoy its legendary peace and prosperity rather than come under Castro's control. For him the reign of the one was not to be compared to the reign of the other.

The reign of grace through the ministry of Christ is as far-reaching as the reign of sin. Through Adam a whole race was reached by sin, but in Christ a complete race is touched by grace. Through birth all are related to Adam; through faith "the many" are related to Christ. Adam's people suffer death, but Christ's enjoy the all-pervading reign of grace, "eternal life," which is related to "righteousness." This means that those who receive the gift of righteousness in Jesus Christ also receive the gift of eternal life in Him. So great is the reign of grace it reaches into eternity and opens it for all people who will come to Christ in faith.

Eternal life has both its qualitative and its quantitative characteristics. Quantitatively, it is the gift of life which is relevant to eternity. It is the kind of life which functions in the realm beyond time as naturally as a fish functions in water or a bird in the air. Without the gift of that kind of life, there would be no more possibility of a human surviving in heaven than of a fish surviving on dry land or a bird under water. Qualitatively, eternal life speaks of the life of the Eternal One. It is related to the quality of life that is His and that is enjoyed only through the new birth. It is experienced only as we realize what it means to be what Peter calls "partakers of the divine nature" and, accordingly, equipped "with all things that pertain to life and godliness" (2 Pet. 1:3–4). The practicalities of this reign of grace are dealt with in the succeeding chapters, but there is another expression which introduces something of the exciting truths which Paul has in store. We will devote the next section of discussion to it.

THE REIGN OF LIFE

Paul says, "Those who receive abundance of grace and of the gift of righteousness will reign in life through the One, Jesus

Christ" (Rom. 5:17). There is a marked difference between this expression and the other three we have considered. The other three reigns speak of powers or principles under which human beings live, but this one speaks of the quality of life which redeemed individuals are to demonstrate. Godet remarks, "Death reigns; it is a tyrant. But life does not reign; it has not subjects; it makes kings."[5]

A chilling but fascinating story in the first chapter of Judges offers insight into our discussion. After Joshua's leadership there was some confusion as to who should deal with the troublesome Canaanites, and the Lord settled the problem by sending the tribe of Judah. Along with Simeon, Judah routed the people of Bezek, captured Adoni-Bezek, and cut off his big toes and his thumbs. He was remarkably philosophical about his mutilation saying: "Seventy kings with their thumbs and big toes cut off have picked up scraps under my table. Now God has paid me back for what I did to them" (Judg. 1:7, NIV).

Big toes give balance and thumbs provide grip. Without either a king cannot walk or grasp his sword. He must wobble about through life unarmed and unrespected. If, in addition to this, he must beg for scraps of food from another's table, he is a king in name only. The possibility of those who have been placed under the reign of grace not reigning in life is always before God's people. For them to hobble through life rather than stride in triumph and to grovel under a tyrant's table rather than feed sumptuously from the table prepared for them is a tragedy of major proportions. Should they be unable to lay hold of the sword given to them and to get a grip on the situations they encounter, their state occasions great concern. This is what is meant by not reigning in life. There are three relevant expressions that clearly state the means whereby God's people reign in life. First, they receive *"the gift of righteousness"*; second, they receive *"abundance of grace"*; and third, they reign in life *"through Jesus Christ."* As we have seen, all those who are redeemed have received the first two, and we need only to mention the third briefly at this point. To live royally is to live related to Jesus Christ.

When I was a small boy I was fascinated by the simple sermon preached in my home church by an old coal miner who had recently been to Buckingham Palace to be decorated by the king for bravery. He had placed his considerable bulk under the collapsing roof of the mine and held it up while his colleagues escaped through his legs. As far as he was concerned, he hadn't done anything particularly noteworthy, and he was far more nervous about going to the palace than about the possibility of facing another mine explosion. I remember his description of the investiture ceremony because of its moving simplicity and humility, and I will never forget how he said, "I couldn't wait to get out of the palace and back to my little miner's cottage in Whitehaven, but there was a young man beside the king who was perfectly at home in the palace and would never have been comfortable in my cottage." He paused and smiled and then added, "You see, he was the Prince of Wales, the king's son, and he was born to the palace".

Those who receive Christ are born to the Palace and have the royal blood in their veins exclusively through Him. It is what He has done and who He is in their lives that alone makes reigning in life a possibility. With Him all things are possible; without Him we can but fail.

NOTES

1. John Milton, *Paradise Lost*, II. 505–16.

2. F. F. Bruce, *Romans* (London: The Tyndale Press), p. 126.

3. Godet, *Commentary on Romans*, p. 204.

4. Joseph Henry Thayer, *Thayer's Greek-English Lexicon of the New Testament* (New York: American Book Co.), p. 200.

5. Godet, *Commentary on Romans*, p. 222.

CHAPTER TEN—SHOULD SAINTS SIN?
ROMANS 6:1–23

Scripture Outline

Saints' Relationship to Sin (6:1–7)

Saints' Relationship to Christ (6:8–10)

Saints' Relationship to Temptation (6:11–14)

Saints' Relationship to Righteousness (6:15–23)

Richard Lovelace was right when he wrote in his book *Dynamics of Spiritual Life:* "Three aberrations from the biblical teaching on justification—cheap grace, legalism, and moralism—still dominate the church today."[1] Moralism is the approach to Christianity that concentrates on the teaching of Christ as moral imperative to be addressed to society without adequate emphasis on the necessity for repentance and faith leading to justification. On the other hand, there are churches that have adopted "legalism" as their approach to Christian experience. Based on a deep commitment to justification by faith and a serious attempt to live as if justified and conscious of the danger of spiritual infiltration or infection, considerable effort has gone into the manufacture of disciplines, rules, and regulations designed to isolate the believer from all that would hinder or mar his spiritual progress. Unfortunately, the emphasis has often switched from Christ to the rules and from the enjoyment of life in Him to a debilitating experience under the load of auxiliary matters the believer is called to shoulder. "Cheap grace," the term coined by the German pastor and martyr Dietrich Bonhoeffer, refers to the sad attitude, displayed in varying degrees of openness, which says, in effect, "I've been forgiven and I will go on being forgiven whatever I do, so I can do whatever I wish." Paul appears to be addressing this type of thinking when he writes:

6:1 What shall we say then? Shall we continue in sin that grace may abound? [2] Certainly not! How shall we who died to sin live any longer in it?

—*Romans 6:1–2*

SAINTS' RELATIONSHIP TO SIN

Having shown clearly that the grace of God "abounded much more" wherever sin abounded, Paul poses the question, which to many would be purely hypothetical but to others may be very real: "If grace is made to abound more as more sin is committed, then why not sin more so that more grace will be released?" In its most common form, this attitude is exhibited in those believers who see in their justification no necessity to go on to experience the sanctification God has in mind for them. Having been forgiven and guaranteed a place in heaven, they feel they can now get on with the business of living as they wish without any concerns or misgivings. Carried to its extreme, this kind of thinking has produced sects that encourage sinning as a prerequisite to salvation. Perhaps the most notorious proponent of this theological aberration was Rasputin, the confidant of the Empress Alexandra of Russia. He defended his profligate lifestyle and scandalous behavior by teaching that it was necessary for salvation. To him and to all others who feel that justification is an excuse to sin and grace is a free ticket to a life of disobedience and licentiousness, Paul would cry, "God forbid!" His vehement rejection of the suggestion is followed by a rhetorical question that states his reasons and introduces a completely new aspect of salvation. Without either introduction or warning, he tells his readers that they "died to sin," a statement so powerful and overwhelming that it requires considerable explanation.

[3] Or do you not know that as many of us as were baptized into Christ Jesus were baptized into His death?
[4] Therefore we were buried with Him through baptism into death, that just as Christ was raised from the dead by the glory of the Father, even so we also should walk in newness of life.
[5] For if we have been united together in the likeness of His death, certainly we also shall be in the likeness of His resurrection, [6] knowing this, that our old man was crucified with Him, that the body of sin might be done away with, that we should no longer be slaves of sin. [7] For he who has died has been freed from sin.

—*Romans 6:3–7*

In contrast to the "cheap grace" people who give little or no thought to sin, the "moralists" who feel that "sin"—if they use the term—is a human problem with human solutions, and the "legalists" who try to conquer sin through legislation, Paul teaches that sin is to be handled through a relationship to Christ.

SAINTS' RELATIONSHIP TO CHRIST

Paul starts his explanation of the believer's death to sin by reminding him of the historical facts of Christ's earthly experience, namely, His death, burial, and Resurrection. Then Paul shows that through baptism the believer is united to Christ and, therefore, is a participant in the experience of Christ. Thus the believer through baptism has died, been buried, and raised again "with Him."

Strange as this may sound to modern ears, there was no problem in understanding this teaching among the people Paul was addressing in Rome. The Jews among them were thoroughly familiar with the rite of baptism through which Gentile proselytes were required to pass before they could be regarded as members of the Jewish fraternity. The initiates were carefully prepared for baptism, then undressed completely and placed in water so that every part of their body was in contact with the water. Then they were required to make confession of their faith in Christ. After receiving instruction from those chosen to officiate at the ceremony, they emerged from the water "new men" in the eyes of the Jewish people. So great was their transformation that everything related to their former life was regarded as an irrelevance and a totally new start was in order. Some rabbis even taught that the new life was so radical that even former family relationships no longer existed and the proselytes were free to marry their own sister or mother if they wished.[2] In the modern church, understanding of the rite of baptism has gone through many changes and has been the subject of numerous debates. But it should be remembered that for the early Christians who came from either a Jewish background or involvement with pagan religions which had their own initiation ceremonies, the act of baptism was a serious step taken by a convinced adult to declare his allegiance to Christ whatever the cost and, also, to announce the termination of his old life and the initiation of the new.

As Christian theology has developed, one section of the church has seen baptism as a sacrament while a second section regards it as a symbol. For the former group baptism conveys grace to the baptized person. Taken to its extreme, this approach can obviate the necessity for repentance and faith and elevate baptism to the lofty status of the means of salvation. On the other hand, those who regard baptism as a symbol of spiritual reality may decide that as rites are relatively unimportant when compared to reality, the rite can be dispensed with without losing any spiritual benefit. This position has been adopted by such groups as the Salvation Army. In their book *The Water That Divides* Bridges and Phypers make the helpful comment, "To the New Testament writers there is no problem. Baptism is integral to the salvation process, of value in itself, bringing with it the full blessing of God. Now, of course, faith saves and in asserting that baptism is a sacrament as well as a symbol, there is no suggestion that Christians should return to the crudely superstitious position of the Middle Ages."[3]

In apostolic times, baptism was administered immediately on confession of faith in Christ. But in later years the practice was modified for various reasons. According to the *Didache,* a second-century document of early church procedures, the believers were required to "rehearse" their understanding of basic Christian truths before being baptized "in living water." They were also told, "If you have not living water, baptize in other water; and, if thou canst not in cold, in warm. If you have neither, pour water thrice on the head in the Name. . . ."[4] Apart from showing how far modern baptism may have moved from the rugged days of cold running water to warm, placid fonts or baptistries, this excerpt also shows that the normal procedure in the early days was for the believers to be immersed. This would be not only a sacrament whereby the believers entered into the merits of their faith relationship with the living Christ but also a striking symbol of the significance of that relationship. As they stepped into the water, they demonstrated the fact that they were *"in Christ";* as they were immersed, they showed they were *"buried with Him"*; and as they emerged from the water, they graphically portrayed their understanding of being *"raised with Him"* before walking from the site of their baptism and showing they were baptized to *"walk in newness of life"* (Rom. 6:4).

Having established the reality of being identified with Christ in death and Resurrection through baptism, Paul proceeds to show the significance of Christ's death, and accordingly, the significance of our relationship to Him.

8 Now if we died with Christ, we believe that we shall also live with Him, 9 knowing that Christ, having been raised from the dead, dies no more. Death no longer has dominion

over Him. [10] For the death that He died, He died to sin once for all; but the life that He lives, He lives to God.

—*Romans 6:8–10*

The key expression in this section is *"He died to sin once for all."* In Paul's thinking we are related to Christ, through baptism, and in that relationship we are in some way sharing in His death and Resurrection. If in His death He died to sin, then we, in Him, died to sin. Therefore, the simplest way to understand what it means to have "died to sin" is to find out what it means that "He died to sin once for all."

When Christ entered the world He came from the glory of heaven sinless, spotless, undefiled, and separate from sin. Immediately upon entering human society, He was confronted on every hand by sin's power and presence. For thirty-three years He lived among the carnage and wreckage of sin. When He went to the Cross, He assumed our sin and bore the wrath of God against our sin; in fact, the apostle says that the Father "made Him who knew no sin to be sin for us" (2 Cor. 5:20). Having come from an environment where sinlessness was normative to a situation where sin is pervasive, and having taken on His sinless self the load of a race's sin, it comes as no surprise to us that He cried exultantly from the Cross at the end of His ministry, "Finished!" and promptly bowed His head and dismissed His spirit. It was all over for Him. The nightmare of sin, the horrors of death and hell, the pernicious tyranny of sin's hold on people had been dealt with, and He could go to the grave anticipating His Resurrection with joy and delight.

In the same way, believers, united to Christ, can exult in the fact that all that must be done about their sin has been done in Christ. They, too, can cry "finished" and breathe a sigh of relief because for them the nightmare of unanswered sin is over and the tyranny of unconquerable sin is broken. But in the same way that Christ did not stay dead but rose to a newness of life to be lived unto the Father, we are raised too! While He was in His body, the Son had an obligation to deal with the sin problem, but when, after death, He arose, having finished with sin, His total concentration was once more upon the Father. In the same way, believers who were previously preoccupied with the remorseless grip of sin on their lives can now concentrate on what they have and who they are in Christ and, accordingly, live new lives.

Paul, who was never less than practical even when at his most theological, outlined three specific results of this divine transaction on our behalf. He said, *"Our old man was crucified with Christ, that the body of sin might be done away with, that we should no longer serve sin."*

Some people have assumed that the "old man" is the sinful nature which, because the Bible says it has been crucified, must be dead and, therefore, no longer operative. When confronted with the obvious unpalatable truth that "it may be dead but it won't lie down," they have tried to make their theology fit their experience or vice versa by many unsatisfactory methods which have produced either nervous breakdowns or blatant hypocrisy. We should not assume that the "old man" is anything more than "the man of old" or the pre-regenerate person. A friend of mine always refers to his life as A.D. and B.C. B.C. is the "old man"; A.D. is the regenerate man raised in Christ. The person you were "before Christ" has been judged, condemned, sentenced, executed, buried, and finished with forever. The new man lives.

But, in addition, there has been a powerful impact on the *"body of sin"* which Paul says in verse 6 has been *"done away with."* Some commentators translate "body" as "mass" and agree with Calvin that "man, when left to his own nature is a mass of sin."[5] Others see no necessity to regard "body" as anything other than the human body which, while not sinful of itself, is very clearly the instrument of sin. Paul states that this body which is so susceptible to sin's domination before union with Christ has, through Him, been placed in a position where this domination might no longer be the norm.

This leads to the third practical fact, namely, that believers *"should no longer serve sin"* (v. 6). Now that the "man of old" has been dealt with in Christ and the new man has, accordingly, been shown that the sin which previously controlled his physical body has been dealt with, he should recognize that he is no longer at the mercy of sin, or, literally, "a slave of sin." In fact, he has been "freed from sin" or "justified from sin." As we have seen previously, "justification" has a legal connotation. But in this context Paul appears to be broadening the use of the word. In the same way that a man who has been exonerated in a court of law has the freedom to walk out of court and take a cab to his home, so the "justified" believer, in addition to his technical justification, has the practical freedom to walk away from the dominating power of sin in his life. To begin to understand this is to see how far those who believe they are saved to live as they wish have strayed from the truth of the all-encompassing gospel.

SAINTS' RELATIONSHIP TO TEMPTATION

In all honesty we have to admit that Paul, so far, has probably raised more questions than he has answered, and this commentator concedes that he has done little to help! But all is not lost, as the next section clearly shows:

> [11] Likewise you also, reckon yourselves to be dead indeed to sin, but alive to God in Christ Jesus our Lord.
> [12] Therefore do not let sin reign in your mortal body, that you should obey it in its lusts. [13] And do not present your members as instruments of unrighteousness to sin, but present yourselves to God as being alive from the dead, and your members as instruments of righteousness to God. [14] For sin shall not have dominion over you, for you are not under law but under grace.
>
> —*Romans 6:11–14*

In the light of all that has been said, the apostle now applies the truth by outlining a path of action that believers must take. The operative words are: "reckon," "let," and "present."

First the believer must do some reckoning. We have already been introduced to this word and seen that it means to "place to someone's account." The Greek word is related to *logos,* which means, among other things, "reason." Paul requires believers to reason through what he has been teaching concerning the believer's relationship to sin and to Christ and then to place to their own account or apply to their own lives that which they have intellectually grasped. He stipulates two things: first, that we are *"dead to sin,"* and, second, that we are *"alive to God"* but only *"in Christ Jesus."*

When Neil Armstrong stepped out of "Eagle" onto the moon's surface on July 20, 1969, and said, "That's one small step for man, one giant leap for mankind," he entered an environment in which it was impossible for him to survive apart from his space suit and its support systems. But because of the capabilities of his unnatural environment—the space suit—and his identification with it, he was able to regard himself as dead to his inhospitable surroundings and alive to his experience of walking around the moon. So the believer must understand that "in Christ" he is no longer totally at the mercy of the inhospitable environment of sin but is alive to all the power and life of God Himself.

When this is appreciated, the believer must make some decisions to *"let not sin reign in your mortal body"* (v. 12). There is nothing very mysterious about this instruction. It means saying "no" in no uncertain terms! Whenever a believer "obeys" the passions of his body and succumbs to temptation, he sins, but he is not obliged to succumb and he does not have to sin. The old Puritans used to say, "God does not take away our ability to sin; He gives us the power not to sin." If television sets were made without on/off switches and we were chained to our seats in front of them and our eyes were held open by mechanical means, we would have no option but to watch everything on the screen. But we all have the option to watch or not to watch. It requires a choice to turn off the set. "In Christ" we have been given the "off" switch—the ability to say "no" and the instructions to do it.

Paul becomes even more specific when he gives instructions concerning individual members of the body. We sin when we "yield" or "present" our tongue to say the wrong word, our hand when we take something that does not belong to us, our sexual organs when we commit adultery, our minds when we harbor uncharitable thoughts. When we take sin seriously, we begin to see how sin cannot operate in our bodies without our giving over a particular member of the body for a specific sin. If the believer is adequately aware of this, he can begin to say "no" to a temptation, not only in a general sense but in the very specific sense of refusing to present the member necessary for the committing of sin. It is important to recognize that Paul gives both a positive and a negative side of this action. When we refuse to present the member as an instrument of unrighteousness, we may feel that we are left in a vacuum, so we need to remember to present the newly redundant member to an action that will further the work of God. When my tongue is required by the old sinful propensity within to engage in critical conversation half the battle is won when I refuse to participate, but the other half is won when I take the opportunity to say something helpful and positive instead.

This way the apostle says, "Sin shall not 'lord it over' you," because believers are living in the benevolent atmosphere of the grace of God, which, in addition to bringing justification from sin, also brings to the sinner the means of no longer sinning.

When as a young teenager I was drafted into the Royal Marines during the Korean War, I came under the control of a particularly imposing regimental sergeant major, who strode around the barracks leaving a train of tough men quaking in their boots.

I didn't realize how dominant this man had become in my life until the day I was released from the Marines. Clutching my papers in one hand, I was luxuriating in my new-found freedom to the extent of putting the other hand in my pocket, slouching a little, and whistling—sins so heinous that if they had been observed by the R.S.M., they would have landed me in all kinds of trouble! Then I saw him striding toward me. On an impulse I sprang into the posture of a Marine until I realized that I had died to him—he and I no longer had a relationship. He was not dead, and neither was I, but as far as his domination of my life was concerned, it was all a matter of history. So I did some reckoning, decided not to yield to his tyranny, and demonstrated it by refusing to yield my arms to swinging high and my feet to marching as if on parade, and my back to ramrod stiffness. Instead I presented my feet, hands, back to my new-found freedom as a former Marine—and he couldn't do a thing about it!

SAINTS' RELATIONSHIP TO RIGHTEOUSNESS

15 What then? Shall we sin because we are not under law but under grace? Certainly not! 16 Do you not know that to whom you present yourselves slaves to obey, you are that one's slaves whom you obey, whether of sin leading to death, or of obedience leading to righteousness? 17 But God be thanked that though you were slaves of sin, yet you obeyed from the heart that form of doctrine to which you were delivered.
18 And having been set free from sin, you became slaves of righteousness. 19 I speak in human terms because of the weakness of your flesh. For just as you presented your members as slaves of uncleanness, and of lawlessness leading to more lawlessness, so now present your members as slaves of righteousness for holiness.
20 For when you were slaves of sin, you were free in regard to righteousness. 21 What fruit did you have then in the things of which you are now ashamed? For the end of those things is death. 22 But now having been set free from sin, and having become slaves of God, you have your fruit to holiness, and the end, everlasting life. 23 For the wages of sin is death, but the gift of God is eternal life in Christ Jesus our Lord.

—Romans 6:15–23

People from a Jewish background who held the law in high esteem were particularly nervous about Paul's insistence that "by the deeds of the law no flesh will be justified" (Gal. 2:16). They believed that Paul's teaching that people cannot fulfill the law for justification would encourage them to disregard the law, to claim to be justified by faith, and then because they accepted no law to embark on a life of lawlessness and sinfulness. To this Paul gives another vehement response and proceeds to show that, far from being lawless, justified believers who were formerly nothing more than "servants of sin" become the "servants of righteousness." He makes the obvious, but no less powerful point, that *to whom you present yourselves slaves to obey, you are that one's slaves*" (Rom. 6:16). Those who revered the law and failed, as did everyone, to keep it, were in their breaking of the law exhibiting their "slavery" to sin. But those who through the grace of God had become united with Christ had been made "free from sin" and had traded their slavery to sin for a slavery to Christ and the righteousness for which He stands.

Bruce paraphrases Paul's thought as follows: "A slave's former owner has no more authority over him if he becomes someone else's property. This is what has happened to you. You have passed from the service of sin into the service of God: your business now is to do what God desires not what sin dictates."[6]

To the sensitive believer, the desire of God is an even more powerful motivational factor than the dictates of sin. He knows from his past history that sin produced those things of which he is *"now ashamed"* and he also knows that *"the end of those things is death."* Pressing home the contrast, the apostle adds: *"For the wages of sin is death, but the gift of God is eternal life in Christ Jesus our Lord"* (Rom. 6:23). On the one hand, there is the law of God which people either treat with benign neglect or with assiduous care. The former sin glibly and freely; the latter seriously and often unknowingly. This sin produces death as just reward for unsatisfactory living. On the other hand, there is the grace of God which brings people in Christ to forgiveness and the position of having taken the stand against sin which Christ took and adopting the attitude that sin, as a lifestyle, is no longer the normative approach. This leads to a life of *"fruit to holiness and the end, everlasting life"* (Rom. 6:22). When seen in such stark contrast, there ought to be no difficulty in recognizing the way to go. But still there is a tendency for people to feel that they have an unshakable, unbreakable obligation to sin and an optional, tentative obligation to righteousness. Exactly the reverse is true! The believer does not have to go on sinning and treating righteous living as something that is good if you can get around to it, but rather he does have to live righteously and take care to live triumphantly over sin in the power of the Lord.

NOTES

1. Richard F. Lovelace, *Dynamics of Spiritual Life* (Downers Grove, Ill.: InterVarsity Press, 1979), p. 100.

2. Barclay, *Romans,* p. 85.

3. Donald Bridge and David Phypers *The Wafer That Divides: The Baptism Debate* (Downers Grove, Ill.: InterVarsity Press, 1977), p. 27.

4. *Documents of the Christian Church,* ed. Henry Bettenson (New York: Oxford University Press, 1963), p. 90.

5. Calvin, *Commentaries on Romans,* p. 125.

6. Bruce, *Romans,* p. 140.

CHAPTER ELEVEN—WHAT ABOUT THE LAW?

ROMANS 7:1–25

Scripture Outline

The Believer's Release from the Law (7:1–6)

The Believer's Respect for the Law (7:7)

The Believer's Revelation Through the Law (7:8–13)

The Believer's Relationship to the Law (7:14–25)

Charles Haddon Spurgeon, the prince of preachers, told his students, "Often when didactic speech fails to enlighten our hearers we may make them see our meaning by opening a window and letting in the pleasant light of analogy."[1] The ministry of the Lord Jesus was liberally sprinkled with apt illustrations which arrested the attention of His hearers and drove the message home to their hearts, but the apostle Paul didn't use many windows! Therefore, his illustration of the woman whose husband died is particularly welcome, even though his application is somewhat convoluted.

7:1 Or do you not know, brethren (for I speak to those who know the law), that the law has dominion over a man as long as he lives? 2 For the woman who has a husband is bound by the law to her husband as long as he lives. But if the husband dies, she is released from the law of her husband. 3 So then if, while her husband lives, she marries another man, she will be called an adulteress; but if her husband dies, she is free from that law, so that she is no adulteress, though she has married another man. 4 Therefore, my brethren, you also have become dead to the law through the body of Christ, that you may be married to another—to Him who was raised from the dead, that we should bear fruit to God. 5 For when we were in the flesh, the sinful passions which were aroused by the law were at work in our members to bear fruit to death. ⁶ But now we have been delivered from the law, having died to what we were held by, so that we should serve in the newness of the Spirit and not in the oldness of the letter.

—*Romans 7:1–6*

In the previous chapter we noted that the striking phrase "we died to sin" was the center of the apostle's argument, but now we are introduced to the added fact that we *"have become dead to the law."*

THE BELIEVER'S RELEASE FROM THE LAW

In Paul's teaching there is a clear connection between "the law" and sin. He told the Roman believers, *"Sin shall not have dominion over you for you are not under law but under grace"* (Rom. 6:14). The person living "under law" is dominated by sin; therefore, if there is to be any realistic release from sin, there must be a corresponding release from the law. That this is all part of the divine provision Paul now seeks to explain through his rare illustration.

Assuming that the Roman believers, both Jew and Greek, were familiar with the law—presumably the Mosaic Law—Paul reminds them that the law has jurisdiction over a man only during his lifetime. For instance, in the marriage contract a wife is required to be faithful to her husband all his life. If she fails in this regard, she is called an adulteress, but as soon as her husband dies, she is free to remarry without there being any suggestion of impropriety. She is *"released from the law of her husband."*

Paul's application of the illustration is not altogether straightforward, but his obvious point is that, in the same way a widow is no longer under any legal obligation to her late husband, so the believer who was formerly married to the law is under no obligation to the law as a means of justification once the law dies. The problem with Paul's illustration is that the picture does not fit, because in real life the law does not die but the believer dies to the law. His point is clear nevertheless.

Those people who see their hope of being justified centered in their relationship to the law do not have happy marriages to the law. Married as they are to a law which is perfect, inflexible, demanding, and all-encompassing, they are soon driven to despair by their own incapability, in the same way that tender young brides have been known to be destroyed by domineering husbands whose rectitude was matched only by their insensitivity. Paul outlined something of the pressures experienced by the brides of the law when he wrote, "Cursed is everyone who does not continue in all things which are written in the book of the law to do them" (Gal. 3:10).

If we may take the marriage analogy a little further, we can imagine what it must be like for a bride to be confronted each day by a husband who has a list of things which must be done thoroughly and perfectly. She must continue to do them; she must not only think about doing them but actually perform them. No half measures will be tolerated; no concessions to weakness will be made. There will be no excuses, no explanations will be asked for or given, and failure in every case will result in the unfortunate bride being cursed for her ineptitude and incompetence. To add insult to injury, the enraged husband will then proceed to live in total inflexible adherence to his own impossible demands, humiliating the bride even more.

It is no surprise when the frustrated bride, living under such pressure, lashes out in anger and fear—or as Paul says, *"The passions of sins which [are] aroused by the law. . . bear fruit to death"* (Rom. 7:5). This does not mean that Mr. Law is breaking his own rules or encouraging his wife to engage in lawless activity. On the contrary, his exemplary behavior is a witness to the perfection of his own demands but also to the imperfection of her abilities. The resultant breakdown of relationship reaches its culmination when upon the death of Mr. Law the bride breathes more sighs of relief than she sheds tears of remorse. No longer must she embark each morning on an impossible task, knowing full well that she must face each evening the inevitable condemnation of Mr. Perfection. She is free!

No doubt in the church at Rome there were many people who had endeavored to keep the demands of the law, seeking thereby to earn the blessing of God. Yet they were conscious that if their blessing depended on their meticulous fulfillment, their failure promised their ultimate condemnation. Through the presentation of the gospel, however, they had learned that through the death and Resurrection of Christ they had been forgiven and reconciled to God, and, at the same time, *"by the body of Christ"* (v. 4) they had been released from the law as a means of reconciliation. Like the bereaved bride of the illustration, they had greeted this death with more relief than grief. In fact, they had rejoiced in their liberty to the extent they had used it to be *"married to another—to Him who was raised from the dead"* (v. 4).

Warming to his theme of marriage as an example, Paul goes on to talk about the "fruit" of the union between the believer and the risen Lord. The previous marriage had been "childless" because of the impotence of the law to reproduce anything but the *"fruit to death"* (v. 5) in a person devoid of the life of God. In complete contrast, the new marriage between the living Lord and the loving disciple has the glorious potential of bearing *"fruit to God"* (v. 4). In much the same way that grandparents keenly await the arrival of grandchildren who are the product of the blended lives of their child and spouse, so the Father awaits the reproduction of a new quality of life in the believer which is the result of the life of the risen Lord being blended with that of the believer.

Another stark contrast is seen in the attitude of the believer when compared to that of the person living under the law. Life under the law is a never-ending list of rules and regulations which produce a never-ending stream of fears and frustrations. But marriage to Christ is a relationship of love which freely submits and obeys with delight. The former attitude, described by Paul as *"oldness of the letter"* (v. 6), is often cold and resentful; the latter, which he calls *"newness of the Spirit,"* is fresh and spontaneous.

Any parent of a teenage boy will remember the days when rules and regulations about scrubbing teeth, combing hair, and washing necks were in force. No doubt they will also recall the remarkable day when, instead of dragging the reluctant adolescent to the scene of ablution, they found that a transformation of attitude had taken place which required new rules limiting the amount of time he could spend in the bathroom. Where once it was a battle to apply a comb to the hair, now it was a battle to be able to afford the exotic shampoos necessary for a young man who was in love for the first time. That is the difference between oldness of letter and newness of Spirit!

THE BELIEVER'S RESPECT FOR THE LAW

It is often hard to maintain a balance of truth, and Paul, in his desire to remind his readers of their emancipation from the law, may have felt that his emphasis was such that a false impression of the law could have been gained. He handles this possibility by adopting a literary device with which we are now familiar:

> [7] What shall we say then? Is the law sin? Certainly not! On the contrary, I would not have known sin except through the law. For I would not have known covetousness unless the law had said, *"You shall not covet."*
> —Romans 7:7

No doubt there were those who, on hearing Paul teach about the inadequacy of the law to reproduce a satisfactory life of righteousness, would leap to the conclusion that the law was sin—bad, contrary to God, the product of yet another human attempt to thwart the purposes of God. But Paul does not allow this conclusion and strenuously sets about showing that he has a profound respect for the law which is not at all diminished by his clear perception of its inadequacies.

In a very real sense, Paul owes his salvation to the Tenth Commandment, "Thou shalt not covet." Like the young man who, with open face, told the Lord that he had kept the commandments from his youth, Paul had lived a life of careful adherence to the law with such success that he could tell the Philippians that, "touching the law," he was "blameless." He had refused to steal, to commit adultery, to lie. Meticulously he had honored the Sabbath and had endeavored to love the Lord in the only way he knew. To all intents and purposes, Paul was a perfect example of a fine young man. But there was one major skeleton in his closet. He was covetous or lustful, but no one would ever have guessed from external appearance. Godet remarks, "'*Epithumia,*' lust, denotes that involuntary motion of the soul *(thumos)* toward *(epi)* the external object which presents itself as corresponding to its desire."[2] Hidden away inside the upright young Pharisee was the dark secret of an "involuntary movement" from God's will to human desire, which, if the law had not described in detail and condemned out of hand, may have been overlooked or dismissed as a normal experience of all men. Thanks to the law, however, Paul had at some stage recognized his covetousness as sin and had moved easily from that discovery to recognize himself as a sinner—which, of course, eventually led him to repentance and faith in Christ. For this reason Paul holds the law in high regard and insists that his readers do the same, for as he has already said, "By the law is the knowledge of sin."

THE BELIEVER'S REVELATION THROUGH THE LAW

In addition to revealing the presence of sin in his life, Paul shows how the law exacerbated indwelling sin and gave him the inestimable gift of seeing himself in reality.

[8] But sin, taking opportunity by the commandment, produced in me all manner of evil desire. For apart from the law sin was dead. [9] I was alive once without the law, but when the commandment came, sin revived and I died. [10] And the

commandment, which was to bring life, I found to bring death. [11] For sin, taking occasion by the commandment, deceived me, and by it killed me. [12] Therefore the law is holy, and the commandment holy and just and good.

[13] Has then what is good become death to me? Certainly not! But sin, that it might appear sin, was producing death in me through what is good, so that sin through the commandment might become exceedingly sinful.

—*Romans 7:8–13*

For centuries, considerable debate has gone on concerning the exact time in Paul's experience to which he is referring. His testimony is that at one point in his life he was *"alive"* because he was not living under the restraints of the law, but this state of affairs came to an abrupt end when he became answerable to the law. Everything changed and he died. One possible explanation is that Paul was referring to the blissful experience of his youth before his bar mitzvah. Prior to becoming a "son of the law," he lived happily in his ignorance both of the demands of the law and the sin within the heart of man. But when he became a responsible member of Jewish society and an earnest seeker after righteousness through the law, he found that the law, instead of leading him to life as promised, was taking him deeper into death.

The age-old statement concerning the law, "This do and you shall live," shows that "life" is available only when the "doing" is being done. Paul found the doing of the law more than he was capable of performing, and so, instead of raising him to the exhilarating experience of the presence of God, it took him farther down the road to despair and dismay. The more he longed for perfection, the more he lacked in performance, and the more sinful he recognized himself to be, the more *"holy and just and good"* the law became in his eyes.

Perhaps one of humanity's greatest needs is to recognize that sin is *"exceedingly sinful."* Paul sees the law as particularly helpful in this regard, because sin took something as wholesome and perfect as the law and made it the means for sin to become rampant. What could be more beautiful than the possibility of human relationships of the highest order and what better way of protecting and promoting these relationships than through instructions to honor father and mother, to abstain from adultery, to refrain from misleading through lies, and to respect other people's dignity by rejoicing in what they have rather than lusting for it ourselves? But it is in the area of human relationships that sin is seen in its worst form as lying and cheating, fornicating and killing, robbing and destroying, and it is through the pure law of God that this sin is brought out into the open. Such is the nature of sin, whether in the heart of the unredeemed or in the life of the believer.

THE BELIEVER'S RELATIONSHIP TO THE LAW

Before looking into the remaining verses of this chapter, it should be pointed out that considerable disagreement exists between Bible students as to the application of this passage. If Paul is referring to his pre-Christian experience, then, of course, the passage is applicable to unbelievers. But if he is relating his struggles after his conversion to Christ, then what he has to say relates to believers. This writer takes the view that Paul is relating the struggles he had with the law of God before he knew Christ and which he continues to have since coming into an experience of the risen Lord. Without going into the pros and cons of the differing positions, none of which is totally conclusive, it should be clear that all earnest people, whether regenerate or unregenerate, find that there has been no final resolution of their intrinsic sinfulness. This is particularly true of those who have so despaired of their sin that they have turned in repentance and faith to Christ and found forgiveness in Him. This state of being forgiven has motivated them to great aspirations after holiness of life. But as many have found to their sorrow, the closer they come to the light the more the cracks and flaws show. One hymn writer expressed the thought beautifully: "Those who fain would serve Thee best, Are conscious most of wrong within."

[14] For we know that the law is spiritual, but I am carnal, sold under sin. [15] For what I am doing, I do not understand. For what I will to do, that I do not practice; but what I hate, that I do. [16] If, then, I do what I will not to do, I agree with the law that it is good. [17] But now, it is no longer I who do it, but sin that dwells in me. [18] For I know that in me (that is, in my flesh) nothing good dwells; for to will is present with me, but how to perform what is good I do not find. [19] For the good that I will to do, I do not do; but the evil I will not to do, that I practice. [20] Now if I do what I will not to do, it is no longer I who do it, but sin that dwells in me.

[21] I find then a law, that evil is present with me, the one who wills to do good. [22] For I delight in the law of God

according to the inward man. ^{23} But I see another law in my members, warring against the law of my mind, and bringing me into captivity to the law of sin which is in my members.

—Romans 7:14–23

It is not uncommon for believers to be unsure about their relationship to the law. On the one hand, they have learned that they have died to the law, that they are not under law but under grace and that they should live as free people. On the other hand, they hear Paul extoling the virtues of the law, calling it "holy, just, and good" and describing it as "spiritual," and they feel a little uneasy about disregarding it all together. The dilemma should be resolved when we remember that God's law reflects the purity of His character and outlines the standards of behavior that He regards as normative. The flaw of the law is that it cannot bring anyone to regeneration, and to die to the law means to die to all efforts to be justified by keeping it. This does not mean, however, that the law is any less true or that God regards it as less important. It still reflects God's nature and continues to outline His standards and, therefore, is relevant to the believer.

The believer who holds the law of God in high regard will, like Paul, find himself in something of a battle. One part of him will give assent to the goodness of the law, but another part of him will rebel against it. In response to the principles of God outlined in the law, one part of the believer will aspire to great deeds, but another part will pull him back from achieving them. Challenged by the law to be done with lesser things, the believer may resolve to change his ways only to find that, like the dog which returns to its vomit, he goes back to do again the things he loathes. Paul, in three great cycles, establishes this to be his own experience and draws some important conclusions. First, the law is good; second, he is bad. (To use the words of the Lord Jesus, he finds that "the spirit is willing but the flesh is weak.") Third, he attributes his failure to the presence of sin dwelling in his members.

Stated in the simplest terms, Paul is describing the sad experience of many a person who believes that the principle "thou shalt not commit adultery" is "holy and just and good" but still has a terrible struggle with adulterous thoughts. Or the person who firmly believes that "thou shalt not covet" is a "spiritual" statement and agrees with it wholeheartedly but has great feelings of resentment toward the person appointed to the position she wanted for her husband (and herself!). They both *"delight in the* law of God according to the inward man," but, unfortunately, they are discovering that the law which could not bring anyone justification cannot bring anyone sanctification either. The law pointed out sin in the unbeliever to bring them to repentance, and it goes on pointing out "sin that dwells" in the believer in order that they may look for ongoing deliverance.

Paul was certainly longing for some kind of release from what he called "the law of sin which is in my members" (Rom. 7:23). He said:

> 24 O wretched man that I am! Who will deliver me from this body of death? 25 I thank God—through Jesus Christ our Lord!
>
> So then, with the mind I myself serve the law of God, but with the flesh the law of sin.
>
> —*Romans 7:24–25*

The picture of the battle of the soul is clearly sketched by Paul as he carefully chooses words with military connotations. He describes sin as "warring" against the law of his mind with the result that he is brought into "captivity." It is fitting that he continues the theme by using the expression commonly employed by soldiers wounded in battle and in need of help when he writes, "Who will deliver me?" No doubt he feels that he has been badly wounded in his struggle against sin and desperately needs help. The phrase "body of death" in verse 24 is clearly related to "the body of sin" (Rom. 6:6) and does not mean that the body is dead any more than the earlier phrase meant the body was sinful. His meaning is that the body, through its susceptibility to the power of sin, can be the instrument of sinful acts which lead eventually to death, and such is his burden that he longs to be released from the bondage. Some commentators, like Calvin, interpreted this to mean a desire to die and be through with sin once and for all, but this hardly seems to fit in with the next things Paul teaches. It would be wiser to see Paul's heartfelt cry as a longing for a fuller life rather than for a quicker death.

His response to his own query is as powerful as it is brief. "Thank God," he says, "through Jesus Christ" deliverance from the ongoing power of sin will be experienced. Without amplifying this electrifying statement, which he will deal with in the next chapter, Paul tempers his exultant cry of promised victory with a balanced reminder: the war is not over and the battle will continue, but with the certainty of victory instead of the inevitability of defeat. The ongoing conflict will feature a mind that serves the law of God and the flesh that serves the law of sin. Without the intervention of the living Christ through His Spirit in the life of the believer, it would be "no contest." But through His power, the law which was powerless can be fulfilled as the power of sin is conquered from day to day.

NOTES

1. David Otis Fuller, *Spurgeon's Lectures to His Students* (Grand Rapids: Zondervan Publishing Co.), p. 337.

2. Godet, *Commentary on Romans,* p. 273.

CHAPTER TWELVE—THE THREE SPIRITUAL LAWS

ROMANS 8:1–13

Scripture Outline

    The Law of Sin and Death (8:1–8)

    The Law of the Spirit of Life (8:9–11)

    The Law of Fulfilled Righteousness (8:12–13)

I n the long history of human affairs there have been few statements more resounding than Paul's assertion: *"There is therefore now no condemnation to those who are in Christ Jesus. . . ."* Having carefully expounded the divine principle whereby God justifies sinners and frees them from all condemnation for their guilt, Paul now shows that the believer has much more to enjoy in terms of freedom from condemnation. The words "therefore now" link his "no-condemnation" statement to the subject with which the previous chapter closed, namely, the deep desire of the justified believer to be delivered from the wretched tyranny of indwelling sin. Paul is pointing out that God does not condemn his redeemed children to a life of wretchedness and defeat. Bruce suggests that the word "condemnation" in this context can mean "penal servitude" or the "punishment following sentence."[1] The explanation of this powerful truth follows his impelling opening declaration:

> **8:1** There is therefore now no condemnation to those who are in Christ Jesus, who do not walk according to the flesh, but according to the Spirit. [2] For the law of the Spirit of life in Christ Jesus has made me free from the law of sin and death. [3] For what the law could not do in that it was weak

through the flesh, God did by sending His own Son in the likeness of sinful flesh, on account of sin: He condemned sin in the flesh, [4] that the righteous requirement of the law might be fulfilled in us who do not walk according to the flesh but according to the Spirit. [5] For those who live according to the flesh set their minds on the things of the flesh, but those who live according to the Spirit, the things of the Spirit. [6] For to be carnally minded is death, but to be spiritually minded is life and peace. [7] Because the carnal mind is enmity against God; for it is not subject to the law of God, nor indeed can be. [8] So then, those who are in the flesh cannot please God.

—*Romans 8:1–8*

It should be noted that the final phrase of verse 1, which also appears in verse 4, is not found in many manuscripts and is regarded by most scholars as an interpolation that anticipates the later verse.

As we have noted earlier, Paul's use of the word "law" varies considerably, and in the key statement about the *"law of the Spirit of life"* in verse 2, there is a further development. In the same way that a law can be either a legal requirement or a scientific principle, so Paul sees the law sometimes as a divine requirement and other times as a spiritual principle. It is the operation of the principle of the *"Spirit of life" in* the believer that sets him free from the operation of the principle of *"sin and death."* The practical experience of deliverance from sin that dwells within is clearly related to an understanding of the dynamic interaction of the opposing principles of the *"Spirit of life"* and *"sin and death."*

THE LAW OF SIN AND DEATH

To understand what Paul means by the *"law of sin and death"* we need to note the link between "the flesh" and "sin" in his thinking. For instance, he concludes the previous chapter with the dismal words *"with the flesh* [I serve] *the law of sin,"* thereby clearly identifying "the flesh" as the means whereby sin operates within the human experience. At this point, considerable confusion can arise because of Paul's habit of using "flesh" (Greek, *sarx*) in a number of ways. In Romans 2:28, "flesh" obviously means the tissues of the physical body; in Romans 1:3, it means natural descent; in Romans 3:20, it is a synonym for the human race, and in Romans 8:30, it refers to human nature. To add to the confusion, the translators of English editions of the Bible occasionally translated *sarx* words by the English word "carnal." But all is not lost if we remember that when *sarx*, whether translated "flesh" or "carnal," appears in contrast to God and His work in human lives, it means human nature with particular reference to its inbuilt sinfulness. Godet defines it as "the inclination to seek self-satisfaction in everything,"[2] and Bruce weighs in with "sinful propensity from Adam."[3] The flesh is an attitude or inclination operating in complete rejection of the divine will that requires self-sacrificial submission, choosing rather the free expression of anything and everything that will bring self-gratification. It is in this flesh that the law of sin and death moves and has its being.

Anyone who reads Romans 8 should have little difficulty grasping the significance of the flesh. The law is said to be *"weak through the flesh"* (v. 3); those who live *"according to the flesh"* set their minds on the *"things of the flesh,"* which we are told is "death" (vv. 5–6); the fleshly mind is *"enmity against God"* and *"is not subject to the law of God, nor indeed can it be"* (v. 7); furthermore, *"those who are in the flesh cannot please God"* (v. 8). To be "in the flesh" means the same as being "in Adam," or unregenerate; to live "according to the flesh" means to live as if unregenerate after becoming regenerate. Paul's cry for deliverance is therefore a longing to be free from the discouraging tendency he has discovered in himself to live, although justified, as if he is not. He finds within himself a sinful propensity which is so powerful that he recognizes he, in himself, is incapable of breaking it; in fact, it is so pervasive that he feels as if he is "sold under sin" because his human nature is so thoroughly imbued with selfishness and self-serving. This is the law of sin and death from which he longs to be free.

Paul carefully outlines the stages of God's dealings with sinful human nature, the flesh in which the law of sin and death operates. First God gave the law which could neither make man right with God nor make him live rightly before God. This lack of ability was no reflection on the law, but rather a condemnation of human nature.

In my youth I attended a school where we had a brilliant musician on the staff. His first and only love was music, and he lived for nothing else than to make music. He longed to join our youthful voices into a choir which would perform the works of the masters. Unfortunately, he was trying to produce music through a bunch of young thugs whose interests were limited to football and rugby. The result was that he, like the law, although brilliant, was weak through our flesh! Nevertheless, by his own musical genius he did expose the total Philistinian lack of his youthful choir—a similar achievement to that of the law.

Second, God then sent *"His own Son in the likeness of sinful flesh, on account of sin"* (v. 3). The precision of Paul's statement should not be missed. If he had said that Christ came "in the likeness of flesh," he would have delighted the followers of docetism who taught that Christ only "appeared" to come in human form, with no physical reality about His Incarnation. On the other hand, if he had said "in sinful flesh," he would have attributed to Christ a sinful nature like ours. He could have limited his statement to "in flesh" and thus avoided both pitfalls, but he would also have avoided making a desperately important point. Christ came into our humanity and assumed our personality, but He was unique in that, while human flesh is consistently corrupt, He lived with and in our nature without in any way succumbing to the sinfulness which goes along with it. It was the inescapable fact of His sinlessness while living in the vehicle of our humanness which roundly condemned the fleshliness of our nature and the sinfulness of our lives.

Third, Christ came *"for sin"* (v. 3)—an expression which in the Greek is found in the Septuagint as a translation of "sin offering" in Psalm 40:6. Having condemned sin in the flesh by His flawless 33 years inhabiting our humanity, He then assumed our sin on the Cross, and in dying for sin, He made the most thoroughgoing denunciation of sin once and for all.

Fourth, those who are "in Christ" have identified with Him in His condemnation of sin in the flesh and in so doing have taken the first step to living free of its dominion. Those who choose rather to excuse their fleshliness by blaming it on heredity or who condone it by pointing out it is "only human" cannot begin to live in liberty. But those who intelligently take their stand in Christ not only lament their sinfulness—cry for deliverance, as did Paul—but also take great interest in the operation of the *"law of the Spirit of life"* which "in Christ" sets them free.

THE LAW OF THE SPIRIT OF LIFE

Up until this point in Paul's painstakingly systematic presentation of the Christian gospel, the Holy Spirit has been conspicuous by His absence. In the early chapters of the epistle, He makes only two brief appearances, and in the crucial seventh chapter, He is not mentioned at all. Presumably this omission can be explained by the fact that the burden of Paul's message so far relating to the believer's sanctification has been to show the hopelessness of the spiritual experience of those who seek to do it on their own, or, as he explains it, on the basis of *autos ego*—*"I* by myself." But when the Third member of the Trinity is given His rightful place in theology and experience, the change is dramatic and radical.

> [9] But you are not in the flesh but in the Spirit, if indeed the Spirit of God dwells in you. Now if anyone does not have the Spirit of Christ, he is not His. [10] And if Christ is in you, the body is dead because of sin, but the Spirit is life because of righteousness. [11] But if the Spirit of Him who raised Jesus from the dead dwells in you, He who raised Christ from the dead will also give life to your mortal bodies through His Spirit who dwells in you.
>
> *—Romans 8:9–11*

The Holy Spirit is given many titles in Scripture—indeed, in the few verses before us—but there can be none more exciting than "the Spirit of life." He emanates from the Father who is the Author and sustainer of life and takes up His abode in the life of the believer, thereby banishing the spiritual deadness with which he had been plagued. Through His intervention in human affairs, dullness and deadness give way to vivacity and vitality; in Him bondage is banished and freedom reigns.

Having described in detail what it means to be "in the flesh" and to live "according to the flesh," Paul now sets out to describe the divine alternatives, which are to be "in the Spirit" and to live "according to the Spirit." *"Those who are in the flesh cannot please God"* (v. 8) either in terms of moving Him to save them because they have been good, or in terms of living such exemplary lives that He delights in watching them do it. But believers do not need to be unduly concerned about this human limitation because they are *"not in the flesh but in the Spirit"* (v. 9) and, accordingly, have the capability of pleasing the One who has redeemed them. The proof that they are "in the Spirit" is to be found in the fact of His indwelling presence. It is apparent that Paul moves freely from one title to another when writing about the Holy Spirit. In the verses we are considering, He is called *"the Spirit of God," "the Spirit of Christ," "the Spirit of Him who raised Jesus from the dead."* While each of these descriptions is synonymous with the others, they all point to a different aspect of His personality and remind us of the Triune God.

The unique Christian truth dealing with the fact of God's indwelling presence was introduced to the disciples by the Lord Jesus. They were definitely unreceptive to what He had to say because He introduced the topic by telling them that He proposed leaving them and that they would be better off without Him. This unpalatable prospect was improved considerably for them when He explained. After He had left them, He said, the Comforter would come to them and make it possible for Him to live in them. With the same kind of free interchange of ideas which characterize Paul's treatment of the truth, the Lord talked about the Holy Spirit's indwelling them, His own indwelling them, and even God's taking up His abode in them. It was the indwelling of their lives which would be far superior to anything they had as yet experienced; therefore, the departure of the Lord which would precede the arrival of the Comforter was to be to their advantage. In the body of flesh which He had assumed, the Lord was subject to the limitations of time and space common to all men. As a result He could not be with Peter in Galilee and at the same time with John in Jerusalem, but when liberated from His earthly body through the Resurrection and Ascension, He would come to them in the Spirit and live in their lives, imparting to them His grace and power.

Because Christ spoke these words to His elite corps of disciples, and because of the remarkable nature of the words spoken, it would be understandable if people, on reading John's account, would assume that the indwelling presence of God was reserved for the supersaints of the apostolic group. But Paul banishes this thought to oblivion by saying, *"Now if anyone does not have the Spirit of Christ, he is not His"* (Rom. 8:9b). In other words, the indwelling presence of Christ through the Spirit, far from being the preserve of the few, is the birthright of all believers and the authentic seal of their redeemed status.

To give the Roman Christians some idea of the significance of the divine indwelling, Paul introduces another of his favorite sets of contrasts. Whereas the human body is subject to death because of sin—a concept already developed—the spirit of man through the presence of the life-giving Spirit possesses life eternal because of justification. While the body of man is not exempt from the corruption common to the race because of Adam's sin, the spirit of man is preserved unto life through the sheer power of the indwelling Spirit. The mortal bodies of the believers which will, of course, return to the dust from which they came, will in a coming day be resurrected to a reunion with their corresponding spirit.

Both the eternal preservation of the human spirit and the ultimate Resurrection of the human body are attributed to the Spirit of God. But of particular interest to us in this context is the fact that the power thus exhibited by the Spirit is the power made available to believers in the present age in order that they, through the Spirit of life, might be set free from the law of sin and death.

This description of the power of the Spirit is advanced even further when we note that His name, the Spirit of God, is introduced in the second verse of the Bible. There He is seen actively engaged in the monumental task of creation *ex nihilo.* It is the Spirit of creation who indwells and empowers the believer. Then Paul's careful use of the *"Spirit of Christ"* in verse 9 reminds us that it is the same Spirit who indwelt Him who indwells us. Jesus, "filled with Spirit," was directed by the Spirit into the Wilderness for His personal confrontation with the Evil One. From this cosmic clash He emerged triumphant "in the power of the Spirit" only to meet him again on Calvary. The result was the same, as He defeated the one who holds humanity hostage to fear and death, but it was "through the eternal Spirit" that He prevailed. This same Spirit is the indwelling Comforter of the contemporary believer, the means of deliverance from the law of sin and death. In case the point of the potential power of the Spirit should escape the Roman reader, the apostle adds, for good measure, the information that it is the Spirit of the One who raised the dead Christ to the heights of glory who is alive in the believer. For the apostles there was no greater demonstration of power than the Resurrection of Christ. They were constantly referring to this act of God as the crowning achievement which justified the claims of Christ and epitomized the power of God available to mankind.

In the same way that Paul's detailed description of sin's abundance set the stage for his presentation of abounding grace, so his stark, searing description of the law of sin and death has set the stage for the understanding of the law of the Spirit of life. If the overwhelming power of indwelling sin is clearly understood, the power of the indwelling Spirit will be magnified in the believer's mind because the latter is more powerful than the former.

THE LAW OF FULFILLED RIGHTEOUSNESS

So far in this chapter we have examined the nature and capabilities of the two mammoth contenders for the inner workings of the believer's life and affection. It may seem to the reader that the chapter has been similar to the interminable introductions before a heavyweight championship, where the opponents glower at each other across the ring while the fans wonder if the fight will every get underway!

The fight takes place in the complex of human experience and thus must not be regarded as a fight in a vacuum. The person in whom the conflict rages is not isolated from the struggle; in fact, although both the principles at war within him are more powerful than he, without his cooperation neither can win. It is true that Paul talks of the struggle between the two laws as if the victory of the law of the Spirit of life over the law of sin and death is a foregone conclusion, but a careful reading of the text will reveal the most important role the believer plays in the struggle.

> 12 Therefore, brethren, we are debtors—not to the flesh,
> to live according to the flesh. 13 For if you live according to
> the flesh you will die; but if by the Spirit you put to death the
> deeds of the body, you will live.
> —*Romans 8:12–13*

There are three things that identify this role. First, the believer must "mind" the things of the Spirit rather than those of the flesh. Second, the believer must choose to "walk" according to the Spirit rather than according to the flesh. Third, the believer is required *"through the Spirit"* to *"put to death the deeds of the body."*

When the apostle talks about the mind, he means more than intellectual capability. The word he uses—*phronein*—stops short of obsession but goes far beyond casual interest. In other words, Paul reminds us that, when it comes to spiritual life, everything is important and nothing is to be taken casually. There is a particular danger for Christians who have worked themselves into a comfortable, undemanding situation where they are confronted with little external challenge and have so come to terms with their own lifestyle that they see little or no necessity for deepening of the spiritual life. Without realizing it, they may have ceased to be ambitious for the things of the Spirit and may have lapsed into a kind of spiritual neutrality which in reality is an ambition for the comfort of the fleshly and an identification with the purely natural.

My younger son, who plays basketball for his high school, came back from practice recently so tired that he went straight to bed. Next morning when I asked how he could be so out of shape halfway through the season, he said, "We are in great shape, but the coach said we had won so many games so easily that we were becoming casual and sloppy in our play and that unless we got our act together we would be beaten by teams far inferior to us." In other words, the young ball players had forgotten to "mind" the essentials of the game and had slipped into an attitude that spelled danger.

The options available to the believer are spelled out clearly. Either we aspire toward the things of the Spirit or those of the flesh. Without a clear understanding of both and the ability to identify each, there is a distinct possibility that the flesh will take over because the secular environment in which we live is dominated by selfish interest and governed by fleshly concerns. The impact of advertising in modern society is a perfect example of this. The modern approach is to make surveys of human thought patterns that clearly identify the hidden longings and aspirations of the average person. Then clever means of presenting painless answers to these longings are developed and presented in such attractive forms that the person subjected to the advertising may unwittingly become totally governed by fleshly attitudes. The principles of the Spirit do not, of course, find their way into most television commercials. The average believer may very well spend more time absorbing commercials than epistles and be exposed to more sales pitches that aim to boost his ego than spiritual principles that promote the Spirit. His aspirations quite understandably may be tarnished without his realizing what has been happening. The mind set on the flesh leads inevitably to estrangement to God and alienation from His Spirit, which is another way of describing spiritual death and deadness. The unbeliever who lives in this way is dead, but the believer who minds the flesh while possessing new life exhibits nothing but dullness and deadness. This is particularly sad when we remember that the human heart longs constantly for life and peace—qualities that are promised by most competitors for human attention but that are delivered exclusively by the Spirit of God. The believer is therefore presented with options that require choices so basic that they operate at the deepest level of desire and ambition, aspiration and intention.

It is worth noting that, although Paul regards the "things" of both flesh and Spirit of the utmost importance, he does not outline what they are. But from the context it would appear that he was thinking of the presence of the Spirit in the believer, which, when borne constantly in mind, has a most salutary impact on the individual's thought processes. The contrast between the holiness of the

Holy Spirit and the things that so easily captivate the believer's thinking is underlined when it has become increasingly normal for the believer to concentrate on the Spirit's presence. No doubt Paul's presentation of the power of the Spirit can be seen as an indication of another effect to be minded. The downward pull of sin and surrounding sinfulness can become such a debilitating force in the believer's life that he may become so defeated that he settles for being a defeatist. But if he is in tune with the power of the indwelling Spirit, this attitude will quickly be banished and replaced by one of positive anticipation that the powerful Spirit will be a factor in daily living. Like the two men who looked through prison bars, those who concentrate on the things of the flesh will see mud while those who mind the things of the Spirit will see the stars.

The "walk" according to the Spirit is a most natural development from minding the things of the Spirit. It means to make definite decisions based on the intelligent appreciation of the Spirit. It is helpful to remember that there is an obvious difference between taking a step and going for a walk. While Christian experience involves taking some massive steps occasionally, the normal Christian experience is the product of a succession of relatively unimportant steps that require varying degrees of decision. When the Holy Spirit reminds me of the unholiness of a particular pursuit I am contemplating, I may choose to disregard His prompting and take a step in the opposite direction. This will, of course, lead to bondage to the flesh and the law of sin and death. But a step of obedience taken in response to the Spirit's prompting will lead to a right decision which in turn will produce a walk in the Spirit. It should not be assumed that the believer will have to concentrate exclusively on "spiritual things" to the exclusion of other legitimate aspects of life. But if the right attitude is nurtured, there will be an unconscious sense of rest in the Spirit which will only become obvious when the pressure of decision becomes imperative. In the same way that a person standing still is not conscious of breathing, the person who is warmly embracing the life of the Spirit will not be concentrating exclusively on Him. But if that person who has been standing still begins to climb twenty flights of steps at a rapid pace he will think of nothing else but breathing. Just so, when the believer is confronted with the old fleshly attractions and the inward response to them, he will become excruciatingly conscious of the step he must take in order to walk after the Spirit.

The negative side of this walk is suggested by the expression *"through the Spirit put to death the deeds of the body"* (v. 9). The decision to do something is inextricably bound up in the decision not to do the opposite. This then may require a courageous act of self-denial that is so difficult that the believer feels incapable of doing it even though he knows it is right. The balanced truth that Paul presents is that we "through the Spirit" perform the necessary spiritual surgery. God knows that it would be an exercise in futility to tell us to put to death these deeds. That is why He insists that we take action through the Spirit. The extreme opposite approach to that of the dedicated self-denier is that of those who "leave it to the Spirit" to do the necessary decision-making. It is as out of order to expect the Spirit to do what we have been told to do as it is to endeavor to do what only God can do. But when the believer cultivates the attitude of the Spirit, takes steps to follow His objective teaching and subjective prompting, and through His power says a loud "no" to the temptations to which the flesh readily and enthusiastically responds, he will then experimentally discover the liberation from the law of sin and death.

Some years ago in California, after I had tried hard to explain this principle to a group of people, I was somewhat discouraged to hear one man say, "Now you've really confused me." When asked if I would have time to talk to him privately, we discovered that the only time I had available was the time he usually spent flying his light aircraft, so he asked me to go and talk and fly. I agreed without any great enthusiasm. To me flying is nothing more than the means of getting from A to B quicker than it should naturally take.

When we arrived at his plane, I feigned horror at its flimsy construction and refused to get on board. He was most perturbed, particularly when I expressed doubt that such a contraption was capable of bearing my weight, let alone lifting it in the air. With great concern, he explained to me that the law of aerodynamics which was stronger than the law of gravity could set me free from earth. But I said that he was only confusing me, until he asked me tentatively if I was "kidding him." I assured him I was, and then as we took off, I explained that in the same way that the law of aerodynamics in the plane was setting us free from the law of gravity on earth, so the law of the Spirit of life in Christ Jesus was setting us free from the law of sin and death. He said that made sense, so I pretended to open the door of the plane as we flew high over Los Angeles, and when he remonstrated, I assured him that I would not fall because of the law which set me free from gravity! By this time he was in tune with my teaching method and said,

"Now you are reminding me that it is as important to abide in Christ to derive the benefits of His life as it is to stay in the plane to be set free from falling."

The quality of life related in the believer through the power of the Spirit is called "the righteousness of the law." But notice that this life is not the product of frustrated self-effort; rather it is the result of human response to the divine Spirit.

NOTES

1. Bruce, *Romans,* p. 159.

2. Godet, *Commentary on Romans,* p. 283.

3. Bruce, *Romans,* p. 43.

CHAPTER THIRTEEN—LIVING IN THE SPIRIT
ROMANS 8:14–27

Scripture Outline

Living in the Good of the Family (8:14–17)

Living in the Midst of Futility (8:18–22)

Living in the Light of the Futurity (8:23–27)

During the last three weeks I have traveled extensively. While this has not helped the production of this manuscript it has given me many opportunities for meeting and observing people. In the Bahamas, I spent time with some fine young pastors who, in addition to their pastoral duties, had full-time jobs and also found it necessary to spend considerable time fishing and diving to supplement their rather meager diets. Under the window of my hotel in Guatemala City I saw pitiful beggars wrapped in rags and old newspapers, trying to keep themselves warm in the cool night air. In Hong Kong I visited refugees from North Vietnam crowded into their transit camps right next to the busy airstrip of the International Airport. On the way home, I stopped off in Honolulu and joined the crowds of well-fed, well-dressed, well-heeled vacationers on Waikiki Beach.

If I were given the choice of being a beggar in Guatemala, a refugee in Hong Kong, a struggling pastor in Nassau, a vacationer in Waikiki, or continuing what I have been doing for years, I would have to admit that the choice would not be terribly difficult! Like most people, I would prefer to live a life of fullness rather than deprivation, of liberty rather than bondage, of purpose rather than aimlessness. The same is true of spiritual life. Sadly, it is possible to see those of us who are "living in the Spirit" behaving more like refugees, beggars, or vacationers than as if we appreciated the fullness of life intended for us. Living in the Spirit as we ought involves:—

LIVING IN THE GOOD OF THE FAMILY

14 For as many as are led by the Spirit of God, these are sons of God. 15 For you did not receive the spirit of bondage again to fear, but you received the Spirit of adoption by whom we cry out, "Abba, Father." 16 The Spirit Himself bears witness with our spirit that we are children of God, 17 and if children, then heirs—heirs of God and joint heirs with Christ, if indeed we suffer with Him, that we may also be glorified together.
—*Romans 8:14–17*

It is quite clear from Paul's use of the words, *"sons," "children," "heirs," "joint heirs,"* and *"Abba, Father"* that he is thinking of the life of the believer in terms of the divine family relationship. In his epistle to the Galatians, the apostle made a clear distinction between sons—*huioi*—and children—*nepioi*. The former he regarded as mature young people who had entered into the benefits due them upon attaining their majority; the latter as children, or infants, who, while members of the family, as minors had not entered into the full benefits of family status. It is open to question whether Paul intends the same distinction in this passage, but there is no doubt about the reality of being both a child of God and a son of God in the sense that the child enjoys the life of the father and the son enjoys his resources. Both are perfectly true of the believer as a member of the family of God.

As is common with all families, life in the family involves many privileges and responsibilities. Sons of God are *"led by the Spirit of God"* (v. 14). This is both an obligation on the part of the son and an evidence of his sonship. The professed son of God who lives in careless indifference to the Spirit or in open defiance of the Spirit is at best a living contradiction and at worst a spiritual impostor. It is unfortunate that such an important aspect of spiritual experience has been so seriously devalued that "to be led" has become, in common usage, an excuse for impulsive behavior, a rationale for lack of careful preparation, or a substantiation for bizarre decisions.

When we bear in mind that the identical expression is used of the Lord Jesus with reference to His experience in the wilderness, we will realize that to be "led by the Spirit" is to come under His control and to be alert to His promptings. The leading of the Spirit which Christ experienced came to Him because He was filled with "the power of the Spirit" (Luke 4:14). The idea of Spirit control and domination is brought out clearly by Paul's use of the Greek word *agontai,* which Godet describes as a "notion of holy violence," adding by way of clarification, "the Spirit drags the man where the flesh would fain not go."

The leading of the Spirit can be experienced in both positive and negative forms, as Paul knew from his own experience. When he and Silas were traveling in the Roman provinces, they tried hard to enter Asia, but the Holy Spirit thwarted their efforts. They then turned their attention to Bithynia only to discover ". . . the Spirit of Jesus would not allow them to enter" (Acts 16:6–7, NIV). But despite the obvious feelings of frustration, they continued to work and explore possibilities until the famous vision of the man from Macedonia.

When they accepted this call as from the Spirit, everything quickly fell into place and they arrived in the place of God's choosing to fulfill the task of reaching the people for Christ. It is important that the sons of God learn so to order their lives in commitment to and dependence upon the Holy Spirit that they can respond to each circumstance they have surrendered to Him, whether it be positive or negative, and interpret it as the leading of the Spirit. Once the son of God is clear about the details and intent of the Spirit's direction, it remains only for him to respond in glad obedience.

Having pointed out the necessity for obedience on the part of those led by the Spirit, Paul hastens to add in verse 15 that this does not mean we have *"received the spirit of bondage again to fear."* There is a marked difference between the experience of one who is bound by malevolent forces leading into all manner of activities that engender phobias and paranoia and the experience of one who because he is a son gladly accepts the responsibilities of sonship, which of necessity, include submission to authority and acceptance of roles. It should be noted that the order of the words is not intended to imply that for the second time we have received a spirit of bondage as if God had already done this to us once, but rather that sons of God do not find themselves in bondage that will lead them into the old paths of fear and trepidation. The "again" relates to "fear," not to "receive."

This means that, in addition to a sense of leading, the believer enjoys a great sense of liberty as a son of God. Paul expressed similar sentiments to his spiritual son Timothy. "God has not given us a spirit of fear, but of power and of love and of a sound mind" (2 Tim. 1:7). While he does not enumerate the fears to which the Romans were susceptible, they were no doubt similar to those with which Timothy struggled. His natural inclination to timidity, his reticence to proclaim the gospel boldly, and his temptation to dis-associate himself from Paul the prisoner were all products of natu-ral fears which bound him and from which the Spirit of God longed to release him. Timothy, like all sons of God, was being called to decide whether his life would be ruled by his fears or whether his fears would be overruled by his response to the Spirit's leading.

As we saw in the previous chapter, the apostle is not at all inhibited in his varied use of names for the Holy Spirit. In a man-ner reminiscent of the Old Testament writers' richly varied use of the names of God to bring into focus different aspects of His nature and work, Paul switches quickly and easily from "Spirit of God" to "Spirit of Christ" to "Spirit of adoption." That he is sim-ply underlining an aspect of the Spirit's ministry rather than introducing another spirit is clear when we note that in a similar passage in Galatians he writes, "God sent the Spirit of His Son" (Gal. 4:6). The Spirit of adoption is, therefore, clearly identified as the Holy Spirit who, among His many ministries, has a ministry of adoption. Bruce remarks that "the term 'adoption' may smack somewhat of artificiality in our ears,"[2] but goes on to show that, in the first century, adoption, far from suggesting inferiority of position in comparison to that of the naturally born child, was actually a means of putting the one not naturally so born into a position of great status and privilege. When it was borne in mind that the one so honored owed his privilege to the choice of the adopting parent, the adopted one, instead of feeling inferior, regarded himself as deeply privileged. Similar sentiments were once expressed to me by a beautiful teenage girl who said, "My sis-ter was born to Mummy and Daddy in the normal way, but I was chosen to be a member of their family, and that to me is special!"

How the adoption process works and exactly what the Spirit does to make us sons of God is a mystery we shall not unravel this side of glory. But the wonder of the relationship can be enjoyed even though the mechanics may well be hidden from our view. This delightful sense of wonder at the relationship is expressed best by cries of loving appreciation which spring to the believer's lips and flow from his heart. Paul expresses this in language which at first sight seems most inappropriate—*"Abba, Father"* (v. 15).

It is a matter of considerable interest that a few words have sur-vived the passage of time and the tender attention of translators and remain today in our language in their original form. The Hebrew "Amen," the Greek "anathema," and the Aramaic "maranatha," for instance, are found in close proximity in 1 Corinthians 16:22–24. "Abba," another of these words, had its roots in the Hebrew *ab*, "father," and developed into the Aramaic *abba*, an affectionate expression similar to our "daddy." This word was in common usage in our Lord's time and was, in fact, the word He used to address His Father in the agonizing prayer in Gethsemane. That this word, which Jews did not use to address God, became a common word in the vocabulary of the Christian church is an indication that the early believers knew it was the Lord's affectionate form of address for His Father, and they adopted it for themselves because they were adopted into a position of intimacy with Him. To pray "Abba" is, therefore, to express unashamedly and joyfully an endearment born of love.

The picture of life in the Spirit begins to emerge here. Through His ministry we can see there is leading, liberating, and loving, but, in addition, the apostle speaks of the learning experience we may have through Him. This learning experience is related to the interplay of the human spirit with the indwelling Holy Spirit. In much the same way that the female ovum, unfertilized, cannot reach its potential, so the human spirit without the penetration of the Holy Spirit is limited to an experience of partial fulfillment and unrealized potential. But as in the case of the ovum penetrated by the sperm, so the human spirit becomes alive with the aliveness of the Spirit and not only reproduces something totally new, but also provides the opportunity for full development and function of the human spirit. This penetrating ministry called by Paul *"the Spirit Himself bearing witness with our spirit,"* has to do with the impregnating of the human spirit with the realization of all that is involved in being "children of God."

Paul's use of the Greek word *summarturein* appears to differentiate between the Spirit's witnessing *to* our spirit in the sense of His being active and the human spirit totally passive, and the Spirit's witnessing *with*, suggesting the cooperative activity of both Holy and human spirit. The objective of the exercise is, of course, the development of status-consciousness. This will be based on the assurance of relationship—a delightful ministry of the Spirit with our spirits which results in an invigorating sense of well-being. It will no doubt also include the fostering of filial pride and the development of family spirit. But, in addition, when we consider the remarkable resilience of the human spirit without the Holy Spirit as seen in the lives of refugees struggling against all odds for survival, or the remarkable creativity of the human spirit in works of beauty and grandeur, we see the glorious potential of the spirits of the sons of God. As they are fused with the power and majesty of the Spirit of God, the result can be great and magnificent acts and activities that will bring great glory to the Father, who, like His earthly counterparts, takes great delight in seeing His children "doing well."

The logical mind of the apostle moves quickly from the idea of *"sons"* to the idea of *"heirs."* While it is true that earthly fathers die and leave their resources to their children, and God Himself will never die, and therefore there must be some limit on the analogy, there is a beautiful thought here in the believer's expectation that he will share in the inheritance that Peter called "an inheritance incorruptible and undefiled and that does not fade away, reserved in heaven for you" (1 Pet. 1:4).

But it would appear that this concept was too vague for Paul, so he adds that as heirs of God we are *"joint heirs with Christ."* While we must conjecture concerning our inheritance, we are left in no doubt about Christ's—He will be clothed with the glory that was His before the worlds were created. This means that in some way we will not only see His glory but share in it too. The glory is His, of course, by right, but will be ours by grace. The young lady whom I mentioned earlier as having been adopted lived in a beautiful home provided for her by a loving father who was a high-ranking business executive. She said to me, "Isn't it wonderful that I share in all the beautiful things Daddy provides just as much as my sister who was born to these things?" She had learned the lesson of sharing through grace the glory of those whose it is by right—a lesson the Spirit of God works hard to teach those whom He indwells.

When Charles, Prince of Wales, met the press after his engagement to Lady Diana Spencer, a nineteen-year-old kindergarten teacher, he remarked that he thought "she was very brave consenting to take me on!" There was a laugh among the reporters, but Lady Diana only smiled for she had already tasted something of the suffering that goes with the glory, having been hounded everywhere she went by newshounds and curious sightseers. There is always a costly side to glory, and the Christian disciple's experience with Christ is no exception, as Paul reminds us in verse 17: *"If indeed we suffer with Him, that we may be also glorified together."*

Writing to the Corinthians, the apostle showed that receiving the glory is a process that takes place over a long period on earth and reaches its culmination in heaven. He explained that "we who with unveiled faces all reflect the Lord's glory, are being transformed into his likeness with ever increasing glory" (2 Cor. 3:18). This transforming process is a metamorphosis not unlike the remarkable process whereby an ugly chrysalis rolls back its unattractive covering to reveal a butterfly in all its fragile, colorful beauty. But the rolling back of that outer skin must be painful, and there is no shortcut for the believer under construction, who must cooperate with the Spirit in laying aside all that is contrary to the glory of the Lord in his life. Living in the Spirit, for all its blessings, includes the basic liability of suffering, from which there is no escape—a lesson Ananias was commissioned to teach the apostle on the day of his conversion. For the Lord determined to "show him how much he must suffer for my name" (Acts 9:16, NIV).

LIVING IN THE MIDST OF FUTILITY

The connection between the sufferings of Christ and His glorification suggested in the phrase *"we suffer with Him that we may be glorified together"* is obvious. But Paul introduces another aspect of human suffering which comes as a complete surprise. He tells us that the creation is suffering too and we with it.

> [18] For I consider that the sufferings of this present time are not worthy to be compared with the glory which shall be revealed in us. [19] For the earnest expectation of the creation eagerly waits for the revealing of the sons of God. [20] For the creation was subjected to futility, not willingly, but because of Him who subjected it in hope; [21] because the creation itself also will be delivered from the bondage of corruption into the glorious liberty of the children of God. [22] For we know that the whole creation groans and labors with birth pangs together until now.
>
> *—Romans 8:18–22*

Paul, with the characteristic understatement he reserved for his own sufferings, says they *"are not worthy to be compared with the glory which shall be revealed"*—a statement with echoes of his remark to the Corinthians about his "light affliction" (see 2 Cor. 4:16–18). We should not assume that Paul was blessed with either a high pain threshold or a slightly masochistic side to his personality but rather that he had carefully looked at his sufferings as an integral part of the glorification process and, accordingly, well worthwhile. This attitude is particularly refreshing in light of the contemporary assumption that we should be free from pain and should be guaranteed pleasantness.

The Christian has the opportunity to view suffering in a much more realistic light than many of his contemporaries because he not only understands the sufferings of Christ but also has keen insights into the suffering creation. He sees mankind as a victim of the travail of earth in flood and earthquake, storm and avalanche, but, more important, sees mankind as a cause of much of creation's agony. When Paul says *"creation was subjected to futility, not willingly, but because of Him. . ."* it is often assumed, by the capitalizing of "him," that God has been responsible for creation's downfall. But there are scholars who believe the "him" should more adequately be interpreted as "mankind"—in other words, mankind was responsible for the fallenness of creation which introduced death along with his own death and disintegration with his own disintegration.

This process has been maintained and exacerbated by man's actions in abusing the creation in many ways. Environmentalists have documented countless examples of man's irresponsible actions that have precipitated innumerable crises in every area of the created order. Indeed, there is no doubt that man's fallenness has done much to subject creation to all manner of disorder, imbalance, abuse, and extermination. Whether Paul means God or man at this point is a matter of interpretation, but there is no doubt that it was because of man's sin that God cursed the ground originally and it is because of man's continued sinning that so much is wrong in God's creation.

There is a glorious note of triumph in Paul's anticipation of new order in the created world. In the same way that man's fall has dragged creation downhill, so man's glorification will not only end that trend but introduce an era in which the new heaven and new earth will demonstrate the glory of God as clearly as will redeemed humanity.

When I spent some time in Southern Africa, I thought I had never seen a more bountifully endowed part of God's creation. Mineral wealth, animal and plant life, landscape and seascape were breathtaking in their variety and beauty. Yet at the same time it was impossible to overlook the fact that the vast mineral resources were a matter for political concern and maneuvering, that some of the wildlife was in danger of extermination because of illegal and unscrupulous hunters, that the fair land was becoming the terrain of the guerrilla fighter and in some areas industrial pollution threatened the survival of some unique species of flora and fauna. My unashamed delight at God's profligate blessing of the area was tinged with a sense of shame for every evidence of our mishandling. Yet my shame turned to joy as I remembered Paul's words that when the sons of God come into the fullness of their redemption so also the creation will be liberated and restored to full untrammeled and untainted perfection. I'm already anxious to visit the new earth equivalent of Southern Africa—it will be fabulous!

LIVING IN THE LIGHT OF THE FUTURITY

Having digressed to talk about the suffering creation and its expectations of full restoration, Paul returns to his consideration of the suffering Christian and his reasonable expectation.

> 23 Not only that, but we also who have the firstfruits of the Spirit, even we ourselves groan within ourselves, eagerly waiting for the adoption, the redemption of our body. 24 For we were saved in this hope, but hope that is seen is not hope; for why does one still hope for what he sees? 25 But if we hope for what we do not see, we eagerly wait for it with perseverance.

> —*Romans 8:23–25*

Christian and creation share two things—they groan together and they anticipate together. Christian groaning should not be confused with childish moaning and selfish grumbling—something which Paul obviously condemns by his positive attitude to his own suffering. The Christian's groaning is related to his new insight into man's fallenness and is as much a sorrowing after what man has lost in terms of God-ordained potential as a sorrowing from a sense of personal deprivation.

But there is also a sense in which the believer is painfully aware of his limitations, both spiritual and physical, and looks away to the time when he will be emancipated from all that hinders and mars. This is particularly true when he considers his experience of the Holy Spirit and recognizes it has only just begun. However much the Spirit has accomplished in his life, he knows it is only "firstfruits." This expression comes from the Old Testament principle of the offering of the first sheaf of wheat or the firstborn lamb, both as an expression of thanksgiving and also a statement of anticipation. No farmer would be satisfied with one sheaf, but he would rejoice in the first one knowing it was just that—the first of many. In the same way, the Holy Spirit as experienced on earth gives a kind of foretaste of what is in store. Knowing this, the believer tends to get a little homesick for glory at times and the inner groaning starts!

The physical limitations that so many believers suffer are also a cause of groaning, not from the point of view of dissatisfaction but from the perspective that in the new heaven and new earth believers will be equipped with new bodies. We do not have much information about the bodies in which we will live eternally, but there is some clue in the body the Risen Lord inhabited before the Ascension, particularly when we remember that we are promised a "body like His glorious body." It would be unwise to venture too far into the realm of conjecture. Perhaps the safest position we should take about *"the adoption, the redemption of our body"* (v. 23), is that the new body will be as ideally suited to the new environment as our old bodies have been fitted for the present environment. I marvel at the versatility and intricacy of the human body and often breathe the psalmist's words with awe, "We are fearfully and wonderfully made." This being the case, I have no alternative but to believe that the One who designed my body for earth in such a superb way will design a body for the new situation that will be as intricately suitable. Those believers who struggle with tiredness, like the young missionary who just took me round the ghettoes of Nassau, and who feel, as he does, that there is so much to be done and so little energy with which to do it, rejoice in the thought of bodies that will not tire out. Those whose aching limbs and arthritic joints hobble them all day and keep them awake at night can be forgiven for groaning with delight at the thought of no more pain, no more doctors' bills, and no more parts that keep wearing out.

Paul insists that this is all part of our salvation and is a legitimate expectation of the believer. *"We were saved in this hope"* (v. 24) and therefore we persevere because when we see we stop hoping, but when we don't see we simply keep on keeping on with patience and perseverance because God has promised.

Continuing with this theme, Paul adds the startling information that there is more groaning than we imagine:

> 26 Likewise the Spirit also helps in our weaknesses. For we
> do not know what we should pray for as we ought, but the
> Spirit Himself makes intercession for us with groanings which

cannot be uttered. [27] Now He who searches the hearts knows what the mind of the Spirit is, because He makes intercession for the saints according to the will of God.

—*Romans 8:26–27*

There is some question whether "weaknesses" should be in the plural or the singular. If the former is correct, we should understand it to cover the full range of human weakness; if the latter, it probably refers to what Paul calls our inability to ask correctly or even know what we should ask at any one time. This experience seems to be close to that of the Lord when He prayed "Now My soul is troubled, and what shall I say? Father, save Me from this hour?" (John 12:27). The sense of uncertainty was only momentary for Him but for us may be extensive and troublesome. But there is comfort in knowing that even the unspoken prayer of the unformed opinion springing from the uninformed mind is valid when prompted by the Spirit who steps in and invests the sigh with significance and the tear with meaning. Moreover, the One "who searches the hearts"—a title both charming and chilling depending on what is going on in the heart—knows what the Spirit is doing in His ministry of intercession and puts His approval upon it because it is in line with the will of God. When we begin to consider these things, we are in the realm of the mystical, an area fraught with delight and danger, and we do well to move with care and reverence, rejoicing in the scope of God's provision for us in our weakness.

Living in the Spirit, therefore, introduces us to a relationship of infinite intimacy with the Father; it draws us into a family of gigantic proportions; it grants us insight into the condition of our natural environment; and it urges us to look forward to the consummation of our redemption when with new bodies we live gloriously in the new heaven and new earth, in the meantime depending on the Spirit to be the Intercessor of our hearts as surely as the Risen Lord is our Intercessor in the throne room of heaven.

NOTES

1. Godet, *Commentary on Romans,* p. 309.

2. Bruce, *Romans,* p. 166.

CHAPTER FOURTEEN—WHAT SHALL WE SAY?

ROMANS 8:28–39

Scripture Outline

> We Are More than Convinced (8:28–31a)
>
> We Are More than Conquerors (8:31b–37)
>
> We Are More than Confident (8:38–39)

There are two ways of looking at stained glass windows. Either you can examine each odd shaped piece of colored glass individually and inspect the way they are fastened together, or you can stand in a quiet church and let the sun shine through all the pieces and bring the whole to life in glorious detail. So far, we have looked at the epistle in the former manner, but now as we approach the conclusion of the doctrinal section we step back with the apostle and bathe ourselves in the glorious glow of the full picture of God's great salvation.

> 28 And we know that all things work together for good to those who love God, to those who are the called according to His purpose. 29 For whom He foreknew, He also predestined to be conformed to the image of His Son, that He might be the firstborn among many brethren. 30 Moreover whom He predestined, these He also called; whom He called, these He also justified; and whom He justified, these He also glorified.
> 31 What then shall we say to these things?
> —*Romans 8:28–31a*

The pieces examined one by one are God's foreknowledge, predestination, call, justification, and glorification, and they all fit together to form what is sometimes called the "plan of salvation." The end result is "the good" to which God is directing His children, and those who are conscious of this plan know what they *"shall say to these things."*

WE ARE MORE THAN CONVINCED

In the beginning God said, "Let us make man in our image. . ." (Gen. 1:26), but man fell, became something considerably less than he was created, and began to reproduce "after his image" (Gen. 5:3). This fallen image was at best a poverty-stricken likeness of the original image, and humanity continued in this vein until Christ came— "the express image of [God's] person" (Heb. 1:3). The Father's objective in Christ's coming was that we might *"be conformed to the image of His Son, that He might be the firstborn among many brethren."*

To know the overall plan of salvation and to realize God's eternal intent produces a deep sense of conviction. Believers increasingly appreciate the ongoing nature of God's craftsmanship in their lives. Even when some of the pieces appear to be too dark or odd-shaped, they "know" that God is fitting lives together which will in eternity resemble His Son. While the finishing date is reserved for the age to come, the process is under way in this present age, and *"those who love God"* have been given a preview of the finished article to encourage them while they live in the age of construction.

There is little doubt that Romans 8:28 has become a favorite verse of contemporary Christians, but care is needed in its application. It must only be applied to those who clearly exhibit a deep sense of the call of God in their lives, demonstrating a love for God by a life of obedience. Neither is it to be seen as grounds for believing that "everything will come out in the wash" because God has committed Himself to sorting out the mess of our lives and relieving us of the consequences of our actions. It is eternal rather than temporal good which God has in mind. He works *"according to His purpose,"* which is far grander than the alleviation of the unpleasantness of the present or a guarantee of plain sailing under cloudless skies in the foreseeable future. He is in the "good" business of making redeemed sinners like their elder brother, the Lord Jesus, and even a cursory glance at the way the Father exposed the Son to the realities of life and death should be sufficient to remind us that we can expect the same kind of processes to work in our lives with the identical and ultimate result—conformity to Him.

Paul's listing of the pieces which God has fitted together is really a summary of the Epistle so far, even though he has not previously used some of the terms that appear at this point. First, there is the foreknowledge of God. There would appear to be no difficulty in the statement that God *"foreknew"* (v. 29), but careful reading will show that Paul is concerned with the *"whom"* of His foreknowledge, not the *"what."* That God knows in advance what is going to happen poses little problem to most people, although some wonder why He let it happen when He knew in advance what would transpire.

But the question that has occupied many believing minds for centuries is "Does Paul mean simply that God knew in advance who would respond to Him or did He know them in advance in the sense that they had a special relationship with Him from a past eternity?" Calvin has no doubt: "The foreknowledge of God here mentioned by Paul is not mere prescience, as some inexperienced people foolishly imagine, but adoption by which He has always distinguished His children from the reprobate."[1] John Wesley evidently would be regarded by Calvin as a member of the category of "inexperienced people" for he "foolishly imagine(d) 'foreknowledge' meant that 'God foreknew those in every nation, who would believe, from the beginning of the world to the consummation of all things.'"[2] Time and space preclude us from pursuing this fascinating subject, which is dealt with thoroughly in Godet, as the editor, Talbot W. Chambers, takes the unusual step of writing a special appendix in an attempt to rebut "the learned author." Whatever conclusions we may reach in this matter, it should be obvious that nothing in the foreknowing of God can deny the necessity for human responsibility and nothing that man can do will ever detract from the omnipotence of God.

"Whom He foreknew, He also predestined" leads us to examine the second piece of stained glass. To "predestine" means literally "to prehorizon" or "to define in advance the limits." This God did in determining that those who are redeemed shall experience salvation to the ultimate in that they will be "like Jesus." While there is debate as to whether "foreknowledge" refers exclusively to God's knowledge, there is no question that "predestine" speaks of the divine will. This predestination is not a predestination to faith but a decision on God's part that glory will be the ultimate of salvation. If my wife invites a friend for dinner and determines that roast beef will be the main course, this fact in no way infringes on the friend's

freedom to accept or reject the invitation, but it does preclude her from choosing to eat roast lamb or turkey. The call of God to respond in faith and repentance to the gospel brings the human will into center stage, but the divine will has already determined what the final result will be.

The third piece we must look at is the call of God, for *"whom He predestined, these He also called."* "To call" *(kaleo)* can mean "to name" or "to invite," or, when used in connection with divine/human experience, "to summon." The context shows God's call refers to the way He, having determined that people through faith in Christ should finally become like Him, intervenes in their affairs and reveals this truth to them. No more dramatic example of this is needed than that of the apostle himself, who, on the road to Damascus, was "apprehended" by God and "called by grace." There is ample evidence that God has not limited Himself to any one method of "calling." We can never escape the sense of mystery involved in His workings, and, accordingly, the whole area should be treated with the greatest reverence.

Paul spent considerable time in the earlier part of the epistle dealing with "justification." This is the next piece he introduces, so it is not necessary for us to spend further time considering it here except to note that *"justified"* and *"glorified"* are both in the past tense and suggest that we should look forward to glorification with the same confidence that we look back to "justification." This can only be done by seeing it in the perspective of the Eternal One who from His special vantage point looks down the annals of time and sees them telescoped into a moment called "now." There is a special joy in knowing the design of God, and in recognizing the sense in which we are already completed in Him. This allows even the most discouraged saint to speak confidently about God's good purposes even in the midst of a "groaning" situation.

WE ARE MORE THAN CONQUERORS

At this stage of the epistle, Paul emerges in a new light. So far we have sat at the feet of the learned teacher and been spectators as he presented his diatribes. His brilliance has dazzled us and his grasp of truth and its orderly presentation have led us along in the train of his thought. But now the preacher takes the podium, and he is looking for response. What are we going to say? What is our attitude going to be? With the rapidity of a machine gun, he fires his questions at us, and we find ourselves being challenged to face the implications of what we have been taught.

> If God is for us, who can be against us?
> [32] He who did not spare His own Son, but delivered Him up for us all, how shall He not with Him also freely give us all things? [33] Who shall bring a charge against God's elect? It is God who justifies. [34] Who is he who condemns? It is Christ who died, and furthermore is also risen, who is even at the right hand of God, who also makes intercession for us. [35] Who shall separate us from the love of Christ? Shall tribulation, or distress, or persecution, or famine, or nakedness, or peril, or sword? [36] As it is written:
> "For Your sake we are killed all day long;
> We are accounted as sheep for the slaughter."
> [37] Yet in all these things we are more than conquerors through Him who loved us.
> —*Romans. 8:31b–37*

As we have seen, Paul was particularly fond of Abraham, and it appears that another part of the Abraham story is in his mind when he speaks in verse 32 of the Father *"who did not spare His own Son."* These words closely follow the LXX (Septuagint) account of Genesis 22 where the Lord put Abraham to the test by requiring him to sacrifice Isaac. Paul appears to be saying that in the same way that Abraham's commitment to the Lord was exhibited by his readiness to give even his son, so the Father's commitment to the human race was clearly expressed in His readiness to give His only Son. This being the case, it is reasonable for believers to assume that God, having given the greatest, will not fail *"to give us all things"* (v. 32), for what could God give that would approach the cost of Calvary? This is the first piece of evidence that God is *"for us."*

He is on our side in another sense in that He has already justified us. This rules out the possibility of anyone being able to bring charges against us before His throne. If the one before whom we are guilty has pronounced us not guilty, what is there to fear from any accusation?

Some years ago a young lady, the wife of a missionary, told a hushed congregation about the way she had robbed her employer of thousands of dollars of merchandise while she was a student in Bible school. She had admitted her sin, sought his forgiveness, learned to paint so effectively that her earnings from painting paid off the debt and led her employer to Christ. When someone asked how she could be so open about her past, she threw her arms wide and with a great smile said, "When all is forgiven, there is nothing to hide, and where there is nothing to hide, there is nothing to fear."

The *"elect"* referred to in verse 33 are, of course, those who have been foreknown, predestined, called, and justified in order that they might arrive at the final status of brethren like the Firstborn. As all judgment has been committed by the Father into the hands of the Son, He alone is the One who may condemn us. The likelihood of this disappears completely when we remember that He is the One who died for us, rose again, and sits at the Father's right hand. Having gone to all that trouble to bring us redemption, there is no thought of His condemning those He died to forgive! When Jesus talked to the woman accused of adultery and gave her accusers the privilege of stoning her provided they themselves were without sin, she remained unstoned. Her adversaries quickly left the scene, and Jesus with rare irony asked, "Woman, where are those accusers of yours? Has no one condemned you?" (John 8:10). If Christ, the Judge, refuses to condemn us, who can be against us?

There is an added joy in remembering the activity in which our Lord is engaged at the Father's right hand: He *"makes intercession"* for us (v. 34). This means that while the Holy Spirit is the Father's advocate pleading His case to us, the Risen Lord is our advocate pleading our case to the Father. So in His capacity as both Judge and Advocate there is no possibility of His condemning us, and no one can throw the first stone because of their own sin!

Turning his attention from judges and advocates, Paul addresses the mighty forces of circumstance that confronted the believers of his day. He asks with the same intensity, *"Who shall separate us from the love of Christ?"* (v. 35). The word "separate" is also translated "put asunder" in Christ's famous statement about the permanence of the marriage bond and man's responsibility not to separate husband and wife. It is interesting that he chose to personalize tribulation, persecution, sword, etc., when he asked, "Who shall separate us?" But this did not hide the reality of these things from those to whom the letter was addressed. They were to suffer "tribulation" (literally, pressure) that would lead to a martyr's death for many.

"Distress" translates a Greek word related to the "narrow" of the famous "broad way" and "narrow gate" of which Christ spoke. The word developed the sense of compression and graphically

speaks of the inner constriction felt by those who come under external tribulation. *"Persecution"* is something with which the early Christians were familiar; in fact, there was a sense in which persecution had been a major contributory factor in the spread of the gospel because the persecuted believers took the opportunity to spread the Good News wherever the fury of their oppressors drove them. Paul's autobiographical passages show that he was personally acquainted with *"famine, nakedness, and peril,"* and his chilling reference to the "sword" reminds us not only that the blood of martyrs was to flow freely in Rome, but also that the apostle himself would eventually pay the supreme sacrifice.

While the literary merit of this glorious passage of Scripture is plain to see, we should not allow its magnificence to blind us to the reality of the situations outlined and the ringing certainty with which Paul speaks of the continuation of the love of Christ to us. Neither should we overlook the challenging tone he uses, as if to dare all the forces of individuals and governments to rob his readers of the greatest of all treasures—the love of Christ.

Quoting the psalmist's similar sentiments to remind his readers that there is nothing new about the persecution of the righteous, he then makes the stirring assertion that *"in all these things we are more than conquerors through Him that loved us."* Oppression and persecution are so distasteful to the human spirit that they produce a reflex action for survival at all costs. But Paul does not talk about God aiding those who wish to escape so that they can be delivered *from* all these things; but rather he is concerned that we should triumph *in* these things. This should not lead to a mindless masochism but to the development of confidence and courage through conviction. The consciousness of the love of Christ and the knowledge of the presence and power of the loved One both in the heart and before the throne make it possible to triumph through Him to such an extent that Paul uses a rare Greek word for the only time in Scripture to describe the experience. We are "super-conquerors"! Paul feels that there are many conquerors and innumerable exploits, but he sets the believers apart from these men and their courageous actions.

WE ARE MORE THAN CONFIDENT

Having challenged sin, sword, and society to do their worst, Paul now directs his attention to the abundant spiritual forces with which he was personally familiar.

> 38 For I am persuaded that neither death nor life, nor angels nor principalities nor powers, nor things present nor things to come, 39 nor height nor depth, nor any other created thing, shall be able to separate us from the love of God which is in Christ Jesus our Lord.
>
> *—Romans 8:38–39*

His message is the same—there is nothing that can possibly affect the eternal purposes of God or the undying love of Christ. Even death cannot rob the believer, because to be "absent from the body" is to be "present with the Lord." For years Paul had shown scant regard for his own safety simply because he lived in the tension of not knowing whether he preferred to live or die. Living to him was "Christ" but to die was "gain." Life with all its pain and problem held no terrors for him for the same reason nothing could change the immutable purpose of God. The *"principalities and powers"* were probably different ranks of angelic powers with whom he was undoubtedly more familiar than we in our contemporary world. Whether he refers to fallen angels or, as Barclay suggests, to unfallen angels who, as the rabbis believed "were grudgingly hostile to men," cannot be stated with certainty. But whoever they are and whatever they do, they cannot affect the love of Christ. Broadening the scope of his thought, Paul includes in a grand sweep everything in the present age and the age to come, which, of course, covers everything not covered!

It is interesting that *"height* [and] *depth"* are included in the list of adversaries the believer is called upon to face. To the Greeks "height" was more than just a spatial measurement. It contained the idea of loftiness and eminence; hence, power and authority. The term was used in astrological vocabulary and was related to the popular concept that man's fate was in the "heights" or the stars. Similarly, "depth" not only referred to deep places and things, but also contained the idea of profundity and mystery. It was also closely related to astrological thought. No doubt there were people in the church at Rome whose lives at one time had been governed by the dread of unseen and unknown powers. To them, as well as to those in our day who suffer from similar misunderstandings, the apostle affirms that no power, real or imaginary, can touch their relationship to Christ. Neither shall *"any other created thing."* The scope of this phrase is boundless, but it has been pointed out that it could be translated "any other creation"—"other" being the Greek *heteros,* which means another of a completely different kind. Paul may have been addressing the fascinating possibility of the existence of other worlds and other peoples. Whether there are such creations we do not know, but, more important, we do not worry, because, if they exist, and if they are more powerful than we (two monumental "ifs"!), they cannot separate us from the love of God in Christ Jesus.

So we arrive at the grand climax of Paul's systematic treatment of the gospel, and we note that, appropriately, it concludes with the words *"our Lord."* It is the reigning and ruling Lordship of Christ that is fundamental to our salvation, but it is the personal aspect of His Lordship, making Him "ours," that brings salvation from the realm of theological possibility into the hearts of men and women in life-transforming power. It was this message that Paul preached and that our world still needs to hear.

NOTES

1. Calvin, *Commentaries on Romans,* p. 180.

2. John Wesley, *Sermons on Several Occasions* (New York: Carlton and Phillips, 1855), p. 39.

CHAPTER FIFTEEN—ISRAEL'S REJECTION OF CHRIST

ROMANS 9:1–33

Scripture Outline

The Word of God is Not Invalidated (9:1–13)

The Sovereignty of God is Illuminated (9:14–19)

The Consistency of God is Illustrated (9:20–33)

The exhilarating experience of the birth of my eldest child was tinged with some of the deepest sorrow I have known. A few weeks before David was born, my father died, and as I held my infant son, I was almost overwhelmed with the thought that he would never know a paternal grandfather and that my father had missed seeing a grandchild of his own. The height of my joy intensified the depth of my sorrow.

Something similar happened to Paul as he exulted in the thought of God's salvation, but in his joy recognized again that his own people, whom he loved deeply, knew nothing of the joy that was his. A cloud passed over his sun as he contemplated Israel's rejection of his Lord.

> **9:1** I tell the truth in Christ, I am not lying, my conscience also bearing me witness in the Holy Spirit, ² that I have great sorrow and continual grief in my heart. ³ For I could wish that I myself were accursed from Christ for my brethren, my countrymen according to the flesh, ⁴ who are Israelites, to whom pertain the adoption, the glory, the covenants, the giving of the law, the service of God, and the promises; ⁵ of whom are the fathers and from whom, according to the flesh, Christ came, who is over all, the eternally blessed God. Amen.
> —*Romans 9:1–5*

There is a striking intensity in the apostle's words as he tries to impress on his readers how genuinely he feels about the condition of his own people. He insists he is telling the truth, adds that he is not lying, appeals to his conscience, and adds the testimony of the Holy Spirit as he speaks of heaviness of heart and continual sorrow.

The degree of sorrow is expressed by a thought so extreme that if it had not been introduced in this way would probably have been dismissed as ridiculous. He actually says that he would gladly be *anathema*—*that* is, "cut *off*" from Christ—if it would help in the blessing of his kinsfolk. It has been pointed out that the verb "wish" is in the imperfect tense and could be translated "I have wished" or "I used to wish," in which case the attitude portrayed would relate to Paul's pre-conversion days rather than his present feelings; but this is unlikely. It would appear that he, like Moses, would gladly suffer the ultimate sacrifice if it were possible and if it would do any good. This, it has been said, is "a spark from the fire of Christ's substitutionary love."[1]

While Paul was justifiably proud of his Greek culture and his Roman citizenship, it was his Jewish heritage that was dearest to his heart. To be a member of the people of God was, to him, the most magnificent privilege, for the name Israelite was itself a reminder of God's special intervention in the life of Jacob leading to the identification of his descendants as a unique people. To be Jewish was to be a part of the "adoption," literally the "placing as sons," or the special invitation by Jehovah to be His family. The Jews alone had seen the glory, or as the rabbis called it, the Shekinah—referring to God's presence with them in the cloud and the fire during the wilderness wanderings. Only with the Israelites had the Lord entered into covenants such as those that promised lands to Abraham and a dynasty to David, and only to them had He also given the privilege of knowing His law. It was to the Israelites alone that the "service of God" or the order of worship in both tabernacle and temple had been revealed, and only to them and through them had promises for mankind been made.

The long line of "fathers" stretched back through the remarkable history of Paul's people, but more than anything in recent history Christ had come from eternity into the turmoil of human history through the people of Israel. Scholars disagree on the correct placing of the phrase *"who is over all,"* some relating it to "God" and others to "Christ." If the former translation is to be preferred, it would mean that "God who is over all" is responsible for Christ coming in such a manner and should be blessed forever. The latter approach would mean that Christ is "God, over all," and should be "blessed." Either way, the emphasis is on God's gracious intervention by sending His only begotten Son.

Israel's rejection of Christ does more than stir deep emotions; it raises profound questions that Paul was continually required to address in his ministry. One question went something like this: "How could Paul's gospel be true when the Israelites had rejected it? Wasn't their rejection proof of its falsity?" Alternatively, "How could God be called faithful if He rejected those He had chosen to be His people simply because they rejected Christ?" Calvin summarized the dilemma as follows: "Either. . . there is no truth to the divine promise, or . . . Jesus, whom Paul preached, is not the Lord's Christ who had been promised to the Jews."[2]

It is clear that Paul felt it necessary to address the problem of Israel's rejection of Christ not only because it weighed so heavily on his own heart but also because the questions being raised were profoundly significant. He tackled the problem in characteristic fashion.

THE WORD OF GOD IS NOT INVALIDATED

[6] But it is not that the word of God has taken no effect. For they are not all Israel who are of Israel, [7] nor are they all children because they are the seed of Abraham; but, "In Isaac your seed shall be called." [8] That is, those who are the children of the flesh, these are not the children of God; but the children of the promise are counted as the seed. [9] For this is the word of promise: "At this time I will come and Sarah shall have a son."

[10] And not only this, but when Rebecca also had conceived by one man, even by our father Isaac [11] (for the children not yet being born, nor having done any good or evil, that the purpose of God according to election might stand, not of works but of Him who calls), [12] it was said to her, "The older shall serve the younger." [13] As it is written, "Jacob I have loved, but Esau I have hated."

—Romans 9:6–13

Paul takes his Roman readers through a little ancient history, starting with God's call to Abraham. God decided of His own will to make Abraham the father of blessing. More than one son was born of the old man, but obviously only one of them could be part of the succession and God decided it would be Isaac. Rebecca, Isaac's wife, became pregnant with twins, and it was clear that only one could be chosen to be in the "train" of blessing. God chose Jacob rather than Esau. By the time Jacob's sons were beginning to establish their families, there were people in many places who had every right, if they wished, to call themselves children of Abraham, but they were far from the mainstream of God's plan. As has the Mississippi in its delta, the children of Abraham had branched in many directions. But God had firmly committed Himself to pursuing His purposes down the channel of Isaac, Jacob, and Judah, through David, until Christ was born. In so doing, He had no more taken away the status of the other channels than a stern-wheeler captain by choosing a certain channel in the delta makes the other channels something less than part of the Mississippi. They just don't fit into the plan.

The Word of God speaks powerfully about God's complete freedom to act as He chooses. This is clearly illustrated in His dealings with Israel in general and the lineage of Christ through Abraham, Isaac, and Jacob in particular. He decided that Isaac rather than Ishmael would be the progenitor of Messiah, the child born of promise rather than natural consideration. Then before the twins in Rebekah's womb came to birth, He chose Jacob rather than Esau despite the fact that Esau was the firstborn and that neither could possibly be responsible for either good or evil actions. Clearly He was choosing as He saw fit, and His choice was based on considerations quite different from those which might have been expected. The result of all this was that there were two kinds of children of Abraham—those who were *"children of the flesh"* and those who were *"children of the promise"* (Rom. 9:8). Paul sees this distinction still operative in the sense that some of the people of Israel had gladly acknowledged Jesus as the Christ while others had rejected Him. There had always been two Israels, and the situation he was dealing with was not new.

To many modern readers the quotation from Malachi, in verse 2–3, *"Jacob I have loved, but Esau I have hated,"* is particularly troublesome. It should be borne in mind that the prophet is speaking of the *people* of Jacob and Esau, with particular reference to the Edomite's refusal to come to Israel's aid at a time of difficulty. The apostle's choice of this statement should be understood first as a comment on God's attitude to a *people* and, second, in light of the fact that "hate" as opposed to "love" is by no means as stark in New Testament usage as may first appear. The remark of the Lord about discipleship recorded in Luke 14:26, "If anyone comes to Me and does not hate his father and mother . . . he cannot be My disciple." bears ample testimony to this fact. For the apostle Paul there was clear evidence throughout Scripture that "they are not all Israel who are of Israel."

We continue by looking at a second reason that Israel's rejection of Christ is important.

THE SOVEREIGNTY OF GOD IS ILLUMINATED

In extreme Jewish thought the fact of election to be the chosen people was tantamount to an eternal guarantee of blessedness, and the corresponding choice of God not to make the Gentiles the chosen people was a guarantee of their inevitable rejection. For the Jews, therefore, to be told by Paul that Gentiles were being accepted while Jews were being rejected because of attitudes to Christ, was totally unacceptable. In the first place, it was a national insult and, in the second, it attributed to God a freedom the Jews did not believe was appropriate—the freedom to reject Jews and accept Gentiles. To attribute this freedom to God was in their eyes to make God the perpetrator of a deeply unrighteous act. Returning to his familiar style, Paul addresses the issue:

[14] What shall we say then? Is there unrighteousness with God? Certainly not! [15] For He says to Moses, *"I will have mercy on whomever I will have mercy, and I will have compassion on whomever I will have compassion."* [16] So then it is not of him who wills, nor of him who runs, but of God who shows mercy.

—Romans 9:14–16

In the touching conversation between God and Moses recorded in Exodus 33:12–23 and quoted here by the apostle, there is clear evidence of God's insistence that He is free to deal even with a Moses as He sees fit. Never has there been a man more in need of divine reassurance than Moses. Confronting impossible odds and battling seemingly endless difficulties, all he wanted was a sense of divine presence and some indication that the Lord was really with him. "Show me your glory," he demanded, to which the Lord replied in effect, "You have been more willing than any man to do my will; you have run when other men would have fainted; and if ever there was a man who could dictate terms to God it is you. But there never was such a man, and you must realize that blessing such as you have demanded is granted not on the basis of merit but on the grounds of what I consider best. I grant graciously and mercifully what I choose to grant, and your demand is not granted."

The apostle moves quickly to another illustration of the divine freedom to act not only in mercy but also in hardening:

> 17 For the Scripture says to the Pharaoh, *"For this very purpose I have raised you up, that I may show My power in you, and that My name may be declared in all the earth."*
> 18 Therefore He has mercy on whom He wills, and whom He wills He hardens.
> 19 You will say to me then, "Why does He still find fault? For who has resisted His will?"
> —*Romans 9:17–19*

The dramatic story of God's dealings with Pharaoh through Moses is replete with references to "hardening." Over and over again, Pharaoh is moved by the momentous events that overtake him, only to revert, once the effects wear off, to his arrogant attitude of resistance to Jehovah's demands. Repeatedly, he hardens his heart until finally God hardens it for him. The history of Pharaoh's heart-hardening should be noted carefully, as should the Lord's explanation of His actions. God claims to have "raised up" this man in order that His power might be made known.

It would be easy to assume by this statement that God had used Pharaoh as a pawn in a cosmic chess game, but neither our knowledge of God nor the study of Scripture warrant such an interpretation. The word "raised up" (Greek, *exegeirein)* and related words can be used to convey many meanings. It describes Christ's Resurrection (1 Cor. 6:14); it can mean "to cure" (James 5:15) or "to establish a position" as in the case of John the Baptist, the prophet (John 7:52). It would appear in Pharaoh's case that God placed this man in his position of international visibility so that when his own hard-heartedness came into conflict with God's purpose he would become an international illustration of the futility of arrogantly opposing the purposes of God. Godet rightly points out that if Pharaoh, with the same natural, sinful, egotistical attitude, had been born in a cabin and lived in seclusion, his sin would have been neither lesser nor greater. But in God's economy He placed this arrogant man in a position where his adamant refusal to accede to God's will would not only lead to his own downfall but also to as broad a demonstration of divine power as possible. The freedom to do this is incontrovertibly God's.

Paul goes on in verse 19 to anticipate the obvious response to this reasoning from his anonymous debating partner. *"You will say to me then, 'Why does He still find fault? For who has resisted His will?'"* Paul answers this predictable objection with a third important point with reference to Israel's rejection of the Messiah.

THE CONSISTENCY OF GOD IS ILLUSTRATED

The most natural way to look at the God/man relationship is from the human perspective, but the most necessary is from the divine. Paul proceeds in the following verses to do this so exclusively that he leaves out completely the balancing aspects of human response and responsibility. This is because his objective is to deal with the nature of God's dealings with mankind rather than the nature of man's involvement in such dealings. This should be remembered when the following verses are read:

> [20] But indeed, O man, who are you to reply against God? Will the thing formed say to him who formed it, "Why have you made me like this?" [21] Does not the potter have power over the clay, from the same lump to make one vessel for honor and another for dishonor?
> —*Romans 9:20–21*

The analogy of the potter and the clay speaks powerfully to the sovereignty of God, who in His glorious power is free to act in the affairs of men. Then they, when considering such authority, know that they have no real grounds for questioning His wisdom and integrity.

It would be a mistake to apply all the qualities of clay to mankind in this context, as can be clearly seen from the fact that Paul speaks of clay that talks! He is not saying that man is a powerless lump of clay that God can mold whichever way He pleases, for to say that would contradict what he has outlined in the early portions of the epistle, namely, that man is responsible. He is stating the unquestioned sovereignty of God to take a rebellious Egyptian and make him Pharaoh and to let Pharaoh live with the consequences of his own arrogance and be a warning not only to his contemporaries but to all posterity.

The same applied to Israel. They had the truth and rejected it. They live with the consequences, and they can't fault God for making them stick. Paul goes on to illustrate his point with a remarkable "What if . . .?"

> [22] What if God, wanting to show His wrath and to make His power known, endured with much longsuffering the vessels of wrath prepared for destruction, [23] and that He might make known the riches of His glory on the vessels of mercy, which He had prepared beforehand for glory, [24] even us whom He called, not of the Jews only, but also of the Gentiles?
> —*Romans 9:22–24*

If God, says the apostle, is prepared to go on tolerating the attitudes and actions of the Pharaohs of this world so that through their own hardness in the end they have come to the place of being hardened by God into "vessels of wrath," that is unquestionably well within God's rights. And if Israel goes on behaving toward the gospel in much the same way that Pharaoh behaved toward the people of Israel, then they must be prepared to accept the fact that if it was right for Pharaoh, it is right for them too. By the same token, God is free to take those who respond to His message and make them "vessels of mercy" even though they come from the ranks of the despised Gentiles.

> [25] As He says also in Hosea:
> *"I will call them My people, who were not My people,*
> *And her beloved, who was not beloved."*
> [26] *"And it shall come to pass in the place where it was* said to them,
> *'You are not My people,'*
> *There they shall be called sons of the living God."*
> [27] Isaiah also cries out concerning Israel:
> *"Though the number of the children of Israel be as the* sand of the sea,
> *The remnant will be saved.*
> [28] *For He will finish the work and cut it short in righ-*teousness,
> *Because the LORD will make a short work upon the earth."*
> [29] And as Isaiah said before:
> *"Unless the LORD of Sabaoth had left us a seed,*
> *We would have become like Sodom,*

And we would have been made like Gomorrah."

[30] What shall we say then? That Gentiles, who did not pursue righteousness, have attained to righteousness, even the righteousness of faith; [31] but Israel, pursuing the law of righteousness, has not attained to the law of righteousness.

[32] Why? Because *they did* not *seek it* by faith, but as it were, by the works of the law. For they stumbled at that stumbling stone. [33] As it is written:

"Behold, I lay in Zion a stumbling stone and rock of offense,

And whoever believes on Him will not be put to shame."

—Romans 9:25–33

Paul quotes at length from the prophet Hosea, showing God's ancient commitment to make those who were "not My people" to be accepted. From Isaiah he substantiates the fact that God has previously turned away from His rebellious people but has always left Himself a "remnant" or a "seed" by way of promise that brighter times lie ahead. This God continues to do in the time of Israel's rejection, as is clearly seen by Paul's own conversion to Christ. God's consistency is therefore maintained, and it remains only for the apostle to reiterate his own exposition of the gospel that "the just shall live by faith," that "by the works of the law shall no flesh be justified," and to apply it to the Jewish people who chose the latter route and the Gentiles who chose the former. Israel, he insists, has stumbled at the idea that they can only be justified by faith in Christ. But even their stumbling shows how thoroughly consistent God has been, for through the prophet Isaiah He had said, *"Behold, I lay in Zion a stumbling stone and rock of offense, and whoever believes on Him will not be put to shame"* (Rom. 9:33).

Paul's arguments are by no means easy to follow and his teaching is far from elementary, plus the fact that interpretations have varied considerably. Nevertheless, it is plain to see that the apostle in this passage, far from capitulating to the criticisms of his gospel, shows how, in fact, it is a thoroughly consistent extension of all that God has been doing through the ages. As a result, God is seen to be superbly sovereign in His dealings with man in ways that wonderfully preserve His control and retain the dignity with which God invested man when He created him in His own image.

NOTES

1. W. H. Griffith Thomas, *St. Paul's Epistle to the Romans* (Grand Rapids: Eerdmans), p. 245.

2. Calvin, *Commentaries on Romans,* p. 190.

CHAPTER SIXTEEN—THE IMPORTANCE OF EVANGELISM

ROMANS 10:1–21

Scripture Outline

The Exposure of Error (10:1–5)

The Exposition of Truth (10:6–13)

The Expression of Faith (10:14–21)

A young pastor colleague of mine, conscious of the many concerns related to my pastoral responsibilities, gave me a special present to hang in my study. It is a simple plaque which says, "When you're up to your waist in crocodiles, remember your objective was to drain the swamp." It is not uncommon for students of the Roman epistle to feel as if they are among the crocodiles by the time they get to chapters 9 through 11. But while we are led by the apostle to consider such profound subjects as the sovereignty of God and the free will of man with particular reference to the nation of Israel, we should not forget that the apostle's purpose in writing the Epistle to the Romans was to give a clear explanation of the gospel in order that it might be more effectively proclaimed. He had no desire for abstruse theological debate but a commitment to a clear enunciation of the Good News of redemption through Christ to all people. Ever the consummate theologian, the apostle was first and foremost the missionary evangelist and church-planter. Accordingly, this passage is not only a development of his theme concerning Israel but also a practical statement concerning the principles and practice of evangelism to which the church is called and in which she must be involved.

THE EXPOSURE OF ERROR

In words reminiscent of the opening verses of Chapter 9 Paul speaks with great emotion concerning Israel:

10:1 Brethren, my heart's desire and prayer to God for Israel is that they may be saved. ² For I bear them witness that they have a zeal for God, but not according to knowledge. ³ For they being ignorant of God's righteousness, and seeking to establish their own righteousness, have not submitted to the righteousness of God. ⁴ For Christ is the end of the law for righteousness to everyone who believes.

⁵ For Moses writes about the righteousness which is of the law, *"The man who does those things shall live by them."*

—*Romans 10:1–5*

The task of the evangelist is not only to point out to people the right way to go but also to explain that they are already heading the wrong way. Because most people have an intense distaste for being told they are wrong, great care should be taken in pointing out error. Paul exhibits three helpful characteristics in this regard. First, he is clearly deeply concerned about the people themselves. He does not see them as statistics but as individuals whose eternal salvation is in question. His *"heart's desire. . . is that they might be saved."* Second, there is no trace of superiority in his remarks about their error, but only a humble reliance upon God to whom he prays for them and from whom alone he looks for blessing. Third, he speaks from a deep understanding of the true position of the people to whom he ministers. For him there is no superficial stereotyping of their beliefs and no inadequate research of their condition. He can *"bear them witness"* or, literally, "speak on their behalf" because he knows what he is talking about.

Israel, Paul says, is in error despite the fact that they are enthusiastic. They are deeply sincere but sincerely wrong. Their zeal for God has the momentum of a freight train, but because it is *"not according to knowledge,"* it is the momentum of a freight train that has come off the tracks. Contrary to popular thought, both then and now, it does matter what one believes and to what one commits oneself because fervency of belief and depth of commitment of oneself may lead to untold tragedy and unmitigated disaster. The error of Israel is also to be seen in that they are fundamentally *"ignorant of God's righteousness."* The ignorance of which Paul speaks is not an academic illiteracy but a basic failure to grasp the significance of data readily available to them in the Scriptures they prize so highly. Ironically, they are ignorant despite the fact that they are informed. The third error is seen in

Israel's persistence in a self-righteous attempt to *"establish their own righteousness"* by keeping the demands of the law regardless of what the law-giver himself wrote: that life through the law comes to those who keep the law and those who do not keep it in its entirety are condemned by the law they thought would bring life. The error is that they are persisting despite the fact that they are perishing.

When Napoleon finally met his Waterloo, one of his soldiers, Chauvin, refused to believe that the little general was defeated and insisted on fighting on even though the battle was lost. This man's name has lived on into our contemporary era because we now call anyone who fights on when the situation is hopeless a chauvinist! Christ, Paul says, *"is the end of the law for righteousness,"* meaning that He is the end (Greek, *telos)* in the sense of the fulfillment of the law, but also in that He terminated the era of the law and introduced the new era where men and women could be delivered from the hopeless task of fulfilling the law and could be invited to be saved through faith. The error of Israel was, in a special sense, that they were chauvinistic despite the fact they had been chosen. Those who endeavor to communicate the Christian gospel should take note of the errors of Israel because they are common to most people in one form or another.

THE EXPOSITION OF TRUTH

Paul proceeds to illustrate both the impossibility of justification through keeping the law and the possibility of being blessed through that which God has made available. He ingeniously uses Moses' farewell speech of encouragement to the children of Israel to realize that through their relationship with the Lord they could find the spirit of His law in their hearts and mouths and live in a way pleasing to Him without feeling the necessity to go to extreme lengths to find in the heavens or the depths the needed strength.

6 But the righteousness of faith speaks in this way, *"Do not say in your heart, 'Who will ascend into heaven?'"* (that is, to bring Christ down from above) 7 or, " 'Who will descend into the abyss?'" (that is, to bring Christ up from the dead). 8 But what does it say? *"The word is near you, in your mouth and in your heart"* (that is, the word of faith which we preach): 9 that if you confess with your mouth the Lord Jesus and believe in your heart that God has raised Him from the

dead, you will be saved. [10] For with the heart one believes unto righteousness, and with the mouth confession is made unto salvation. [11] For the Scripture says, *"Whoever believes on Him will not be put to shame."* [12] For there is no distinction between Jew and Greek, for the same Lord over all is rich to all who call upon Him. [13] For "whoever calls on the name of the LORD shall be saved."

—Romans 10:6–13

The apostle's free application of Moses' words reminds us that we do not have to ascend into heaven to discover salvation. It has been made available in the Lord Jesus through whose Incarnation heaven came down to earth. In the same way we must not search the depths for our deliverance, because Christ, having descended into death, rose again from the dead and in His Resurrection made the fullness of salvation ours. This message of salvation through faith in the living Lord could not be closer to them, as it had been proclaimed in their hearing. All that was necessary for them to do was to believe in their hearts and confess with their mouths. But for the Jewish person deeply steeped in the idea that salvation came through the fulfilling of the law through their own efforts, this message seemed so simple as to be simplistic and so free as to be insulting.

Similar attitudes confront the proclaimer of the gospel in today's world. While the religious systems of self-effort vary in many degrees from those Paul wished to counter, the fundamental attitude of many people is that they must do something to merit or earn their salvation. This attitude is perfectly understandable in those societies where people have learned all their lives that "there is no such thing as a free lunch." The task of the modern-day evangelist is still the same, namely, to explain the impossibility of salvation through self-effort and the availability of salvation through faith in Christ.

There is a most important definition of faith at this point in the apostle's argument. Faith is, first of all, heart belief in the reality of Christ's Resurrection. It would, of course, be possible to believe firmly that Christ had died without in any way implying in that belief anything other than belief in the demise of a mere man. But Paul in his insistence in belief in a risen man points to the uniqueness both of the Person and the work of Christ. That thousands have died, even been crucified, is beyond dispute, but no one would suggest that their deaths were in any sense propitiatory for the sins of the world. But in the Resurrection of Christ there is evidence of the validity of His claims to deity and, accordingly, the unique efficacy of the death of the Deity to bring salvation. Furthermore, this clearly defined belief required a clearly stated confession. At some point in the heart-believer's experience, there had to be a simple but profound statement, which was probably the first and most adequate creed of the Christian church—"Jesus is Lord." Some have felt that this referred to baptism when those who had turned from their paganism to Christ would, on confession of their faith in Him as Lord and Savior, be immersed in water typifying their death, burial, and Resurrection in Him. Others see no necessity to limit this confession to a particular event but rather see it as an ongoing articulation of faith. Whatever the facts of the matter, there is no avoiding the necessity for believers to be articulators of their faith.

Paul proceeds to explain why. He differentiates between "righteousness" and "salvation," attributing the acquisition of the former to heart belief and the latter to mouth confession. Some commentators see in this an example of Paul's love of hebraic parallelism, but it would appear that this does not satisfactorily explain his meaning. There is a difference in the believer's experience between being "justified" or being "declared righteous" and the other aspects of salvation. In the previous chapters we have seen something of the full scope of salvation which is instituted by the reception of forgiveness and justification and goes on through the whole of life, through death and into ultimate glory. The ongoing process is sanctification, and, while faith is all that is necessary for justification, clear commitment which finds expression in articulation is necessary if the ongoing experience of growth in Christ is to be known.

The person who believes thoroughly enough to make confession of that faith in situations which may not be conducive to such testimony, is of necessity a convinced person. The basis of such conviction comes from the clear statement of Scripture in verse 11: *"Whosoever believes on Him will not be put to shame."* Faith being the basis of assurance, it becomes clear that everyone is capable of assurance because everyone is capable of exercising faith. When the fulfillment of law is seen as the basis of justification and forgiveness, only those initiated in the law can hope to be saved, but faith transcends all limitations and makes salvation a possibility for all people. This means that there is *"no distinction between Jew and Greek"*— a concept the Jews had not been prepared to accept even though the prophet Joel had proclaimed the fact that "whoever calls upon the name of the Lord will be saved." The Jews had misunderstood the message of salvation not only in the fact that it became available through faith but also in the vastness of its scope. They had failed to realize that the message of grace, as opposed to law, was also a message of universal relevance, as opposed to one of limited national application.

In the debate over the Jewish situation as it related to their lack of acceptance of the gospel Paul preached, the apostle wishes to make it clear that the Old Testament had consistently reiterated the principle of faith and the intention of Jehovah to make His salvation available on a universal basis. These factors must, therefore, be included in any discussion of the credibility of the message and the integrity of God. For the contemporary evangelist, these factors are highly motivating because they continually remind him that whoever he meets in whatever circumstances there is a message of hope, summarized in the great words of Joel's prophecy, "Whoever calls on the name of the Lord will be saved."

THE EXPRESSION OF FAITH

The relationship between the hidden belief of the heart and the open confession with the mouth deduced by the apostle from Moses' farewell speech is further developed in the following verses:

> 14 How then shall they call on Him in whom they have not believed? And how shall they believe in Him of whom they have not heard? And how shall they hear without a preacher? 15 And how shall they preach unless they are sent? As it is written:
> *"How beautiful are the feet of those who preach the gospel of peace,*
> *Who bring glad tidings of good things!"*
> *—Romans 10:14–15*

Having established the universal relevance of the Christian gospel, Paul engages in some relentlessly logical rhetorical questioning. Starting with the fact that faith is necessary, he asks how anyone can possibly call on the Lord for His promised salvation without believing the promise. Then he asks how anyone can come to this belief without being told what is available to believe. He follows with a question as to how people can hear without someone telling them. This in turn leads to a question as to how people can tell others about the promised salvation of

God without being sent as those who will tell. In the context of Paul's argument, his point is that if the gospel is available to the whole race, the whole race must know about it, and the telling of it to the whole race will require considerably more involvement in Gentile ministry than has been evidenced by the Jews of Paul's day. Godet summarizes as follows: "A universal apostolate is therefore the corollary of a free and universal salvation."[1] The expression "apostolate" is used not in a limited sense but as a description of those who are "sent," the English word "apostle" being a direct derivative of the Greek word meaning "to send."

Once again Paul draws from the rich poetry of Isaiah to underline his point. He sees the one sent to preach in the same light as the prophet saw the herald who, returning from the field of battle, brought "glad tidings of good things." The picture seems to be that of the watchman on the gates seeing the returning soldier on the mountaintops silhouetted in the rising sun as he makes haste to return home to share the news of great victories won on far-off fields of battle.

> [16] But they have not all obeyed the gospel. For Isaiah says, *"LORD, who has believed our report?"* [17] So then faith *comes* by hearing, and hearing by the word of God.
> [18] But I say, have they not heard? Yes indeed:
> *"Their sound has gone out to all the earth,*
> *And their words to the ends of the world."*
> [19] But I say, did Israel not know? First Moses says:
> *"I will provoke you to jealousy by those who are not a nation,*
> *I will move you to anger by a foolish nation."*
> [20] But Isaiah is very bold and says:
> *"I was found by those who did not seek Me;*
> *I was made manifest to those who did not ask for Me."*
> [21] But to Israel he says:
> *"All day long I have stretched out My hands*
> *To a disobedient and contrary people."*
>
> —*Romans 10:16–21*

To his own people, the Jews, who are upset at his ministry and scandalized by his message of God's grace to the Gentiles, Paul is saying, "Come join me in the exciting acceptance of salvation through Christ and the ensuing sharing of the message of glad tidings and good things with those who have never heard." The same emphasis is necessary to those who sit comfortably in Christian pews, untouched by the condition of more than half the world's population which has no knowledge of God's Son. The apostle's words ring true and clear. How will these people call on the Lord if they don't believe, and isn't their believing dependent on hearing? And surely hearing is related to telling, and the telling is exclusively in the hands of those who sense that Christ has commissioned His people to take the message to the uttermost parts of the earth.

There is a sense in which the unreached populations of our world are a scandal to the name of Christ and His church. In the two millennia which have passed since the Master commissioned His servants, superb efforts have been extended and major victories have been won which have resulted in Christianity becoming a truly universal religion. Yet at the same time it must be clearly understood that so much has not been attempted and so many need to be reached.

The key to the relative failure of the church appears to be in the "sending" of those who can reach the unreached. There is no possibility that the principles of speaking, hearing, believing, calling, and saving do not work because the Lord, Himself, has promised that they will function in blessing. The only possible flaw in the system must lie in the sending, and it would appear that perhaps the church has failed to understand in some measure the link between "confession with the mouth" and being sent as a herald so that people can hear, believe, call, and be saved. If Christian preachers and evangelists could stress the necessity for articulate expressions of faith from those who believe, those within earshot of the articulators would, themselves, become hearers. They, in turn, would then be required, before God, to believe or disbelieve, if they should believe to the point of justification, they should be encouraged to confession of Christ, which would not only lead to a deeper experience of salvation but also to the possibility of others hearing and starting the process off again. This constant motion of salvation, experienced and expressed, would produce an environment in which spontaneously and effectively all those who believe would sense the privilege and joy of being sent to tell. Once new believers taste the thrill of sharing the glad tidings, they develop a hunger for ministry and a burden for those who have not heard, believed, called, or been saved, and, as time goes by, they find themselves directed by the Spirit of God into broader avenues of service and increasing opportunities of witness.

Isaiah's beautiful poems relating to the suffering Servant, which the New Testament applies on numerous occasions to Messiah, predict the unbelief of some who hear, for Isaiah says, *"Lord, who has believed our report?"* (Rom. 10:16). Paul pounces on Isaiah's word "believed" to show once again the message to his own people was one of the necessity for faith, which he explains *"comes by hearing and hearing by the word of God"* (v. 17). According to Isaiah, the unbelief of Israel came as no surprise, although some might not be prepared to accept that they were guilty of unbelief but wondered if Israel had not heard properly. Paul raises and answers the possibility: *"But I say, have they not heard? Yes indeed: 'Their sound has gone out to all the earth, And their words to the ends of the world'"* (Rom. 10:18).

Then perhaps they did not understand, suggests the apostle for the sake of argument. But this he also rejects with quotations from Moses and Isaiah, showing once again that the Lord of the Universe, whose heart is open to all people, will not be limited by the failure of His own people to believe as they ought and to act as they should. On the contrary, He is committed to seeing that even though His people may be a *"disobedient and contrary people,"* this in itself will not hinder His purposes of making salvation available to all people in all ages through the preaching of the gospel.

Paul's words, addressed primarily to the peculiar problems raised by Jewish failure to respond to the message of a suffering and exalted Christ, are also pointedly relevant to the church in all ages which must constantly re-evaluate the ways and means by which the message of Christ might be made known through whatever means are available. The church cannot, in the light of Christ's sacrifice and the Father's purposes, afford to miscalculate the importance of evangelism. She must not repeat the fatal error of the ancient people of God.

NOTES

1.   Godet, *Commentary on Romans,* p. 385.

CHAPTER SEVENTEEN—GOD AND ISRAEL
ROMANS 11:1–36

Scripture Outline

    God's Preservation of a Remnant in Israel (11:1–10)

    God's Purpose in the Rejection of Israel (11:11–15)

    God's Power with Regard to Israel (11:16–25)

    God's Promise of Restoration for Israel (11:26–36)

The long history of Israel's rejection of God and their trampling underfoot of His grace quite naturally leads to the thought that He may eventually decide that "enough is enough" and terminate His relationship with His people. Paul raises and answers the possibility:

11:1 I say then, has God cast away His people? Certainly not! For I also am an Israelite, of the seed of Abraham, *of* the tribe of Benjamin. 2 God has not cast away His people whom He foreknew. Or do you not know what the Scripture says of Elijah, how he pleads with God against Israel, saying, 3 *"LORD, they have killed Your prophets and torn down Your altars, and I alone am left, and they seek my life"?* 4 But what does the divine response say to him? *"I have reserved for Myself seven thousand men who have not bowed the knee to Baal."* 5 Even so then, at this present time there is a remnant according to the election of grace. 6 And if by grace, then *it is* no longer of works; otherwise grace is no longer grace. But if *it is* of works, it is no longer grace; otherwise work is no longer work.

7 What then? Israel has not obtained what it seeks; but the elect have obtained it, and the rest were blinded. 8 Just as it is written:

"God has given them a spirit of stupor,
Eyes that they should not see
And ears that they should not hear,
To this very day."
⁹ And David says:
"Let their table become a snare and a trap,
A stumbling block and a recompense to them.
¹⁰ Let their eyes be darkened, so that they do not see,
And bow down their back always."

—*Romans 11:1–10*

GOD'S PRESERVATION OF A REMNANT IN ISRAEL

Paul declares there is not the slightest possibility of this termination taking place despite the fact that Israel has rejected the Savior. Paul is himself a powerful proof of this fact, for he is a thoroughgoing Jew, as much a member of the family of Abraham as anyone with the perfect pedigree of a son of Benjamin, yet there is no doubt about his knowing the Savior. So long as there is a man like Paul there is no such thing as a rejection of Israel. Furthermore, the principle "whom He foreknows He predestines" applies. Knowing everything in advance, God has the advantage of seeing the end from the beginning, and with this knowledge His determining of the final outcome is sure. Therefore, with God's having foreknown and predestined, there is no thought of casting off the foreknown and predestined.

At a time of national apostasy, Elijah, the prophet of God, became most discouraged and engaged in a pity party. He thought he was the only believer left, and, having seen what had happened to the other prophets, he didn't hold out much hope for his own survival. As the only one left, he had a feeling of high visibility and peculiar vulnerability! God, however, pointed out to His man that he was not alone; in fact, there were seven thousand others who had not betrayed the Lord. These people God claimed to have reserved for Himself. They were part of the unfailing remnant which runs like a thread through the bewildering tapestry of Israel's history—at times highly visible as the children of faith, at others practically lost from sight in the apostasy of the nation, but always surviving, because God, having chosen by His grace that Abraham would be the father of all that believe, is committed to seeing that His line is not broken.

The remnant, having been saved by grace through faith, are clearly discernible among those natural-born sons of Abraham who, unlike their father, choose to seek justification through their works rather than the way ordained by God. The more they have resisted the grace of God, the harder their hearts have become, until, like Pharaoh, their hearts have arrived at such a state that God has hardened them. In the same way that there has always been a faithful remnant, there have always been those whose hearts have been hard, as can clearly be seen in the Old Testament record of God's dealings with His people. In the days of Moses' struggle with the rebellious wilderness wanderers and in the days of Isaiah's powerful ministry, there were those who had "eyes that they should not see and ears that they should not hear for God has given to them a spirit of stupor." David wrote, *"Let their eyes be darkened, so that they do not see, and bow down their back always"* (Rom. 11:7–10).

The situation in Paul's day differed only in detail from the days in which his great predecessors lived. Then, as now, there was a believing remnant characterized by eyes wide open to the truth and ears unstopped to hear the word, while many had dimmed eyes that could not see and ears that grasped nothing of the significance of Christ. But the existence of the remnant through the years was proof positive that God had not cast away His people.

GOD'S PURPOSE IN THE REJECTION OF ISRAEL

11 I say then, have they stumbled that they should fall? Certainly not! But through their fall, to provoke them to jealousy, salvation has come to the Gentiles. 12 Now if their fall is riches for the world, and their failure riches for the Gentiles, how much more their fullness!

13 For I speak to you Gentiles; inasmuch as I am an apostle to the Gentiles, I magnify my ministry, 14 if by any means I may provoke to jealousy those who are my flesh and save some of them. 15 For if their being cast away is the reconciling of the world, what will their acceptance be but life from the dead?

—Romans 11:11–15

The nation of Israel at the time of Paul's ministry was a stumbling nation that had not completely fallen. Or, to use boxing parlance, they were "down but not out," and God had no intention of letting His people be "counted out." What, then, was His purpose in allowing Israel to openly reject His Messiah and live on in the resultant darkness and hardness? Paul's answer is as striking as it is unexpected. God is trying to make Israel jealous by turning to the Gentiles to offer them what Israel has refused. Paul knew this was true from his experience of evangelism in such places as Corinth. After he had ministered in the synagogue for some time, the people there opposed him and became abusive, so he "shook out his clothes" and told them, "Your blood be upon your own heads. I am clean. From now on I will go to the Gentiles" (Acts 18:6).

It seems that God has to deal with His children literally as children on occasions. Most parents can remember when they have offered something to a child only to have him refuse, but when the offer has been made to a sibling, the original child has become very upset and obviously deeply regretful that he passed up the first opportunity. Paul hopes, personally, that his highly visible and highly beneficial ministry to the Gentiles will be so striking to his kinsmen that they will be attracted to what is going on in the purposes of God and be saved along with the Gentile believers.

Warming to his theme of the Gentile opportunity which became possible through the Jewish rejection of the gospel, Paul thinks aloud about the "riches" that have reached the world through the fall of Israel and then begins to dream about the possibilities of blessing when the people of Israel finally come to acknowledge the Savior. If the fall of Israel means revival for the world, the "fullness" of Israel can mean nothing less than "life from the dead," or, as Bruce suggests, "a veritable resurrection."[1] In his enthusiasm the apostle has introduced a thought of monumental significance without bothering to give us any warning. He is telling us that Israel, which was down but not out, will, in actual fact, rise again. Her failure will give way to fullness; her rejection will be replaced by reception. There will indeed be a day when Israel is seen to be, on a grand scale, the people of God, through faith.

GOD'S POWER WITH REGARD TO ISRAEL

By drawing a sharp contrast between Jew and Gentile and by showing how he was trying to provoke the Jews to jealousy, Paul was running the risk of provoking both Jew and Gentile to more than jealousy. He seems to sense this because, having spoken to the Jews in terms which they could readily have found offensive and having addressed the Gentiles in such a fashion that they might well become arrogant, he promptly sets about redressing the balance. He speaks warmly of the privileged position of the

Jewish people and reminds the Gentiles of their relatively inferior position, thereby in one fell swoop pricking the potential Gentile balloon and smoothing the potentially ruffled Jewish feathers. Then he gathers both Jew and Gentile together by the use of two deft illustrations.

> [16] For if the firstfruit is holy, the lump is also holy; and if the root is holy, so are the branches.
>
> —*Romans 11:16*

The first expression is no doubt a reference to the ancient practice of presenting to the Lord a loaf or cake baked from the first flour to come from the threshing floor. The idea behind the ceremony was that if the first cake was offered to the Lord, the whole batch would be special in the Lord's eyes and, accordingly, in the people's stomachs. The second illustration draws from the common Old Testament picture of Israel as the vine, and it points out that because root and branch are one, thus if the root is holy so also is the branch. There is some question as to Paul's exact meaning concerning the identification of the root and the first cake. Some believe he is referring to Abraham from whom the family of God has come; others incline to the belief that he meant the patriarchs. Either way it is clear as the illustration develops that he is speaking of Jewish roots and origins which alone have made Gentile blessing a possibility.

That the purposes of God in salvation were first revealed through His chosen people goes without saying, as also does the fact that His Son was, according to the flesh, a member of the Jewish people. Despite all her faults, Israel has never been less than God's chosen means of bringing blessing to the world, and everything else that He has chosen to do must be seen in that context. This truth Paul makes abundantly clear through developing the illustration of Israel as the Vine.

> [17] And if some of the branches were broken off, and you, being a wild olive tree, were grafted in among them, and with them became a partaker of the root and fatness of the olive tree, [18] do not boast against the branches. But if you do boast, remember that you do not support the root, but the root supports you.
>
> [19] You will say then, "Branches were broken off that I might be grafted in." [20] Well said. Because of unbelief they

were broken off, and you stand by faith. Do not be haughty, but fear. 21 For if God did not spare the natural branches, He may not spare you either. 22 Therefore consider the goodness and severity of God: on those who fell, severity; but toward you, goodness, if you continue in His goodness. Otherwise you also will be cut off. 23 And they also, if they do not continue in unbelief, will be grafted in, for God is able to graft them in again. 24 For if you were cut out of the olive tree which is wild by nature, and were grafted contrary to nature into a cultivated olive tree, how much more will these, who are natural branches, be grafted into their own olive tree?

25 For I do not desire, brethren, that you should be ignorant of this mystery, lest you should be wise in your own opinion, that blindness in part has happened to Israel until the fullness of the Gentiles has come in.

—Romans 11:17–25

There is something awesome about Paul's description of God's dealings with His Vine. He shows the mighty power of God as He relentlessly works according to His own righteous principles and will continue to do. Paul speaks of God's power to establish Israel as the Vine purely on the basis of His own choice. But then he adds that He will use His power to break off some of the branches if they refuse to come to Him in humble faith. At the same time, God has no reluctance at all in taking wild branches and grafting them into the old stock, provided, of course, that the wild branches would do what the natural branches refuse to do—namely, come to Him in faith. But the wild branches must not overlook the fact that when natural branches refused to believe, God reserved the right to remove them, and He will not hesitate to do the same with wild branches. So there is no room for complacency, only humble trust. It is the continuance in belief that is the true evidence of genuine faith in the same way that the "perseverance of the saints" reminds us that true saints do persevere.

God in all His majestic power is thus seen to be a God of "goodness and severity," and it is the behavior of the people that determines which aspect of His nature becomes most dear then. If they fall, severity in judgment is a reality. If they continue, only the goodness of God will be their portion. In the same way that those who do not continue in faith reveal the spurious nature of their faith and are thus broken off, so those who previously were hard to the gospel but subsequently believe will be grafted in. In other words, Gentiles should no more presume on the goodness of God than the people of Israel, because God has the power to graft in any who believe and to break off all who will not—Jew or Gentile—and He will use this power.

There are numerous evidences of God's power at work in this way. When I became a pastor in a middle class suburban church in the United States, there was an influx of young people from the counterculture. To the chagrin of the regular attenders who were respectable, upright citizens, many of the newcomers wore tattered blue jeans, long hair, sandals and various pieces of chunky jewelry around their necks. One girl raised the ire of the congregation by wearing jeans patched with the flag of the U.S.A. The old vine struggled with the wild branches for some time, and the wild branches found it hard to settle in to the ways of the old vine. But God's power was seen in our midst, and slowly the steady flow of life from the experienced believers flowed into the experience of the youngsters, while the "wild life" of the young people began to spark the enthusiasm of the more mature. Both profited and God was honored, for only He could have worked out such a tricky grafting operation.

GOD'S PROMISE OF RESTORATION FOR ISRAEL

On a limited scale, the foregoing is a remarkable occurrence. How much more, therefore, is Paul justified in saying that, on a worldwide scale which incorporates Jew and Gentile, this action of God is a mystery. Particularly is this the case as we remember that, once the fullness of the Gentiles has come in, there will be a revival in Israel as they come to faith in Christ.

> 26 And so all Israel will be saved, as it is written:
> *"The Deliverer will come out of Zion,*
> *And He will turn away ungodliness from Jacob;*
> 27 *For this is My covenant with them,*
> *When I take away their sins."*
> 28 Concerning the gospel they are enemies for your sake, but concerning the election they are beloved for the sake of the fathers. 29 For the gifts and the calling of God are irrevocable.
> 30 For as you were once disobedient to God, yet have now obtained mercy through their disobedience, 31 even so these also have now been disobedient, that through the mercy shown you they also may obtain mercy. 32 For God has committed them all to disobedience, that He might have mercy on all.
> —*Romans 11:26–32*

The fullness of the Gentiles (v. 25) refers to the time when the full complement of non-Jews will have believed and found their way into the kingdom. This fact has significance for Israel in that as Israel's hardening gave opportunity for Gentile blessing so the conclusion of Gentile blessing will give rise to the new day of opportunity for Israel so great that *"all Israel will be saved"* (v. 26). The exact timing of this predicted revival is of course not stipulated; neither is the exact meaning of "all Israel" universally agreed upon. But there is no doubt that something unusual should be expected in terms of Israel's future response to the Messiah whom they reject to a great extent at this time.

Israel's condition is therefore partial in that there are genuine believers, and it is temporary in that there will be a restoration of the fortunes of the people of Israel. In His divine wisdom, God chose to use the rejection of Christ by His people as a means of reaching the Gentiles so that through His abundant demonstration of grace to them Israel might be brought to a realization of the grace of God in Christ. The tragedy of Israel's unbelief is therefore used by God to bring about the victory of Gentile evangelization, which, in turn, will lead to Jewish restoration. God has not altered His principles, violated His laws, besmirched His character, altered His plans, forsaken His people, nor ignored the Gentiles. In fact, He has shown that even in the midst of human obduracy and rebellion, He can and will use all things to bring about His eternal purposes. No wonder Paul breaks out in praise:

> 33 Oh, the depth of the riches both of the wisdom and knowledge of God! How unsearchable are His judgments and His ways past finding out!
> 34 *"For who has known the mind of the LORD?*
> *Or who has become His counselor?"*
> 35 *"Or who has first given to Him*
> *And it shall be repaid to him?"*
> 36 For of Him and through Him and to Him are all things, to whom be glory forever. Amen.
> —*Romans 11:33–36*

It is sometimes said that knowledge is the accumulation of information, and wisdom is knowing what to do with it. Paul is deeply impressed by God's unique grasp of both. God's information concerning human behavior in general and response to the gospel in particular is unique in that it incorporates foreknowledge, and His wisdom in handling the human problem as demonstrated by both Gentile degradation and Jewish obduracy is shown to great effect by the way He used Jewish hardness to bring about Gentile blessing and then used Gentile blessing to bring about Jewish revival. His knowledge and wisdom truly do qualify for the adjectives *"unsearch-able"* and *"past finding out."*

It is particularly fitting that Paul's lengthy exposition of the Christian gospel which started with a description of human failure should finish with a shout of appreciation for divine capability. By doing this Paul demonstrates the truth of the centrality of the Lord in all things, which he then articulates in one of the greatest of all statements: *"For of Him"*—a reminder that He is the source of all things—*"and through Him"*—a reminder that He is the sustainer of all things—*"and to Him"*—a reminder that He is the significance of all things. It is He who has originated us, in order that He might perpetuate us so that when He is ready He might terminate us. As the One from whom we come, we know Him as Source; as the One who keeps us alive in every dimension, we recognize Him as the Force; and because it is to Him that we are inexorably moving, we gladly acknowledge Him as the Course of our lives. It is to Him that glory rightly belongs.

To glorify God is, as we know, the chief end of man, but the *"all things"* (v. 36) of which Paul speaks and which should therefore glorify Him includes all aspects of the created Universe. When eventually we stand in glory, we will no doubt be given a tour of human history and be shown how in one event after another God was at work. His working in no way violated human freedom or exempted human beings from the consequences of their actions; nevertheless God was working to bring things to their predetermined conclusion. To understand this fully will be the greatest possible stimulus to praise and worship. There will be such acknowledgement of His wisdom and knowledge, His grace and mercy, His holiness and His justice that all of creation will be needed rightly to express the wonder and glory of His Being.

In the meantime, humans who understand in some measure the things of which Paul has written join him in articulating their sense of wonder and take every opportunity to express their appreciation to God for God. In addition, they take seriously the necessity not only to speak His praise but also to show forth His glory by the very lives they live. It is to this practical expression of appreciation for God's glory that the apostle now turns in the conclusion of his epistle.

NOTES

1. Bruce, *Romans,* p. 212.

CHAPTER EIGHTEEN—A SENSE OF VALUES
ROMANS 12:1–8

Scripture Outline

The Reality of Your Commitment (12:1–2)

The Estimation of Yourself (12:3)

The Functions of Your Church (12:4–5)

The Exercise of Your Gifts (12:6–8)

The word "therefore" is one of the most underrated in the English language. "Therefore" is like a hinge on a door that acts as the link between the wall and the door and enables the one to relate to the other. In Scripture, "therefore" holds together doctrinal principles and practical application. It is therefore vitally important when we consider the dangers of theory unrelated to practice and practice unrelated to theory. Paul's use of the word is pivotal in the Roman epistle:

> **12:1** I beseech you therefore, brethren, by the mercies of God, that you present your bodies a living sacrifice, holy, acceptable to God, which is your reasonable service. ² And do not be conformed to this world, but be transformed by the renewing of your mind, that you may prove what is that good and acceptable and perfect will of God.
> —*Romans 12:1–2*

The exposition of Christian truth requires a response in the enlightened heart, and with this in mind the apostle asks his readers to do some realistic evaluation of their application of spiritual truth.

THE REALITY OF YOUR COMMITMENT

Christians are to demonstrate their commitment by presenting their bodies, refusing to conform to this world, and by being transformed through renewed minds. Paul's use of the words *"present"* (the verb used is the technical expression for presenting a victim for sacrifice) and *"sacrifice"* show clearly that he expects the believers to hand over their bodies to God in a manner resembling the way the people of Israel presented their offerings to the Lord. There were, of course, two main kinds of offerings: first, those which led to reconciliation; and, second, those which were an expression of celebration after reconciliation had been accomplished.

In the epistle to the Romans, the sacrifice of Christ as the means of reconciliation has been clearly described, and Paul specifies that in response the believer is to offer his body to the Lord out of appreciation and celebration. The body may be seen as the "whole person" or perhaps as the means whereby the whole person is expressed symbolically in a physical setting, in much the same way that the defeated general in a military situation would hand over his sword, thereby demonstrating the surrender of his whole being. The sacrifice is to be unique in that it will be "living" as opposed to the normal dying experience of the victim. This points to the fact that believers when committed to the Lord show in the lives they live in the body the genuineness of that commitment. The body then is also *"holy* [and] *acceptable to God."* We have seen the body as the agent of sin in previous chapters, but now it becomes the instrument of holiness which, of course, is totally acceptable and well-pleasing to the Father. It is possible to engage in mighty sacrificial acts which, like Cain's costly sacrifice, are totally unacceptable to God because of the attitude in which they are presented. But when the body is intelligently yielded to the Lord to be the means of expressing a living, vital holy experience, the Lord is as well pleased as He was with the sacrifice of Abel.

The *"world"* of which Paul speaks is not the physical or geographical location in which we live. Rather, it is "the age" of which we are a part in contrast to "the age which is to come." Believers have the unique privilege and tension-filled opportunity to live in the present "evil age" as members of the age to come. Therein lies the thrill of much Christian living. It is relatively easy for Christians who are aware of the tension to handle it by withdrawing from their contemporary society and protecting their spirituality by developing a ghetto mentality and a greenhouse environment. Conversely, others simply identify with their age and culture without thought or question and become totally indistinguishable from the pagans among whom they live. Because human beings are inveterate conformists, the temptation to simply fit into the picture and fade into the scenery can be practically overwhelming. The committed life, however, is shown by the degree in which the believer stays in the secular world without being trapped by it and without failing to be a witness to it. The tension is aptly described by the Master's words explaining that we are "in the world but not of it."

In complete contrast to the conforming tendency, the believer experiences a transforming dynamic in his life. To be "transformed" is to be literally "metamorphosed" or changed into another form. We may draw an analogy with the way caterpillars shed their crinikly skins to become transparent butterflies, or we may relate the experience to that of Christ, Himself, being "metamorphosed" on the Mount of Transfiguration when the pent-up glory of heaven suddenly burst through the confines of His physical body. The inward power of this transforming experience is the renewed mind. We have already been shown the tragic influence of the carnal mind and its invidious consequences, but the mind renewed by the truth of God mediated by the indwelling Spirit produces results as beneficent as the works of the flesh are malevolent.

It is because of the *"mercies of God"* outlined in the previous eleven chapters that Paul exhorts or encourages the Roman believers to evaluate their spiritual lives in these three categories, but he gives another reason also. To respond in committed lifestyle is *"reasonable service."* "Reasonable" translates the Greek *logikos*. This word in Greek thought belonged to the *logos* family of ideas, which contained such concepts as word based on reason; reason as a function of the mind, the reasonable or rational activity of the mind, the relationship of the mind to spirit, and the link between reasonable and spiritual. "Service" contains the idea of acts of worship and other religious functions. When coupled with "reasonable," the beautiful principle is produced that those who are rightly related to the Father through the Son will engage in all manner of activities which by their very nature will exhibit the committed life as a consequence of their spiritual, logical, moral, and reasonable consideration of the wonder of their salvation.

The result of such living is stated with disarming simplicity: we will *"prove what is that good and acceptable and perfect will of God."* Most believers do not question the truth of the "will of God," but many regard it as such an obscure mystical reality that they despair of knowing it with any certainty or of doing it with any deep sense of assurance. For many the will of God is as confusing as an Agatha Christie mystery story—an idea that finds unfortunate confirmation in the use of the word "mystery" in many versions of the New Testament. Paul would strongly resist this concept. He rightly insists that the will of God is to be discovered and done with such relish that it will be proved to be good, acceptable, and perfect. He does not promise that the careless, the casual, and the uncommitted will somehow land on their feet and find out that they did God's will by accident. Rather he states that those who genuinely do what is required will find in their own experience the reality of the sweet will of God.

THE ESTIMATION OF YOURSELF

> ³ For I say, through the grace given to me, to everyone who is among you, not to think of himself more highly than he ought to think, but to think soberly, as God has dealt to each one a measure of faith.
>
> —*Romans 12:3*

It is worth noting that in the previous verses Paul "beseeches" as a brother, but in the third verse he "says"—a strong word—"through the grace" given to him—a reference to his apostolic status, which is the gift of God to him for the church. There is a note of authority in his words as he reminds the Christians at Rome that they must be very careful in their evaluation of their own lives. This evaluation will come from a renewed mind, as opposed to the common secular evaluation. But it will also be in direct relationship to the particular calling of each Christian, which is discernible through *"the measure of faith"* that *"God has dealt to each one."* By this expression Paul means that God equips each believer for a particular task and expects him to discover and fulfill his special role in the context of the believing community. Once this is understood, the believer is delivered from a number of potential miscalculations. He will not aspire to be more than God intends him to be, but he will not settle for being less than he was created and redeemed to be. Accordingly, he will be delivered from an arrogance which is destructive of harmony in the body of believers and will be content to make a "sober" evaluation of his own gifts and calling.

While it is not uncommon to think *"more highly"* than we ought, it is equally possible for some people to look at themselves in such a defeated manner that they do not think of themselves as highly as they should. Paul himself illustrates this by his insistence on his apostolic office—something for which he takes no credit, because it was a gift, but at the same time something which he will not deny for the same reason, that it is God's gift! The reminder that all we have is ours through the grace of God is most appropriate to those who have a tendency to arrogance. Reminder that they are sons of God, gifted for His purpose that they might be to His glory, is equally appropriate to those who grovel in their own inadequacy under a cloak of false humility.

I came across a most unusual illustration of realistic evaluation recently. A friend of mine was singularly successful in launching a special ministry in the church of Christ in such a way that it became extremely beneficial in a very brief period of time. After developing the ministry for five years, however, he resigned his position as president, stating that he knew that his gifts were such that he could take the ministry only so far, that it had grown to such a size that he was becoming a hindrance to its development, and that he felt his former deputy was the man to take over. His decision was made in response to his own convictions, confirmed by his friends and colleagues who loved him and the ministry, and who were unanimous in their desire to see the work of the Lord continue and to see him functioning in the setting for which he was most suited. He was thinking soberly as God had dealt to him the measure of faith.

THE FUNCTIONS OF YOUR CHURCH

The apostle has spent much time in this epistle explaining how individuals can be reconciled to God and become recipients of the life of Christ in order that they might live in a new relationship to Him. Another important dimension in spiritual experience is related to the fact that if many people become related to Christ, they must develop their relationship with each other. When believers become heirs of God and joint heirs of Christ, they also become fellow heirs with each other. The environment in which these relationships operate is the assembly of believers— the local church. Paul, whose ministry to the Gentiles was characterized by the formation of churches, loved to use the human body as a striking analogy of the functions of the church:

⁴ For as we have many members in one body, but all the members do not have the same function, ⁵ so we, being many, are one body in Christ, and individually members of one another.

—*Romans 12:4–5*

On a recent visit to Brazil to speak to pastors and Christian workers, I took the opportunity to watch the National Soccer Championship Final between Sao Paulo and Gremio. Only one goal was scored, but it was a masterpiece of skill and execution. As the ball was centered high by the right winger of Gremio, the center forward, Baltazar, seeing his opportunity, slipped between two defenders. Leaping high in the air, he trapped the ball on his chest, dropped it on his left foot, flipped it on to his right, glanced at the goal, and with tremendous power shot into the far left corner out of the goalie's reach. It would be interesting to know how many members of Baltazar's body were utilized in scoring the winning goal in such superb fashion, but as I will never know, I am satisfied to enjoy his athletic skills, marvel at the wonder of the human body, and ponder the reality of the functioning of the body of Christ—the local church.

Our natural tendency to selfishness and individualism militates against the concept of the body of Christ, but the renewed mind produces a different attitude. Those who are instructed from the Word of God by the Spirit of God recognize the uniqueness of the believer's position in the church and also are committed to being a part of the body of Christ. When Christ was on earth, He inhabited a body similar to our physical bodies and, accordingly, knew something of our physical limitations. But after His Resurrection, He was free to come again in the Person of the Spirit and inhabit numerous individuals who, together, would become the means of His continued activity on earth. So varied were the abilities and ministries of the Lord that it would be ludicrous to expect any one individual to begin to emulate His ministry. But when many people come together as His body, they can collectively begin to demonstrate the multiplicity of ministries which He longs to perform through their united efforts.

This basic concept of the church is quite different from many which govern the activities of the contemporary believer. Because we live in a specialized world, we have tended to form churches around the specialist and have encouraged the congregation to participate more as spectators and critics than as participants in ministry. This not only robs the church of her vitality and versatility, but also tends to produce a dull uniformity where there should be a cohesive, coordinated diversity.

Whenever differences of function, outlook, and ministry arise, there is always the possibility of friction. Perhaps it is because we have been reluctant to risk the friction and work on the differences that we have preferred instead to allow a few people to become dominant and the majority passive. It should be pointed out, however, that if the renewed mind is in control, there is no reason why we should fear diversity and give up on the coordination of a multiplicity of outlooks and ministries. And when the sheer delight of mutual support and inter-related gifts is experienced, there will be no desire to experience anything less than the special life of the body of Christ where the members are not only members of Christ but also *"members of one another."* What is required to do this is the topic of the next section.

THE EXERCISE OF YOUR GIFTS

6 Having then gifts differing according to the grace that is given to us, let us use them: if prophecy, let us prophesy in proportion to our faith; 7 or ministry, let us use it in our ministering; he who teaches, in teaching; 8 he who exhorts, in exhortation; he who gives, with liberality; he who leads, with diligence; he who shows mercy, with cheerfulness.
                                                            —Romans 12:6–8

While Paul does not state explicitly that his apostleship is a gift, it is clear that he regarded it as such when we note that he uses the phrase *"the grace that is given"* both to describe his own position and that of the other believers who had received the gifts of the Spirit. The grace *(charis)* of God which brings salvation through faith also brings gifts *(charismata)* to the saved believer which he must utilize in the context of the body of believers. That these gifts will differ from each other is as fascinating as it is challenging. The fascination comes from the understanding that in a normal, healthy group of believers we can reasonably expect to discover a variety of capabilities specially imparted by the Holy Spirit for the good of the body and the ongoing of the work of the Lord. The challenge comes from the necessity to respect and encourage those whose gifts and personality may, because of their differences, threaten our position or draw attention from our ministry.

It is noteworthy that Paul does not spend time describing the functions of the different gifts and the corresponding responsibilities but rather concentrates on the spirit in which the gifts are exercised. His overriding concern is that the believers utilize to the full the grace of God in their corporate life. To do this, they must overcome all potential attitudinal problems. The only way for this to happen is through the individual believer's accepting the apostolic injunction to behave in a manner that befits the renewed mind.

After apostleship, the ministry of prophecy heads the list. Considerable discussion concerning the exact nature of the prophetic gift in New Testament times and in the modern era has led to some confusion. Shedd quotes Philippi as follows: "The New Testament idea of the prophetic office is essentially the same as that of the Old Testament. Prophets are men who, inspired by the Spirit of God, remove the veil from the future; make known concealed facts of the present, either in discovering the secret will of God, or in disclosing the hidden thoughts of man, and bringing into light his unknown deeds; and dispense to their hearers instruction, comfort, exhortation in animated, powerfully impassioned language going far beyond the ordinary limits of human discourse."[1]

If Philippi is right, it is plain to see why the apostle warns against believers thinking more highly of themselves than they ought, for such a man with such superlative gifts would need to guard carefully against using his remarkable powers for his own advantage. The safeguard, as we saw earlier, is to exercise the gift of the Spirit with a deep sense that it is a gracious gift attributable to the Giver and, therefore, something for which the recipient can take no credit.

Paul appears to suggest that other believers may abuse their gifts by simply not using them. There is little doubt that, because of the unfortunate tendency of churches to underemphasize the truth of the giftedness of all believers, there are many who have no concept of their gifts while others who know their gifts are given little or no encouragement to exercise them. It is the responsibility of the believer to see that if his gift is "ministry" (diakonia) or teaching or exhorting (paraklesis—an obvious relative of the beautiful name "Comforter" which our Lord gave the Holy Spirit) that he be actively involved in serving, teaching, comforting, and encouraging, and not allowing the gift of the Spirit to be a buried talent.

The attitude in which the gift is exercised is also important. There are those who have a special gift of giving—presumably because they have a particular gift for producing—and they should take extraordinary care to see that their special ability is exercised in above-average giving. Leaders can become casual and careless, but if they see their abilities as divinely granted gifts and their charges as the flock of God, they will lead with diligence. Those who are particularly endowed with the ability to show mercy should not become disgruntled by the heavy demands that will be made on their time and energy when their beautiful gift becomes known. They should cheerfully respond. When Churchill cabled Roosevelt and said, "Give us the tools and we'll finish the job," he was echoing the cry of the church of Christ which so often feels inadequate for the demanding task of being Christ's body on earth. But the church should be reading the Scriptures as if they were the cabled response from the Throne: "I gave you the tools (the gifts); now finish the job."

NOTES

1. William G. T. Shedd, *Romans* (Grand Rapids: Zondervan Publishing House), p. 363.

CHAPTER NINETEEN—GOOD AND EVIL

ROMANS 12:9–21

Scripture Outline

Good, Evil, and Fellowship (12:9–12)

Good, Evil, and Stewardship (12:13–16)

Good, Evil, and Hardship (12:17–21)

The cosmic struggle between good and evil as it relates to mankind's relationship to God has been graphically portrayed by Paul in the doctrinal sections of the epistle, but once he turns his attention to practical application of doctrine, the apostle quickly reminds believers that the conflict still rages.

The series of staccato, ethical instructions that he presents are built around a framework of statements relating to "good and evil." *"Abhor what is evil." "Cling to what is good." "Repay no one evil for evil" "Have regard for good things. . . ." "Do not be overcome with evil, but overcome evil with good."* In summary, the believer is required to make a decision about good and evil and to come down firmly on the side of good and in opposition to evil. (The words "cling" and "abhor" are powerful.) This takes away from the believer the commonly held assumption that those who suffer evil are free to respond in kind. Moreover, the believer's commitment to "good" will require that his weapons for the fray, both in terms of defense against and opposition to evil, will always be "good" and never "evil." This attitude, the product of the renewed mind, is succinctly described in verse 9 as *"love without hypocrisy."*

Love as an attribute of God, manifest in His relations with man through Christ, has figured prominently in the epistle, but now the love of which Paul speaks is a response to God worked out in the crucible of human relations. Without "hypocrisy" translates the Greek *anupokritos,* which means literally "without play-acting or pretending" and, accordingly, "genuine." In a nut-shell, to combat evil with good is genuinely to love—a response of a renewed mind which has grasped something of the genuine love of God.

GOOD, EVIL, AND FELLOWSHIP

The characteristics of this love are to be shown in the fellow-ship of believers in the following ways:

> ⁹ Let love be without hypocrisy. Abhor what is evil. Cling to what is good. ¹⁰ Be kindly affectionate to one another with brotherly love, in honor giving preference to one another; ¹¹ not lagging in diligence, fervent in spirit, serving the Lord; ¹² rejoicing in hope, patient in tribulation, continuing stead-fastly in prayer;
>
> *—Romans 12:9–12*

Paul's reminder to believers that they are not free from evil leads to another intensely practical thought—that there is no lack of opportunity for evil to triumph in the fellowship of believers where only good belongs. The Greek word *philostorgos* reminds us of our family relationships as believers and of the need for special attention to filial love, without which all manner of evil attitudes and tensions will inevitably arise. More often than not, trouble erupts in the fellowship because people are offended when they perceive, rightly or wrongly, that their posi-tions have been usurped or their personhood has been slighted. The insistence on position and rights rather than privilege and responsibility is the seedbed in which a variegated crop of evil flourishes. But where love is expressed in glad acknowledgement of the achievement of others and genuine appreciation of the deficiencies of ourselves, it is hard for evil to triumph. A simple formula to follow requires the reversal of the natural tendencies and the institution of the supernatural, as follows: "Concentrate on his good points and my bad points rather than on my good points and his bad points."

Once evil is hated rather than treated with courteous civility, and good is firmly embraced rather than regarded merely as a desirable concept, all possibility of casual Christianity evaporates and in its place a life that is *"not lagging in diligence, fervent in spirit"* takes over. Both expressions denote an all-out attack on anything that savors of lethargy or lukewarmness and present the exciting picture of zealous, white-hot believers acting lovingly out of firm conviction and deep commitment.

"Serving the Lord" could just as easily be translated "serving the times" in the sense of grasping the opportunities that present themselves. Both, of course, are true and necessary and in a real sense need to be combined in the life of the believer. *"Rejoicing in hope, patient in tribulation"* are further instructions that relate clearly to the teaching of the earlier chapters of the epistle. *"Continuing steadfastly in prayer"* is a command that believers are to obey in light of the special understanding Paul has given concerning the ministry of the Spirit in times of difficulty.

It is impossible to estimate the potential of a fellowship in which believers take seriously the injunctions outlined by Paul. But we can be sure of the serious intent of Scripture in this regard, and also we can be certain that the evil which so often rears its ugly head in the family of God can only be banished when it is overcome with good—the good of genuine love demonstrated in tangible actions and attitudes.

GOOD, EVIL, AND STEWARDSHIP

The list of instructions continues with more powerful requirements:

> [13] distributing to the needs of the saints, given to hospitality.
> [14] Bless those who persecute you; bless and do not curse.
> [15] Rejoice with those who rejoice, and weep with those who weep. [16] Be of the same mind toward one another. Do not set your mind on high things, but associate with the humble. Do not be wise in your own opinion.
> —*Romans 12:13–16*

The resources with which we have been supplied can be the means of blessing or cursing, the instruments of good or evil. The determining factor is whether we regard our resources as our personal possessions to be used as we desire, or as gracious gifts entrusted to us to be used for God's glory and man's benediction.

To be aware of the needs of others, particularly the "saints," and to fail to share is the essence of evil. Not only does it demonstrate hardness of heart but it clearly shows deficiency of understanding of the true nature of possessions. What is true of possessions, in general, is particularly true in relation to the use of homes. To be *"given to hospitality"* means, literally, "to pursue strangers with love." The emphasis is on the glad sharing of the resources of home and family with those in particular need of shelter and succor. The need for this was particularly apparent in the days of the early church. Those who traveled with the message of Christ were totally dependent on the generous hospitality of others if they were to be able to carry on. The infant churches were dependent on homes being open to them as places of worship, and those who became ostracized from home and family because of their newfound faith in Christ were in danger of destitution unless the generous spirit of believers opened both heart and hearth. While the circumstances have changed, the readiness to regard our homes as places of support and strengthening for those in need rather than as castles reserved exclusively for our own pleasure is one of the most obvious acts of stewardship and one of the greatest aids to evil being thwarted and good being done.

One of the Christian's greatest resources is the unique example of the Master. He, *"when He was reviled, did not revile in return; when He suffered, He did not threaten. . ."* (1 Pet. 2:23). This example, like that of homes and wealth, is to be used judiciously for the well-being of those among whom we live. To hit out in reflex action against those who hit out at us is to perpetuate problems rather than resolve them. The history of the human race is so full of illustrations of this principle that it is clear that the world has not benefited from Christ's example; neither, for that matter, has the church in many instances.

Human beings are equipped with a great capacity for giving and receiving love. Even the hardest heart melts before the innocent smile of a child or the antics of puppies and lambs. But this capacity for love, sympathy, and empathy is often strangely locked up in the confines of selfishness. This may be because genuine, loving, empathetic involvement is debilitating and costly. To weep when you are more interested in having fun or to appreciate another's gain when you are suffering loss is hard, but necessary, if the evil of selfishness is to be overcome by the sheer goodness of selflessness.

Another precious resource is the gift of uniqueness, of our individuality. Created by an intelligent God for an intelligent purpose, only one of each of us exists. To believe this is to be introduced to the possibility of living a life that contributes uniquely to the fulfilling of the divine purpose and sensing the special value of the individual in the eyes of God. But the abuse of this resource can lead to untold evil.

When the thinking of the individual becomes individualistic, tensions arise, schisms develop, and relationships are fractured. The drive of the highly motivated individual, which of itself can be the means of great progress, may easily be directed into channels of personal ambition and self-aggrandizement which do all manner of evil to the underprivileged and the needy. And should the highly talented individual become enraptured with his own ability to the extent that he disregards the abilities and sensitivities of others, great harm results. The only answer to the potential abuse and the resultant evil of the God-given resource of uniqueness is the humble submission of uniqueness to the equally humble oversight and direction of the community of believers. When that community is operating properly, the potential for evil—schism, division, estrangement, conflict, and destruction—is avoided and the blessing of cooperative and balanced living is ensured.

GOOD, EVIL, AND HARDSHIP

Having briefly mentioned the unpleasant possibility of having to deal with persecution, the apostle returns to his subject in more detail:

> [17] Repay no one evil for evil. Have regard for good things in the sight of all men. [18] If it is possible, as much as depends on you, live peaceably with all men. [19] Beloved, do not avenge yourselves, but rather give place to wrath; for it is written, *"Vengeance is Mine, I will repay,"* says the Lord. [20] Therefore
> *"If your enemy is hungry, feed him;*
> *If he is thirsty, give him a drink;*
> *For in so doing you will heap coals of fire on his head."*
> [21] Do not be overcome by evil, but overcome evil with good.
> *—Romans 12:17–21*

The realistic practicality of the apostle's instructions concerning conflict in human relations should be carefully noted. Evil will persist and Christians will not be exempt from its painful encroachment. But while they are subject to the same attacks as the rest of society, they are not free to handle them in the manner common to that society. "Getting even" is a natural response but according to Paul— and, of course, his Master, as expressed in the Sermon on the Mount—something better than "getting even" is the spiritual response. Two factors need to be underlined—one negative, the other positive. The former is the Christian's refusal to regard an evil response to an evil action as legitimate. While the spontaneous response or the reflex reaction may move in that direction, the Christian has settled in his mind that he will *"repay no one evil for evil."* The positive response comes from a commitment to doing what is good in the sight of all men. There is not agreement in our society as to what exactly constitutes good, but there is a deep-rooted sense of what is fair and decent, even though these values may not always be prized or maintained. But the Christian has a keenly developed sense of fairness and rightness which, at its lowest level, is at least as high as the commonly held "good," and to this he has committed himself in the bundle of his commitment to the Son of Righteousness.

It is vitally important that Christians arrive at a specific position with regard to their response to evil when it attacks their lives. It is equally important that they take active steps to work out the practical ramifications of their position. There is no real difficulty in arriving at positions that may be totally idealistic and thoroughly unrealistic, but to deal with hardship in a uniquely Christian manner is one of mankind's greatest challenges.

Paul's advice is most helpful. First, steps should be taken to *"live peaceably"* with everyone. No doubt, when the Roman believers read the apostle's words, there was a similar reaction to the one elicited by contemporary readers—"How can I be expected to live at peace with those who are intent on making war?" The answer is, "You are not expected to do the impossible. You are to do what *'is possible, as much as it depends on you.'"* In other words, we are all responsible for our own actions but cannot be held responsible for the actions of others. Therefore, do what you can, attempt what is possible, and leave the consequences of the other person's reaction to God. Second, we are to recognize that, while evil actions must be punished, that does not mean that we are the punishers. The key thought is expressed by Paul's quotation of Deuteronomy 32:35. "'Vengeance is Mine, . . .' says the Lord." The temptation to take matters into our own hands and to see to it that evil is repaid with evil must be resisted at all costs.

This thought was expressed by one of the former hostages when she was released from Iran. Asked about the actions she proposed to take against Iran, she answered that she proposed no action but preferred to leave matters in the hands of the "One to whom vengeance belongs."

The third practical step is to look for ways to *"overcome evil with good."* This requires more than a willingness to walk away from what many people would say is our right of recompense. It introduces an obligation to look for steps to work actively for the good of the one who did the evil action. Recently I read of a middle-aged couple who over a period of years worked for the rehabilitation of the young man who had raped and killed their daughter. This remarkable story of loving forbearance and gracious ministry reflected nothing less than the love of Christ in the power of the Spirit.

The apostle quotes a striking passage from Proverbs to underline his point, and it is interesting to note that this particular proverb probably originated in Egypt in the "teaching of Amenhotep." Derek Kidner writes, "If Proverbs is the borrower here, the borrowing is not slavish but free and creative. Egyptian jewels, as at the Exodus, have been re-set to their advantage by Israelite workmen and put to finer use." The "finer use" reminds us that when a reaction that promotes good is made in response to an action born of evil, the evildoer has "coals of fire" placed on his head, which, while unpleasant at the time, are much to be preferred to the possibilities of burning condemnation at a later date. Better the flame of shame today than the blast of judgment tomorrow.

There is an unusual tenderness in the way Paul reminds his readers of their special responsibilities as Christians, particularly in their response to evil, and this explains his use of the rather uncommon "Beloved." We are not to feel that there is any degree of insensitivity on the part of the inspired apostle as he instructs the disciples of the Lord in the practicalities of the life of the renewed mind. On the contrary, he knew what it meant, as did his Master, to feel the heat of adversity and so to use it that the dross in his own life was burned up and the melting power of the Spirit moved in the hard hearts of evil men. No doubt in later years many a hard soldier of Rome would know firsthand what it meant to be literally chained to a man who repaid their evil with good and who contentedly committed himself to the One to whom the final judgment belongs.

NOTES

1. Derek Kidner, *Proverbs* (London: The Tyndale Press), p. 24.

Chapter Twenty—The Christian Attitude to Authority

Romans 13:1–7

Scripture Outline

The Principles of Authority (13:1–2)

The Purpose of Authority (13:3–4)

The Problems of Authority (13:5–7)

Having outlined the believer's behavior in the church, Paul goes on to deal with the way in which the person with the renewed mind is to function in secular society. The Christian, he insists, will have a high view of authority and will be submissive to it as a matter of Christian conscience.

> **13:1** Let every soul be subject to the governing authorities. For there is no authority except from God, and the authorities that exist are appointed by God. ² Therefore whoever resists the authority resists the ordinance of God, and those who resist will bring judgment on themselves.
> —*Romans 13:1–2*

THE PRINCIPLES OF AUTHORITY

Throughout the epistle Paul has described God in authoritative terms. It was His authoritative word that created things that were nonexistent; it is through the obedience of nature to His laws that the visible things portray something of the invisible God; His dealings with His chosen people clearly demonstrate that He is their God and demands their allegiance; and His freedom to deal with them and others as He chooses is defended vigorously, as is

His absolute right to judge the world in righteousness. That ultimate authority rests with God is beyond question, but it should be noted that God exercises His authority on earth and in heaven through delegation. The most obvious illustration of this is His appointment of the Risen Lord as Judge. But Paul surprises us by adding that God also delegates His authority to man and appoints *"governing authorities"* to whom mankind must submit as they submit to Him. In fact, failure to do this is seen as resistance of God's principles and merits divine judgment. Paul does not specifically identify the appointed ones, and this omission has led some commentators to assume, with some justification, that the apostle had in mind those heavenly powers specifically commissioned to oversee the affairs of earth. But the context does not lend support to this interpretation, because Paul goes on to show that respect for authority, among other things, means paying taxes—something which, fortunately, only earthly powers can impose.

Elsewhere in his writings, Paul teaches that God has delegated His authority to parents, employers, elders, and husbands, but his emphasis here is on the role that government plays in the administration of divine authority.

The apostle's view of the privileged position and responsibility of the secular authorities is illustrated by the fact that the word translated "appointed" was also used by Paul, himself, when he described his encounter with the Risen Lord on the Damascus Road. "Arise and go into Damascus and there you will be told all things which are appointed for you to do" (Acts 22:10). For Paul, the "appointing" of the magistrates by God merited the same word as the "appointing" of apostolic duties by the same God.

Furthermore, the designation "minister" (v. 4) translates the word he uses in the same epistle to describe the work of Christ on behalf of the "circumcision" (Rom. 15:8), and that of Phoebe, the deaconess in the church of Cenchreae. In addition, the description of the governmental authorities as "God's minister" (v. 6) is perhaps even more striking as *leitourgoi* is a word usually reserved for those giving service of a priestly nature.

In the light of the exalted position of divinely appointed secular authority, the Christian should "be subject" to such authority, and the extent to which his submission is shown will be some indication of the extent to which his mind has been renewed, for only the mind enlightened by the Spirit of God would see secular powers in such a light.

THE PURPOSE OF AUTHORITY

It is clear that man cannot survive on his own and must, therefore, establish a community in which to live. His involvement in community provides certain things which individualized living would not furnish, but this provision requires a sense of responsible cooperation, particularly with the necessary powers appointed to administer the community. That Christians do not cease to be members of the secular community when they are born into the kingdom of Heaven needs to be reinforced, because throughout the history of the church there have been those who have failed to recognize the benefits the state has provided them and the reasonable expectations the state has of them. The Preamble of the Constitution of the United States outlines some of these privileges: "In order to form a more perfect Union, establish justice, insure domestic tranquility, provide for the common defense, promote the general welfare, and secure the blessings of liberty. . . ." Paul uses different language to spell similar concepts in more general terms:

> 3 For rulers are not a terror to good works, but to evil. Do you want to be unafraid of the authority? Do what is good, and you will have praise from the same. 4 For he is God's minister to you for good. But if you do evil, be afraid; for he does not bear the sword in vain; for he is God's minister, an avenger to execute wrath on him who practices evil.
> —*Romans 13:3–4*

God's concern for individuals is seen in His concern that society should operate in such a way that man may be free to live as He intended. Authority is necessary if such an environment is to be provided and preserved, so it follows that God-ordained authority is a natural prerequisite for God-ordained order. It is interesting to note that the role human authority is called to play is clearly linked to a realistic appraisal of man's sinfulness. Society will be spoiled where sinful man is allowed to engage in all manner of evil, and society will never flourish for the common good where man is allowed to squander his life on himself and pursue relentlessly his own self-centered course. Accordingly, the authorities are required by God to punish the evildoer and reward the one who does right. Both actions provide incentives to proper societal behavior without which man would destroy his own environment and totally pollute his own community.

The extent to which punishment is to be meted out to the evildoer can be seen from Paul's use of the phrase *"he does not bear the sword in vain"* (v. 4). At least, this is an indication that the apostle saw the necessity for the use of some kind of force as a deterrent to those intent on evil. There is little doubt that he envisioned occasions when the authorities would act as *"an avenger to execute wrath"* (v. 4). It should be borne in mind that, while Paul expressly forbids the individual's taking matters into his own hands as far as retribution for evil is concerned, quoting, "'Vengeance is mine,' says the Lord," he does see the need for the administration of punishment by the state authorities. Clearly he sees such punishment as part of God's administration of wrath. At the same time, the authorities have the responsibility to offer incentives to those who would live righteously in society. They are "ministers for good."

Paul concludes that the Christian must respond to God's institution of civil authority as the means of working out His purposes in society, as follows:

> ⁵ Therefore you must be subject, not only because of wrath but also for conscience' sake. ⁶ For because of this you also pay taxes, for they are God's ministers attending continually to this very thing. ⁷ Render therefore to all their due: taxes to whom taxes are due, customs to whom customs, fear to whom fear, honor to whom honor.

> *—Romans 13:5–7*

Fear is a great motivator, but, while Christians are not exempt from either the possibility of doing wrong or bearing the consequences of wrongdoing, they should be motivated to responsible respect for authority as a matter of conscience. They, of all people, should have the highest view of the authority structures of society because they understand better than others how the purposes of God for society require the institution of authority.

Many people pay their taxes for no other reason than that they are terrified of an audit by the Internal Revenue Service. The Christian has no such fear because he knows that he has declared his income properly, taken his legitimate deductions, and acted well within the law as a matter of conviction. He knows the collector of taxes is doing what is necessary to provide the funding for that which will make his society the place it should be and, therefore, he accepts his responsibility to bear his share of the burden. Some people sweat their way through Customs because of the game they are playing with the Immigration Service, but the Christian as a matter of principle declares his purchases, shows his receipts, pays what is necessary, and may even stuff his clothes back in the bag and zip the zipper with a smile on his face!

It may be that the Christian will not appreciate the politics of a person holding high office, and he may even deplore the official's private life, but this does not exempt him from the responsibility to show respect and honor. The man is a mere mortal, but the office he holds is one ordained of God and the good of the society. The Christian, because he knows this, will always be on his guard concerning the way he expresses his disapproval and voices his dissent. As a matter of conscience, his behavior will never take anything away from the person who is God's minister.

THE PROBLEMS OF AUTHORITY

The Romans had little time for the Jews, whom they regarded as troublesome zealots, religious oddities, and thoroughly difficult subjects. But this did not stop them from treating their unwilling subjects with fairness and respect. For instance, the Jewish law that forbade a Gentile to enter certain parts of the temple on pain of death was enforced by the Romans to the extent that they would execute a Roman citizen for such a contravention. Paul, himself, had many reasons to be thankful for the Roman treatment of the Jewish people. On more than one occasion he was literally rescued from the mobs by the Roman soldiers; he was given freedom to speak by Roman proconsuls, and he even got a free ticket to Rome from the government!

Some people have suggested that this benevolent treatment had led Paul to adopt a position toward secular authority which was understandable under his circumstances but which he could not lay down as a rule for all people under all circumstances. There is no doubt that in later years, when the fury of the Roman emperors was unleashed on defenseless Christian heads, that Rome was described in most uncomplimentary terms by Christian writers. But it is worth noting that, even through the persecutions, the Christians were encouraged to have respect for their persecutors and to see even in their extremity that God was still in control.

235

Perhaps the major difficulty that Christians encountered was related to the dilemma that faced them when the divinely appointed Government acted in ways that directly contravened divine law. The rule of thumb enunciated by Peter before the Council—"We ought to obey God rather than men"—applied in those early days and still applies today.

In an era when respect for authority is at low ebb, it is necessary to point out that Christians must be very careful to ensure that any act of civil disobedience is a matter of conscience inspired by divine principle, because there is an unfortunate tendency for Peter's dictum to be applied in a manner far removed from the original intent. Further, it should be pointed out that when the Christian has a duty to disobey the civil authority as clear cut as he would normally have an obligation to obey, his disobedience should be seen as a striking act of conscience because it is so different from his normal attitude of compliance, cooperation, and support. The habitual troublemaker is easily recognized as troubled even when he may have a valid point to make. The consistent Christian whose regular law-abiding stance is suddenly shattered by a conscience-inspired action is bound to cause a stir and to get his message across. The refusal of the early Christians to worship Caesar was striking not only because of its inherent bravery but also because of its remarkable contrast to their regular position of "rendering to Caesar what was Caesar's."

The distinctive message of Paul concerning the Christian's response to secular authority is to be seen as a call to Christians to demonstrate their renewed lives by responsible behavior. By honoring authority structures because they are divinely established and by challenging corrupt systems because they are aberrations of the divine intention, the Christian living in secular society is uniquely equipped to glorify God and enrich society.

NOTES

1. Barclay, *The Letter to the Romans*, p. 234.

CHAPTER TWENTY–ONE—ROUSE TO REALITY

ROMANS 13:8–14

Scripture Outline

The Reality of Practical Obligation (13:8–10)

The Reality of Eternal Orientation (13:11–12a)

The Reality of Spiritual Operation (13:12b–14)

When the apostle wrote in Romans 13:11, "It is high time to awake out of sleep," he was introducing a note of urgency to the epistle. This was evidently necessary either because he thought his readers might have dozed off during the public reading or, more likely, because the believers in Rome had fallen into a state of spiritual lethargy and ineffectiveness. He exhorted them to "rouse to reality" *(Amplified NT)*—a word that is always appropriate to people living in a world where fantasy is sometimes more pleasant than reality and the dream world more comfortable than the real world.

THE REALITY OF PRACTICAL OBLIGATION

⁸ Owe no one anything except to love one another, for he who loves another has fulfilled the law. ⁹ For the commandments, *"You shall not commit adultery," "You shall not murder," "You shall not steal,"* "You shall not bear false witness," "You shall not covet," and if *there is* any other commandment, are *all* summed up in this saying, namely, *"You shall love your neighbor as yourself."* ¹⁰ Love does no harm to a neighbor; therefore love *is* the fulfillment of the law.
                    —*Romans 13:8–10*

Having spoken about the Christian obligation to pay tax and tribute, Paul turns his attention to private financial concerns. He insists that Christians meet their commitments in this area, too, as a matter of spiritual and moral obligation but then, surprisingly, adds the instruction concerning the obligation to love. Love is a theme found throughout Scripture; it is the theme of countless hymns and secular poetry; literature and music are permeated with its message. "Love makes the world go round," we are told, and there is little doubt that all people hold the idea in high regard, respond to love's attractive embrace, and in their noblest movements distinguish themselves by acts of love. But love seems to reside in peoples' minds as something between a noble ideal and a pleasant optional extra. The apostle insists, however, that love is an obligation as real as taxation and personal debt repayment.

Not only must we grasp the reality that love is an obligation, but we must awake to the reality of the nature of love. There is no doubt that love has its romantic and its sentimental aspects. That love has sexual connotations goes without saying, but the love of which Paul speaks is a choice to behave in a certain way, not necessarily because of romantic, sentimental, or sexual feelings, but simply because it is right. To love means to refuse acts of adultery because they are unloving by nature. They show total lack of concern for the married partner, no respect for the sexual partner, and complete lack of restraint and discipline. They give evidence of a lack of self-respect and proper self-love.

Selecting other commandments from the Mosaic Law, Paul underlines his point and summarizes by reminding his readers of the statement of the Lord that the divine requirement is fulfilled in loving the neighbor. It is necessary to remember that God requires love to be shown first to Himself and then to the neighbor, but Paul's emphasis at this juncture is on the interpersonal relationships which are to be a matter of prime concern to all believers. This is particularly important for those who may have fallen asleep on the job either because they were lulled into a sense of spiritual ease and relaxation or because their thinking was warped by the secular approach to love to which they were exposed in their everyday lives.

The two main questions related to loving our neighbor have to do with defining what is love and discovering who is our neighbor. The first is answered by the complete biblical statement—we are to love as we love ourselves. This means that minimally we are to have the same concern for the preservation, protection, and respect of our neighbors as we have for ourselves. A normal, healthy person loves himself enough to be concerned about his own safety, security, and station in life. Normal love for the neighbor has at least the same concerns. The second question was answered once and for all by the Lord in the parable of the Good Samaritan: my neighbor is any man in the sphere of my influence whose needs I am in a position to meet or whose sufferings I am in a position to alleviate. To love him is to take action and do something on the understanding that God in Christ loved me first and did something about me.

THE REALITY OF ETERNAL ORIENTATION

When we talk about orientation, we usually mean to "get our bearings." It is interesting to remember that the word originally meant to point toward the East and was used particularly in the building of churches where the high altar was placed at the East end of the edifice. There is a special sense in which orientation is the right word for getting our spiritual bearings, because Paul speaks of a coming event with special Eastern connotations:

> 11 And do this, knowing the time, that now it is high time to awake out of sleep; for now our salvation is nearer than when we first believed. 12 The night is far spent, the day is at hand.
>
> —*Romans 13:11–12a*

He was referring, of course, to the climactic event to which all Christians eagerly look forward—the Second Coming of our Lord Jesus. To Paul this event was going to be as dramatic as the daily advent of dawn and the resultant banishment of darkness. Many times as I have flown on long overnight journeys I have seen the darkness slowly, imperceptibly give way to subtle hints of light until suddenly, with a blaze of glory, the sun appeared over the horizon and a new day dawned. When Christ returns, as He promised He would, the night will give place to day and darkness will be lost in the light of His presence. It is to this overwhelming event that all believers look forward. It is to the dawn of the new day that they are orientated.

The return of Christ will, of course, signal the finalization of our salvation. That is what Paul means when he says, *"Our salvation is nearer than when we first believed"* (v. 11). At the moment of justification the repentant believer is introduced to salvation that is far from complete—it is initial. At that same moment he also becomes an heir to salvation that is potential, but he must wait till he meets Christ face to face to experience salvation that in the fullest sense is actual. His initial salvation delivers him from the penalty of sin; he is an heir to the salvation that gives him the promise of ultimate freedom from sin's power and presence. And one day when Christ takes him to glory, his salvation from sin's penalty, power, and presence, which were potentially his from the moment of justification, will be his in actuality. To this great day the believer looks forward. This is his orientation.

The problem with living on earth is that the things of earth which clamor for so much attention can become totally absorbing. The Christian can begin to think like secular man, imbibe his philosophies, adopt his attitudes, and emulate his lifestyle. But the believer must be reminded that his reality is not down here— it is up there. He is a citizen of heaven and merely a resident alien on earth. It is the reminder of the certainty of Christ's return and the resultant consummation of earth's history that acts as a constant stimulus to the believer with regard to his lifestyle on earth. Paul goes on to remind his readers of:

THE REALITY OF SPIRITUAL OPERATION

Therefore let us cast off the works of darkness, and let us put on the armor of light.

13 Let us walk properly, as in the day, not in revelry and drunkenness, not in lewdness and lust, not in strife and envy.
14 But put on the Lord Jesus Christ, and make no provision for the flesh, to fulfill its lusts.

—*Romans 13:12b—14*

As we saw in the Introduction these words were used by the Spirit of God to bring Augustine to faith in Christ, and if for no other reason they are of profound importance. But it should also be noted that Paul is summarizing the basic aspects of human spiritual experience in a way that is memorable for its simplicity. We are to be fundamentally concerned with two things: "putting off" and "putting on." In the light of the coming consummation, Christians need to take steps to be done with all that is antithetical to the coming era of light and truth. With great determination we are to throw off those things in our lives that will have no place in eternity and with the same distaste that we would throw off filthy garments when preparing for a formal occasion. Then with equal enthusiasm we are to clothe ourselves with those graces that belong to the realm of light and glory, and that are suitable to our new life.

The apostle goes on to specify the kind of things that were particularly relevant to the Christians living in first century Rome. If Christians were to live as citizens of the eternal age, their *"walk"* would have to be proper or consistent and that would mean no more involvement in much of contemporary Roman life—the excesses of drunkenness, sexual immorality, partying, and general ill-disciplined capitulation to the base instincts of the sinful nature. It is interesting to note that he adds "strife and envy" to the list, perhaps because there were those believers who, while they no longer engaged in the overt expressions of sinful living that were common to secular Rome, were now guilty of more civilized expressions of the same sinful indulgence. Many Christians have *"put off"* the external evidences of selfish excess and indulgence but have failed to recognize that the unresolved conflicts and the intolerable frictions of their Christian relationships are simply the same fleshly attitudes dressed up in more acceptable garb. When recognized as such, they are to be "put off" with equal distaste.

Finally, Paul makes two exceedingly helpful, practical remarks. The first is remedial and the second is preventative. To *"put on the Lord Jesus Christ"* (v. 14) is a similar expression to *"put on the armor of light"* (v. 12). This injunction conveys the idea that we are to arm ourselves with the resources of Christ Himself. These include His example, His teaching, His expectations, but primarily His divine power.

The preventative action that needs to be taken is to *"make no provision for the flesh"* (v. 14). Some people make things much harder for themselves by failing to take suitable steps to avoid problems. For instance, the believer who knows he has in the past been guilty of drunken behavior and excessive living is not helping himself if he continues to stock up his cocktail cabinet and regularly throws parties for his old cronies. By so doing, he is making provision for the flesh, and in all probability he will eventually avail himself of that provision and return to "the works of darkness." I have counseled with not a few young believers who prior to their conversion to Christ were living sexually active lives without the benefit of marriage. Recognizing the necessity of "putting on Christ," they had made commendable efforts to do so but subsequently had slipped back into their old ways. When we examined the situation, it was obvious that the problem lay in their failure to obey the instruction about not making provision for the flesh. They had continued to meet with the same people in similar seductive circumstances and eventually succumbed to the powerful drives they were not able to combat. Their ability to overcome in this area was impaired, because when they ought to have been drawing on Christ's resources, they were sadly out of touch with Him and dangerously surrounded with malevolent forces to which their indwelling sinful nature gleefully responded.

Recently my elder son was married. He didn't sleep very well the night before his wedding, and he arose early and dressed in his grubby jeans and tee shirt. He busied himself with a number of jobs until the time of the wedding drew close. We suggested to him that as his clothing was hardly suitable perhaps he ought to think of showering and changing—a suggestion to which he warmly responded. The transformation was dramatic. Washed, shaved, and dressed in immaculate morning suit, he suddenly seemed to be ready for his big moment. Casting off the unsuitable and putting on the clothes which were appropriate, he went to meet his bride.

There is a sense in which the believer should constantly be alive to the possibility that his salvation might be completed before nightfall. Accordingly, he will take steps to ensure that he is appropriately dressed at all times to meet his Lord.

CHAPTER TWENTY-TWO—ONE MAN'S FAITH IS ANOTHER MAN'S POISON

ROMANS 14:1–23

Scripture Outline

The Inevitability of Differences of Opinion (14:1–5)

The Importance of the Discernment of Essentials (14:6–14)

The Imperative for Discipline in Attitudes (14:15–23)

The church of Rome, like many of the churches founded as a result of Paul's ministry, was made up of both Jews and Greeks. This was particularly significant to the apostle as he firmly believed that one of the greatest arguments for the validity of Christianity was its ability to bring together people from segments of society that would normally be estranged from each other. He insisted that "in Christ" societal, cultural, economic, and sexual barriers were broken down, and the resultant unifying of peoples from all manner of groups was not only a preview of heaven but also a practical means of bringing a measure of peace on earth.

The tangible evidence of this was the local assembly of believers which operated on the basis of mutual love between people whose only common denominator was relationship to Christ as Savior and Lord. The practicalities of this situation, however, demanded careful attention, because while in theory the walls of partition were broken down, in practice the walls had a nasty habit of putting themselves up again. Paul uses two examples, neither of which seems particularly important to us but both of which were sore points in the church at Rome. The first had to do with food and the second with holy days.

THE INEVITABILITY OF DIFFERENCES OF OPINION

14:1 Receive one who is weak in the faith, but not to disputes over doubtful things. [2] For one believes he may eat all things, but he who is weak eats only vegetables. [3] Let not him who eats despise him who does not eat, and let not him who does not eat judge him who eats; for God has received him. [4] Who are you to judge another's servant? To his own master he stands or falls. Indeed, he will be made to stand, for God is able to make him stand.

[5] One person esteems one day above another; another esteems every day alike. Let each be fully convinced in his own mind.

—Romans 14:1–5

There were in the church those whom Paul describes as *"weak in the faith."* By this he means that there were areas of immaturity in their relationship to Christ and His church. This was particularly evident in those who felt it necessary to maintain certain rules and regulations in their Christian lives that were neither taught nor encouraged by the Lord Jesus. For instance, those who came from a Jewish background were fastidious about their eating habits. This was undoubtedly related to the dietary laws that had been part of their religious heritage from time immemorial. They would never eat certain animals and would not eat others unless they were sure that they had been killed in the correct way. Because they lived in areas where they could not be absolutely sure about the suitability of the meat they were eating, some had taken the position that they would not eat any kind of meat.

This position, while understandable, was not biblical and, moreover, was very hard for those from different backgrounds to understand and accept. They were used to buying meat in the stores of merchants who had obtained it in the pagan temples after meat had been offered to the temple gods. The priests kept some for themselves and sold the rest to the store owners nearby. Pious Jews and concerned Jewish Christians were appalled at the thought that they might be eating something that had been part of a pagan festival, so they soothed their scruples by abstinence.

Meanwhile, many of the believers from different backgrounds had no such problem. To them the meat was meat—nothing more or less—and the fact that it had possibly been in a pagan temple did not alter that fact. They also felt it was the best meat in town! The two different attitudes—"to eat or not to eat"—created a highly volatile situation, because those who felt free to eat sometimes treated their brothers with utter contempt, while those with scruples were highly critical of those who were more free. Criticism and contempt were equally unacceptable in the fellowship of believers, and Paul sets out to deal with both.

The same kind of conflict swirled around the issue of the commemoration of certain days in the calendar. The Jewish reverence for the sabbath was so profound that they had hedged it around with many rules lest they contravene the sabbath laws by chance. The result of their attention to minute detail was a kind of tyranny which they applied to all and sundry, including the Lord Jesus, whose more relaxed approach they deeply resented. Some of the same attitude had remained with some of the believers, and it is not hard to imagine the feelings that would be aroused by the differing views of the observance of the Lord's Day. One solution to the problem would have been simply to put the conservatives in one group and the liberals in another and keep them away from each other. But to do this would not only have been a concession to human obduracy; it would have robbed the body of Christ of its unique characteristic of unity in diversity.

Paul is committed to a nobler, albeit more difficult solution.

THE IMPORTANCE OF THE DISCERNMENT OF ESSENTIALS

First, Paul requires the believers to act out of conviction.

> 6 He who observes the day, observes it to the Lord; and he who does not observe the day, to the Lord he does not observe it. He who eats, eats to the Lord, for he gives God thanks; and he who does not eat, to the Lord he does not eat, and gives God thanks. 7 For none of us lives to himself, and no one dies to himself. 8 For if we live, we live to the Lord; and if we die, we die to the Lord. Therefore, whether we live or die, we are the Lord's. 9 For to this end Christ died and rose and lived again, that He might be Lord of both the dead and the living.
>
> —*Romans 14:6–9*

There is a major difference between doing things out of a sense of convention and doing them from a sense of conviction. The former approach is often a capitulation to the pressures of external factors while the latter should be the product of deep thought and careful evaluation. Paul wants the believers to deal with their controversial issues on the solid base of commitment to Christ rather than surrender to pressure. He does not mind, personally, if they eat meat or not, provided they have decided on the basis of what they understand the Lord's will to be. Provided they do it or don't do it in the light of Christ's lordship over their lives, he has no problem.

Care should be taken at this point to remember that he is not saying that it does not matter what Christians believe or how they behave. In many matters Christ was explicit and the apostle dogmatic, and in such cases Christians have no option but to obey. But in many areas of spiritual experience there are no hard and fast rules and a certain degree of freedom has been granted. It is in the areas of spiritual freedom and scriptural silence that Paul does not mind what conclusions are reached, so long as the conclusion is compatible with the lordship of Christ.

Second, Paul requires the believers to terminate their criticism.

> [10] But why do you judge your brother? Or why do you show contempt for your brother? For we shall all stand before the judgment seat of Christ. [11] For it is written:
> "As I live, says the LORD,
> Every knee shall bow to Me,
> And every tongue shall confess to God."
> [12] So then each of us shall give account of himself to God. [13] Therefore let us not judge one another anymore, but rather resolve this, not to put a stumbling block or a cause to fall in our brother's way.
>
> —*Romans 14:10–13*

When differences of opinion arise concerning deeply held traditions, reactions are usually quite extreme. Feelings of anger and resentment, frustration and bitterness spill over. Usually the people involved in acrimonious dispute become more entrenched in their position and increasingly isolated from those with whom they disagree. Before long it becomes necessary for those who hold strong positions not only to strengthen their own but also to weaken the other. Criticism becomes the order of the day.

This Paul flatly condemns with words reminiscent of the Lord. His point is that every Christian is ultimately responsible to the

Lord, and while we do have the responsibility to encourage, correct, and edify each other, we do not have the freedom to take over the work of evaluation. This only the One who will eventually sit on the Judgment Seat is qualified to do. Therefore, judgmental attitudes in matters of scriptural silence and freedom are totally out of order, and those of us who are guilty of them will answer for them at the Judgment Seat as surely as those with whom we disagree will be evaluated by their Lord.

Third, Paul requires believers to see the other point of view.

14 I know and am convinced by the Lord Jesus that there is nothing unclean of itself; but to him who considers anything to be unclean, to him it is unclean.

—*Romans 14:14*

The apostle makes a surprisingly strong affirmation of his conviction that in the matters he is discussing there is nothing fundamentally right or wrong about the meat or the day. But if the other person has a strong conscience about the wrongness of participation in the meat or the rightness of recognition of the day, then to that person it is a matter of right or wrong. From a purely biblical point of view, it is not possible to argue the "teetotal" position. If a person feels that partaking of alcoholic beverages is wrong, then it would be wrong for him to partake. But he cannot and must not impose that view on his brother. At the same time it would be wrong for the brother who has no scruples in this matter to bring pressure to bear on his more scrupulous brother. When understood, the apostle's words are clear in their direction.

THE IMPERATIVE FOR DISCIPLINE IN ATTITUDES

The attitudes we have already noted are warm acceptance of those with whom we may differ, openness to ideas other than our own, and rejection of a censorious and critical spirit. All of these portray that most beautiful of all Christian virtues—love—but Paul has more to say on this subject:

15 Yet if your brother is grieved because of your food, you are no longer walking in love. Do not destroy with your food the one for whom Christ died. 16 Therefore do not let your good be spoken of as evil; 17 for the kingdom of God is not eating and drinking, but righteousness and peace and joy in

the Holy Spirit. [18] For he who serves Christ in these things is acceptable to God and approved by men.

[19] Therefore let us pursue the things which make for peace and the things by which one may edify another. [20] Do not destroy the work of God for the sake of food. All things indeed are pure, but it is evil for the man who eats with offense. [21] It is good neither to eat meat nor drink wine nor do anything by which your brother stumbles or is offended or is made weak. [22] Do you have faith? Have it to yourself before God. Happy is he who does not condemn himself in what he approves. [23] But he who doubts is condemned if he eats, because he does not eat from faith; for whatever is not from faith is sin.

—Romans 14:15–23

The one who has scruples is described by the apostle as being the weaker brother, and it is interesting to bear in mind that usually when we hold tenaciously to traditions and feel deeply about the things that scripture may treat with silence, we regard ourselves as strong on that point. By the apostle's definition the strong person is the one who is free in areas of God-given freedom and sees no need to build regulations around his freedom, while the weak brother is the one who feels that he needs help in the area of freedom and adds principles which of themselves may be quite right but which are not biblical in origin.

In the examples he has given Paul shows himself to be clearly on the side of the stronger brother but insists that his commitment is to love and peace. This requires willingness to refuse to act in the area of freedom if by so doing one would be offensive or unhelpful to his brother. He is ready to deny himself that which he feels deeply he is free to enjoy because his concern is more for the building up of his Christian brother than for his own fulfillment, and his concern is more for the unity of the fellowship than for the liberty of himself.

Meanwhile the brother who has scruples must live within his own limits because if he contravenes them he must remember *"he who doubts is condemned if he eats"* (v. 23). The inevitability of differences and the possibility of controversies in the Christian church can be viewed either positively or negatively. Some believers are not prepared to allow for differences of position in matters of secondary importance and insist that everything must be spelled out so that unity might prevail. This approach avoids the unpleasantness of controversy but does nothing to enhance diversity or produce maturity. Other groups allow for freedom of conviction but become so embroiled in feuding that they never achieve a unified position of strength and stability. Paul teaches the Roman believers that they must allow for differences but they must avoid division. In summary, they must commit themselves to working in love to produce a unified body that demonstrates the diversity of God's wonderful handiwork.

CHAPTER TWENTY–THREE—THE MINISTERING MENTALITY

ROMANS 15:1–33

Scripture Outline

The Ministry of Edification (15:1–14)

The Ministry of Proclamation (15:15–21)

The Ministry of Administration (15:22–29)

The Ministry of Intercession (15:30–33)

One of the greatest motivational factors is the inbuilt desire that all people have to please themselves. This quite naturally leads to all kinds of selfishness and independence which, in themselves, are responsible for many of society's ills. The renewed mind of the believer leads to a different motivational factor, which is the development of a ministering mentality.

THE MINISTRY OF EDIFICATION

As we saw in the previous chapter the peculiar difficulties facing the church at Rome because of the disparate nature of the membership required mature and careful handling. Paul summarizes this as follows:

> **15:1** We then who are strong ought to bear with the scruples of the weak, and not to please ourselves. ² Let each of us please his neighbor for his good, leading to edification.
> ³ For even Christ did not please Himself; but as it is written, *"The reproaches of those who reproached You fell on Me."*
> ⁴ For whatever things were written before were written for our learning, that we through the patience and comfort of the Scriptures might have hope.
> *—Romans 15:1–4*

The onus of responsibility rests squarely on the shoulders of those who are "strong," meaning those who in areas of spiritual freedom are free to enjoy such liberty. A conscious decision on the part of the strong is necessary—a decision to refrain voluntarily and sacrificially from the enjoyment of legitimate freedom if it is necessary for the "pleasing" of the neighbor. To make such a decision and to adopt such an attitude requires remarkable and commendable strength and maturity. This comes from a variety of sources.

First, there is the understanding that Christian life in the community of believers involves concern for the edifying or the "upbuilding" of both the individual and the body. A commitment to these goals will, of necessity, preclude a commitment to pleasing oneself.

Second, there has to be a desire for the glory of God. There is little that brings honor to the Lord in a feuding, fighting fellowship. Paul's prayer to this end is extremely important:

5 Now may the God of patience and comfort grant you to be like-minded toward one another, according to Christ Jesus, 6 that you may with one mind and one mouth glorify the God and Father of our Lord Jesus Christ.

7 Therefore receive one another, just as Christ also received us, to the glory of God. 8 Now I say that Jesus Christ has become a servant to the circumcision for the truth of God, to confirm the promises made to the fathers, 9 and that the Gentiles might glorify God for His mercy, as it is written:

"For this reason I will confess to You among the Gentiles,
And sing to Your name."

10 And again he says:

"Rejoice, O Gentiles, with His people!"

11 And again:

"Praise the LORD, all you Gentiles!
Laud Him, all you peoples!"

12 And again, Isaiah says:

"There shall be a root of Jesse;
And He who shall rise to reign over the Gentiles,
In Him the Gentiles shall hope."

13 Now may the God of hope fill you with all joy and peace in believing, that you may abound in hope by the power of the Holy Spirit.

—*Romans 15:5–13*

The likemindedness of which he speaks in verse 5 becomes reality not by sweeping differences under the carpet or by destroying the fellowship by fragmenting it into various pressure and interest groups. It is, on the one hand, the product of careful sacrificial action on the part of the strong, and, on the other hand, the result of God's graciously granting through the living Christ that which only He can accomplish in the hearts of His fractious people.

Third, there is the factor of the Word of God, which produces "patience and comfort" in trying times and which outlines the principles to which God is committed in His dealings with mankind. The major relevant principle Paul states at this point in his argument is the oft-repeated and clearly stated purpose of God to bring Jew and Gentile together in the body of Christ. To know this is to be committed to building up people to accept it and to building up the church to reflect it.

Fourth, there is the working of the Lord Himself, as outlined in the apostle's positive and exhilarating benediction of verse 13.

"Hope, joy, and peace" are ingredients needed in great measure by those whose commitment is to edifying those who are locked in conflict.

Fifth, there has to be some degree of confidence in the people involved in addition to the confidence placed in the "God of hope." Paul's expression of this is outstanding.

> 14 Now I myself am confident concerning you, my
> brethren, that you also are full of goodness, filled with all
> knowledge, able also to admonish one another.
> —*Romans 15:14*

The apostle not only had a sense of confidence in the Roman believers but he also expressed it to them, no doubt recognizing the importance of overt statements of encouragement in all areas of ministry.

THE MINISTRY OF PROCLAMATION

Paul, the theologian, teacher, pastor, and apostle, was always the evangelist. His heartbeat for those who had never heard of Christ was always clearly discernible. Having opened the epistle with a statement concerning his call to the ministry of proclamation, he returns to the theme in the concluding verses:

> 15 Nevertheless, brethren, I have written more boldly to
> you on some points, as reminding you, because of the grace

given to me by God, [16] that I might be a minister of Jesus
Christ to the Gentiles, ministering the gospel of God, that the
offering of the Gentiles might be acceptable, sanctified by the
Holy Spirit. [17] Therefore I have reason to glory in Christ Jesus
in the things which pertain to God.

—*Romans 15:15–17*

The Greek language has a number of words that are translated
"minister." The one used here has the special connotation of
"priestly" ministry, although it also has secular applications. Paul
talks about his evangelistic ministry as if it is the activity of a priest
bringing his offering to the Lord in order that the heart of God
might be gladdened. There are many motivations to evangelism
that are detectable in Paul, but overriding even the concern for the
lostness of the lost is the deep desire that the Lord might be honored and glorified by the reconciliation of men and women
through the work of Christ on the Cross. While he never hesitates
to affirm his position of authority and responsibility as the one to
whom "grace [was] given," there is a humble aspect to his statement
as he affirms also his complete dependence on the Lord. He writes:

[18] For I will not dare to speak of any of those things
which Christ has not accomplished through me, in word and
deed, to make the Gentiles obedient— [19] in mighty signs and
wonders, by the power of the Spirit of God, so that from
Jerusalem and round about to Illyricum I have fully preached
the gospel of Christ.

—*Romans 15:18–19*

The mighty preaching, the powerful living, the remarkable
conversions are all attributable to the work of God in him and the
flow of blessing through him. If Paul did not believe that, he
would not even dare to talk about his ministry or to exert his
authority in speaking so firmly to the believers in Rome and elsewhere.

Finally, in the heartfelt words about his proclamation ministry, he speaks of a deep-rooted desire (Greek, *philotimeomai,*
which means literally "love of honor," or "ambition"):

[20] And so I have made it my aim to preach the gospel,
not where Christ was named, lest I should build on another
man's foundation, [21] but as it is written:

*"To whom He was not announced, they shall see;
And those who have not heard shall understand."*
—*Romans 15:20–21*

In churches where all types of ambition motivate all types of behavior, it is salutary to remember the ambition of the aging evangelist.

THE MINISTRY OF ADMINISTRATION

22 For this reason I also have been much hindered from coming to you. 23 But now no longer having a place in these parts, and having a great desire these many years to come to you, 24 whenever I journey to Spain, I shall come to you. For I hope to see you on my journey, and to be helped on my way there by you, if first I may enjoy your company for a while. 25 But now I am going to Jerusalem to minister to the saints. 26 For it pleased those from Macedonia and Achaia to make a certain contribution for the poor among the saints who are in Jerusalem. 27 It pleased them indeed, and they are their debtors. For if the Gentiles have been partakers of their spiritual things, their duty is also to minister to them in material things. 28 Therefore, when I have performed this and have sealed to them this fruit, I shall go by way of you to Spain. 29 But I know that when I come to you, I shall come in the fullness of the blessing of the gospel of Christ.

—Romans 15:22–29

The undying enthusiasm of the apostle for his ministry which had led him to claim, *"from Jerusalem and round about to Illyricum I have fully preached the gospel of Christ"* (v. 19), had its drawbacks, as he acknowledges in verse 22.

He goes on to outline his travel plans, which include a missionary journey to Spain in keeping with his commitment to the unreached people, a brief stop in Rome as much for his benefit as theirs (his desire to *"enjoy your company for a while"* is literally a deep longing to be "filled" or "saturated" with their fellowship), and a trip to Jerusalem to deal with some business there. In addition to all the traveling he was contemplating, he had a number of different things on his mind. First he had to complete his work in Corinth; then he had to deliver personally the collection he had organized for the impoverished church in Jerusalem; then he had to make plans for the evangelization of Spain, bearing in mind the necessity to visit the established church in Rome. The collection had necessitated a considerable amount of organization with the churches of Macedonia and Achaia, with much correspondence, encouragement, and personnel administration.

The spiritual aspects of Paul's ministry are easy to identify, but it is important that we recognize the administrative expertise that he exhibited in the many and varied ministries in which he participated. The balance of the apostle is particularly welcome when we are confronted with the tensions that exist in the contemporary church of the Western world—the tension between organization and inspiration and the balance in seeing the church as an organism and organization. Those who think of the church as a business whose problems can all be solved by better organization need to remember that the church is an organism whose secret is life. But those who eschew organization for the reason that the church is a living body should remember that every organism is organized. The apostle could never be accused of overlooking the fact that the churches were the body in which the Spirit moved, but this did not affect his careful attention to matters of detail in a responsible and organized way. His balance is further seen in his recognition of the absolute necessity for everything to be under "the will of God" and his own ministry being exercised *"in the fullness of the blessing of the gospel."*

THE MINISTRY OF INTERCESSION

The way in which the apostle opens his heart to the Roman believers in the following verses is most enlightening:

> 30 Now I beg you, brethren, through the Lord Jesus Christ, and through the love of the Spirit, that you strive together with me in prayers to God for me, 31 that I may be delivered from those in Judea who do not believe, and that my service for Jerusalem may be acceptable to the saints, 32 that I may come to you with joy by the will of God, and may be refreshed together with you. 33 Now the God of peace be with you all. Amen.
>
> —*Romans 15:30–33*

First we note his special request for prayer on his own behalf. There was no doubt about his commitment to intercessory prayer for those to whom he ministered, but he wanted the believers to know how dependent he was on their prayer support. The intensity of this is seen in his use of the word "appeal," which he also employed at the beginning of the practical application in the latter part of the epistle and will later use when asking the believers to do something about those who are disrupting the order of the church. His appeal for intercession invokes the name of *"the Lord Jesus Christ and. . . the love of the Spirit"* and is, of course, directed *"to God."*

Paul is not indulging in clichés when he asks for prayer, but he specifically outlines the matters he wants the recipients of his letter to bring before God. He is apprehensive about his chances of surviving the attentions of the unbelieving (literally, "disobeying") Judeans whose antipathy to him is well documented. He has no guarantee that the church of Jerusalem will be receptive to him or his gift of love to them. There is doubt in his mind as to whether he will ever make it to Rome, and he frankly admits he is in dire need of refreshment.

With all this on his mind it is not surprising that he sees prayer as a struggle and, accordingly, asks the believers in Rome to engage in the ministry of intercession with him to the extent of striving with him. He concludes with his own brief prayer of intercession and blessing for them: *"Now the God of peace be with you. . . ."*

The variety of ministries dealt with in the latter part of the epistle serves to encourage all believers actively to develop their own ministering mentality and to find specific outlets of service while it also recognizes the place for a plethora of ministries in the body of believers. This recognition of variety serves not only to meet numerous needs and glorify God in a variety of ways but also gives opportunity to add diversity in operation to the existing diversity of background, maturity, and experience that makes the church uniquely the body of Christ.

CHAPTER TWENTY–FOUR—THE IMPORTANCE OF BEING CAREFUL

ROMANS 16:1–27

Scripture Outline

> The Care of Giving Encouragement to People (16:1–16)
>
> The Care of Giving Attention to Problems (16:17–20)
>
> The Care of Giving Glory to God (16:21–27)

The apostle is full of surprises. After the soaring theology of the early chapters and the striking and challenging practicality of the latter section of the epistle, he concludes with a delightful personal and intimate series of greetings which show a number of things that he wanted to do.

THE CARE OF GIVING ENCOURAGEMENT TO PEOPLE

16:1 I commend to you Phoebe our sister, who is a servant of the church in Cenchrea, ² that you may receive her in the Lord in a manner worthy of the saints, and assist her in whatever business she has need of you; for indeed she has been a helper of many and of myself also.

³ Greet Priscilla and Aquila, my fellow workers in Christ Jesus, ⁴ who risked their own necks for my life, to whom not only I give thanks, but also all the churches of the Gentiles. ⁵ Likewise greet the church that is in their house.

Greet my beloved Epaenetus, who is the firstfruits of Achaia to Christ. ⁶ Greet Mary, who labored much for us.
⁷ Greet Andronicus and Junia, my countrymen and my fellow

prisoners, who are of note among the apostles, who also were in Christ before me.

8 Greet Amplias, my beloved in the Lord. 9 Greet Urbanus, our fellow worker in Christ, and Stachys, my beloved. 10 Greet Apelles, approved in Christ. Greet those who are of the household of Aristobulus. 11 Greet Herodion, my countryman. Greet those who are of the household of Narcissus who are in the Lord.

12 Greet Tryphena and Tryphosa, who have labored in the Lord. Greet the beloved Persis, who labored much in the Lord. 13 Greet Rufus, chosen in the Lord, and his mother and mine. 14 Greet Asyncritus, Phlegon, Hermas, Patrobas, Hermes, and the brethren who are with them. 15 Greet Philologus and Julia, Nereus and his sister, and Olympas, and all the saints who are with them.

16 Greet one another with a holy kiss. The churches of Christ greet you.

—Romans 16:1–16

It should be noted that this final chapter has been the basis of much debate, particularly with regard to the fact that the apostle could hardly have known so many people in a church he had never visited. It has been suggested, therefore, that the letter was really sent to Ephesus. The response to this theory has been that the apostle was asking for trouble in mentioning only twenty-six people by name in a church where he had recently spent two and a half years! In the light of such arguments, we may assume that Paul knew a lot of Christian people all over the world and had the ability to keep track of them as they moved from place to place. It is clear that he was careful to remember names and details of the people he met.

Phoebe, the bearer of the letter, is warmly commended as she makes her journey to Rome expecting to enjoy the normal hospitality extended by the believers in the early church. She is described as *"sister," "servant"* (Greek, *diakonos—deaconess), "saint,"* and *"helper"*—credentials of the highest order.

The apostle's beloved co-workers, Priscilla and Aquila, who have braved innumerable dangers with Paul, are described graphically in verse 4 as those who *"risked their own necks for my life."* The fact that Priscilla almost always precedes her husband in the Scriptures may be attributable to her superior social station or more likely to her being the more striking and gifted person in the joint ministry they exercised.

Numerous people are commended for their *"labor,"* and not a few are simply described as *"beloved,"* while the apostle repeatedly uses the expression *"in the Lord"* to identify the bond that holds them together.

It is clear that some of the believers are of Jewish origin, that some of them knew Christ before Paul, that some were slaves and others came from the household of Herod, that some had shared prison cells with Paul and others had cared for him and even "mothered" him. But all were remembered and all were appreciated.

Barclay[1] points out that Tryphena and Tryphosa were probably twins, that their names mean "dainty and delicate," but they were described as those who "labor," with Paul purposely choosing the word that suggests labor to the point of exhaustion. Of such stuff was the church of Rome made!

As his mind teems with remembrances of dear friends and courageous fellow-workers, the apostle shows his concern as he gives them an important warning.

THE CARE OF GIVING ATTENTION TO PROBLEMS

17 Now I urge you, brethren, note those who cause divisions and offenses, contrary to the doctrine which you learned, and avoid them. 18 For those who are such do not serve our Lord Jesus Christ, but their own belly, and by smooth words and flattering speech deceive the hearts of the simple. 19 For your obedience has become known to all. Therefore I am glad on your behalf; but I want you to be wise in what is good, and simple concerning evil. 20 And the God of peace will crush Satan under your feet shortly.

The grace of our Lord Jesus Christ be with you. Amen.

—Romans 16:17–20

The authoritative apostle appears at this juncture as he takes steps to warn the believers in Rome about the possibility of people moving into the fellowship with perverted doctrine delivered with considerable expertise and less than honorable motives. He refers to these people as those who *"deceive"* and cause *"division"* and who serve *"their own belly."* They are committed to their own appetites, resist the ministry of Paul, and deny the fundamentals of the faith as outlined in the apostolic teaching. They are, therefore, to be regarded as agents of Satan, and the believers should *"avoid them."* Under no circumstances should the believers be afraid of these people, for while they are to be watched and avoided, they cannot prevail ultimately. As was promised in the Garden, the enemy of souls will eventually be crushed, and the Romans will enjoy their special place in this promised victory as *"the God of peace will crush Satan under [their] feet shortly."* As always, Paul strikes a fine balance as he warns Christians not to ignore Satan but at the same time not to be paranoid about him. That he is real and dangerous goes without saying, but that he is defeated and his days are numbered is equally true. The devil is like a roaring lion seeking whom he may devour, but he is on a short leash and the hand that holds it is the hand of God. Careless ignoring of satanic infiltration is foolish, but chronic oppression by satanic influence does no justice to the victory which is ours in Christ.

THE CARE OF GIVING GLORY TO GOD

21 Timothy, my fellow worker, and Lucius, Jason, and Sosipater, my countrymen, greet you.

22 I, Tertius, who wrote this epistle, greet you in the Lord.

23 Gaius, my host and the host of the whole church, greets you. Erastus, the treasurer of the city, greets you, and Quartus, a brother. 24 The grace of our Lord Jesus Christ be with you all. Amen.

25 Now to Him who is able to establish you according to my gospel and the preaching of Jesus Christ, according to the revelation of the mystery kept secret since the world began 26 but now made manifest, and by the prophetic Scriptures made known to all nations, according to the commandment of the everlasting God, for obedience to the faith— 27 to God, alone wise, be glory through Jesus Christ forever. Amen.

—Romans 16:21–27

It is quite possible that Tertius, who had taken down the epistle at Paul's dictation, read the finished document to the apostle, who then picked up the pen and wrote these final words of doxology. They ring with similar sentiments to those with which the letter opened and direct the attention of the readers to God and His ability to "establish" them. In the light of the great themes of salvation that have been unfolded, the believers in Rome are to live as people who will be part of the team who will present the gospel to all corners. This will require great strength and fortitude but God would not call them to the task if He were not able and willing to "establish" them. Accordingly, they must look up continually to Him and see in the gospel and the preaching of Jesus Christ, the revelation of the mystery, and the Scriptures of the prophets, the message that God has intervened in the human arena and that, having called people to faith in and obedience to Christ, He will strengthen them for the task ahead.

He is the One who intervened; His was the wisdom that devised the glorious blending of grace, mercy and justice; it was His Son who died and it was His power that raised Him from the dead; it was from His right hand the Spirit was dispensed and through Him that the redeemed believer lives the life that honors the Lord and crushes Satan. Therefore, to Him all glory rightly belongs!

BIBLIOGRAPHY

Barclay, William. *The Letter to the Romans.* Edinburgh: St. Andrews Press.

Bettenson, Henry, ed. *Documents of the Christian Church.* New York: Oxford University Press, 1963.

Bridge, Donald and Phypers, David. *The Water That Divides: The Baptism Debate.* Downers Grove, Ill.: InterVarsity Press, 1977.

Bromiley, G. W. *Historical Theology.* Grand Rapids: Eerdmans, 1978.

Bruce, F. F. "Epistle to the Romans." *Zondervan Pictorial Encyclopedia of the Bible,* vol. 5. Grand Rapids: Zondervan Publishing Co., 1975.

_____. *Romans.* London: The Tyndale Press.

Calvin, John. *Calvin's Commentaries on Romans.* Grand Rapids: Eerdmans, 1947.

_____. *Calvin's Institutes.* Institutes of Christian Religion I. III. 1. Grand Rapids: Associated Publishers.

Fuller, David Otis. *Spurgeon's Lectures to His Students.* Grand Rapids: Zondervan Publishing Co.

Godet, Frederick Louis. *Commentary on Romans.* Grand Rapids: Kregel Publications, 1977.

Green, Michael. *Evangelism in the Early Church.* London: Hodder and Stoughton.

Guthrie, Donald. *New Testament Introduction.* Downers Grove, Ill.: InterVarsity Press, 1973.

Keil, Carl F., and Delitzsch, Franz. *Nehemiah to Psalm LXXVII.* Old Testament Commentaries, 10 vols. Grand Rapids: Eerdmans.

Kidner, Derek. *Proverbs.* London: The Tyndale Press.

Kittel, Gerhard, and Friedrich, Gerhard, eds. *Theological Dictionary of the New Testament.* Grand Rapids: Eerdmans, 1964–1976.

Leighton, Robert. *Commentary on First Peter.* Grand Rapids: Kregel Reprint, 1972.

Lovelace, Richard F. *Dynamics of Spiritual Life.* Downers Grove, Ill.: InterVarsity Press, 1979.

Luther, Martin. *Luther's Works,* Weimar ed vol. 54.

Milton, John. *Paradise Lost.*

Prior, Kenneth F. W. *The Gospel in a Pagan Society.* Downers Grove, Ill.: InterVarsity Press, 1975.

Shedd, William G. T. *Romans.* Grand Rapids: Zondervan Publishing Co.

Thayer, Joseph Henry. *Thayer's Greek-English Lexicon of the New Testament.* New York: American Book Co.

Thomas, W. H. Griffith. *St. Paul's Epistle to the Romans.* Grand Rapids: Eerdmans.

Wesley, John. *The Journal of John Wesley.* Chicago: Moody Press.

_____. *Sermons on Several Occasions.* New York: Carlton and Phillips, 1855.

Williams, Don. *The Bond that Breaks.* Ventura, Calif.: Regal.

Wuest, Kenneth S. *The New Testament: An Expanded Translation.* Grand Rapids: Eerdmans, 1961.

_____. *Word Studies in the Greek New Testament, for the English Reader, Romans.* Grand Rapids: Eerdmans.

Zondervan Pictorial Encyclopedia of the Bible, 5 vols. Grand Rapids: Zondervan Publishing Co., 1975.